DUPLICITY

DUPLICITY

BASKETBALL, DRUGS, AND MY DOUBLE LIFE

CURTIS MALONE

Post Hill PRESS

A POST HILL PRESS BOOK
ISBN: 979-8-89565-132-2
ISBN (eBook): 979-8-89565-133-9

Duplicity:
Basketball, Drugs, and My Double Life

Cover design by Cody Corcoran

This is a work of nonfiction. All people, locations, events, and situations are portrayed to the best of the author's memory and knowledge. While all of the events described are true, many names and identifying details have been changed to protect the privacy of the people involved. Although adequate research was undergone concerning criminal cases, real-life people and perceptions, and authentic situations and incidents, the author and publisher do not assume and hereby disclaim any liability concerning any legal or criminal details present in this book.

Post Hill Press
New York • Nashville
posthillpress.com

Published in the United States of America
1 2 3 4 5 6 7 8 9 10

This book is dedicated to the game—
to the wins that lifted me, the losses that taught me, and the journey that shaped me.

Contents

Part 3
The Rise of DC Assault
1992–2000

Part 4
The Trouble with Guys like Gary Williams
2001–Present

Preface

Unless a man goes on trial and is able to defend himself, his prosecutors may depict him in any manner they choose.

Standing in a courtroom, prosecutors go out of their way to destroy a man's reputation. Regardless of what good the man may have done in his life and ignoring who he loves and who loves him, the prosecutor paints a picture of evil malice and flagrant disregard of society's expectations. The newspapers and television personalities repeat those ideas presented in the courtroom. The man becomes a pariah.

In 2013, I pled guilty to one count of conspiracy to distribute or possess with intent to distribute 500 grams or more of cocaine and one hundred grams or more of heroin. For this, I was sentenced to one hundred months in federal prison.

Because I pled guilty, I never went to trial and never challenged the prosecutor's depiction. The press portrayed me as a selfish manipulator who used my youth basketball program and the talented players it produced as commodities to trade for my own benefit, all while leading a double life as a drug trafficker who poisoned his own neighborhood.

I don't challenge the veracity of their description, but I do take issue with the exaggeration used to sell newspapers and magazines. They demonized my greed to make a buck for themselves. They were hypocrites—all of them.

I gave whatever I could to my players: food, clothing, an education, a home. Pushing, training, mentoring, and guiding them, I was a father when they didn't have one.

I kept their eyes on the goal, urging them to get a college education and succeed in whatever professional field they chose, be it in the NBA making money off their God-given talent, or making money otherwise.

But as they pursued their goals, I had dreams of my own. As those dreams faded away, time and time again, I was left with nothing but my own resources on which to live. I had grown up surrounded by hustlers. When I couldn't do what I wanted, I resorted to what I knew.

Ultimately, I decided to write this book because I wanted to tell my story without the added narrative of anyone else. I wanted to set the record straight on numerous events, conversations, and relationships others have speculated about. And I wanted to do so in my own voice.

Writing a memoir is difficult. So many influences exist in life. How do I know which to capture on the page and which to ignore? Tracing my own personal development from childhood until now, at age fifty, was both revealing and painful. I gained so much insight into how and why I think the way I do. I realized just how arrogant I often acted.

Recreating and recording my life also presented other, more practical challenges. Memories fade. People die. Throughout the book, I have tried to accurately represent conversations I had with others. If those conversations are not exactly verbatim, the nature and context are true. Some may take exception to my chronology or specific details in my retelling. Though I cannot claim every detail is exact, I do stand by the intention, sentiment, and results of the events I relate in this book.

A memoir is a retracing of one's life—but it is not just an autobiography. I have learned lessons from the mistakes I have made. My intent with *Duplicity* is to share my story with young men, husbands, and fathers. I hope they can learn the lessons I did not learn until I landed in prison: Lessons on loyalty and greed.

Curtis Malone, July 2018

Part 1

The 1320 and Rare Essence at Palmer Park

1973–1986

Roots

Dr. James Naismith, a white man, invented the game of basketball in 1891. For over 125 years, young Black men have perfected it: Julius Erving, Abdul-Jabbar, Russell, Magic, Jordan, Bryant, LeBron, Curry. Basketball provides a fortunate few the opportunity to escape poverty, crime, drugs, broken homes, and dead-end dreams. But if you're not a star, then you don't escape. Instead, you go back to your hood and become a hustler. Palmer Park, Maryland, thrives on those kinds of ballers.

The neighborhood began as one of those post-WWII subdivisions where every house looks the same, all on identical postage-stamp-sized lots surrounded by chain-link fences. Over the decades, the white servicemen the neighborhood originally housed gave way to increasing numbers of Blacks. The houses were ideal starter homes, and by the late '60s, Palmer Park became an African-American neighborhood.

Each house featured three bedrooms, one bath, a kitchen, and a living room. Some offered basements; most did not. My family's house on Muncy Road had green aluminum siding. My parents had their own bedroom. My oldest sister Sharon demanded privacy and received a bedroom. My other two sisters, Brenda and Beverly, shared the third. That left me, the baby of the family, to sleep wherever I found room—be it the sofa, the floor, with my parents, or on Sharon or Brenda's bed, if either stayed out.

But the house beat our previous apartment at 1320 Missouri Avenue in DC. There, our family of six shared a one-bedroom. Palmer Park represented a major step up. An achievement for my father Herman, who worked long hours at Trailways, and for my mother, Rosa.

I think back upon my parents at that time. One memory surfaces; my mother, brown-skinned and just tall enough to see out the window above the kitchen sink with her back to me as she washes dishes; my father, just home from work, still wearing his light-blue uniform, wrapping his arms around her from behind, moving his hands to her hips, swaying to Marvin Gaye playing on the radio. The ebbing humidity of a summer's evening clings to the air. A lawn mower hums down the street. The house is quiet except for "Let's Get It On," and I watch from the doorway as my father kisses my mother's neck. I'm sure it is a Friday or Saturday, and I know they will soon head into DC, back to our old apartment building at 1320 Missouri Avenue—where my grandmother, Ella C., now lives—to play cards, drink, and party. Both will dress to impress. Both are young, classy, and smooth. A friend will see my mother at the party and tell her she looks fly. Although I won't be there to overhear the compliment, I know this with absolute surety.

This memory, my favorite of my parents, represents a paradox. They have always loved one another, although they've argued like demons. My father: a player who ran the streets, womanizing with abandon. My mother: laid-back until her anger exploded. At times, I feel they played parts in some staged production—the happy Black couple—especially in public. They loved parties and excelled in social settings. Two charmers, quick with smiles or a wink. So, my best memory of that one moment in time, both swaying to the music, represents the best of their life together, if not the actual reality of their relationship.

In many ways, my parents epitomized Palmer Park. The neighborhood was divided into two halves, separated by Barlowe Road and the Palmer Park Shopping Center. Our neighborhood offered a pool, basketball courts, a recreation center, and an actual park. From a bird's-eye view, I'm sure the neighborhood appeared to be an idyllic suburban environment, full of young families. Zoom in and one found an open-air drug market full of hustlers selling reefer, heroin, PCP, and, eventually, crack. The strip mall offered much more than liquor and convenience stores: It offered drugs and stolen clothing.

Craps games surrounded us. We all knew one another, and we quickly challenged strangers. It seemed every night offered a party on our block. The fun lasted all hours unless a fight broke out.

Our family moved to Palmer Park in 1973 when I started first grade. I had enjoyed living in DC and did not want to move away from friends and family who lived in the 1320 apartment building. I imagine moving hit my sisters harder. Sharon, the oldest, would've just started high school, which is an awkward age to change schools. Sharon could be tough and mean, but she worked hard. She didn't hesitate to throw down if pushed, and her petite stature disguised a fierceness within. Brenda, five years older than me, acted like a mother, always bossing our sister Beverly and me around. Brenda and Beverly couldn't have been more different. Brenda was always smart and independent. She never got into the street life. She cared for all of us, taking a parental role, especially when my mother and father went out. While Beverly...well...Beverly and I are the most alike. Her personality growing up mirrored Sharon's. She was a tough, mean fighter. But unlike our older sister, Beverly ran the streets, always had a thug for a boyfriend, and avoided home as much as she could.

Then came me: light-skinned with curly hair and a dimple in my cheek. When I smiled, I charmed people. Little girls loved me, while mothers warned one another to keep an eye on me, lest the devil inside should cause trouble.

Like Beverly, I saw Palmer Park as my playground and quickly learned the rules. Being the only boy, I hung out with my dad a lot. He'd take me around different neighborhoods introducing me to everyone, even some of his lady friends mom didn't know about. Back then, I thought a man needed to dress well and have lots of girlfriends. When alone, I rode my bike through the neighborhood and hung out with older guys. I thought I was the shit.

"Coach's gonna put you in?"

"Yeah, on the kickoff."

"Shit, Curtis, just run around. Don't try to tackle anyone."

I glared at my friend, Steve Williams. "I'll be fine."

"I'd listen to him, Curt. You'll get smashed," added my other best friend, Albert, whom we called Loopy.

I'd met both when my father signed me up to play football through the Palmer Park Boys and Girls Club. He used football as leverage to improve my behavior in school. At eight years old, I weighed forty pounds soaking wet, and my head just barely came past the kitchen counter. I played on a sixty-five-pound-and-under team. Though annoying, Steve gave sound advice.

"Special teams! Let's go!" yelled our coach.

I gamely fastened my chin strap and jogged onto the field. I only got into the game on kickoffs, but I loved football. At first, I did not want to play, but being part of a team really appealed to me.

The whistle blew and we kicked off. I ran down the far sideline, swiveling my head to the left to try and spot the return man. By the time I reached our opponent's twenty, the play had been blown dead on the other sideline.

No one had tried blocking me. I hadn't touched a soul. And that's how it went all season. I ran onto the field picturing myself making a heroic tackle, just to be ignored by the bigger kids. I must have looked ridiculous with my tiny body and an oversized helmet. But my father's strategy paid off: I loved the game enough that a threat of "no football" prevented me from landing on the hot bench in the principal's office.

Steve and Loopy quickly became my best friends at that time. Steve, though three years older than me, excelled at sports. He always kept out of trouble and now works for Wonder Bread. He introduced me to basketball, and we all discovered go-go music.

Loopy, who was dark-skinned, slim, and hyper, looked up to his older, straight-up gangsta brothers. Loopy always caused trouble but was great fun to be around. He loved to box. Loopy and our friend Sean Harris introduced me to the sport.

"Yo, Curtis? You comin' over tonight?" Loopy asked after our last football game of the season. "Parents won't be around…"

"They never around! But Imma go uptown to my grandma's."

Every weekend she hosted card games to earn money. When we arrived at her place, we walked into a room full of cops, taxi drivers, the mailman, neighbors, and friends. Clouds of cigarette smoke hung above the heads of gamblers and hustlers looking to win an ante. Motown played on the radio, drowned out by constant arguments. The people dressed up, and the dim light of her living room caught flashes of gold off chains and earrings.

At the center of it all stood Ella C. One moment she fixed a dinner, the next dealt a hand of Tonk. She gave orders when a friend's drink ran low while carrying on conversation or cursing out Uncle Monk, the building's maintenance man. My grandmother amazed me. She spoiled me with attention and provided for me when she could. Yet, she could not be charmed, and she showed a hard backbone when it came to bullshit. She turned feisty when challenged and had a hidden cunning a stranger would not immediately perceive. Like my mother, my grandmother had a fiery temper, a trait Sharon and Beverly inherited.

My grandmother's longtime partner, Coles Terry, allowed her to bask in the attention these weekend parties provided. Growing up, we thought Coles was our maternal grandfather and found out much later our real grandfather never left South Carolina when Ella C. moved to DC. Coles worked as a custodian at the National Institute of Health, and he treated her well.

I loved those parties, which usually lasted all night. The fish, chicken, music, and booze flowed freely. More than once I'd crash in my grandmother's bedroom only to wake up the next morning and find the party still raged. I watched my grandmother closely as she monitored the card game. She'd cut the pot every time someone won.

"Curtis, mind your damn business," she scolded after catching me watching her skim off the proceeds, stuffing cash into her bra. I blushed. "Actually, your mama told me you think you're that damn boy from the Jackson Five. Why don't you show us?"

"No, that's okay," I practically pleaded.

"Everyone! My grandson is going to put on a little show now. Coles, put the Jackson Five record on," she shouted. The whole apartment went quiet. I wanted to haul ass, yet part of me enjoyed being the center of attention. Well, I knew I could not get out of the situation without performing. A space cleared and "Dancing Machine" played on the stereo. I danced my ass off. A little curly-haired, eight-year-old Michael Jackson, who understood none of the song's meaning, but reveled in the attention and adulation of those cheering me on. When the song ended and the applause died down, I was sweating but pleased with myself and the tips I'd earned.

"Now, go get your grandpa a beer," my grandmother told me as she skimmed the pot. I eagerly moved into my other role at these parties: waiter. I'd fetch drinks, plates of fried fish, or anything anyone asked for. I enjoyed the responsibility, as it made me feel older, needed, and like I was one of them. Plus, I often received tips.

I cannot emphasize enough just how important 1320 Missouri Avenue served in my childhood and in my life as a man. The building acted like one big family, with my grandmother as the muscle. Every door always opened, everyone always shared with one another. It had a sense of togetherness. Uncle Monk and my dad acted like brothers. They would always wrestle and horseplay. I remember one time they went at it fierce until my dad fell through a glass-topped coffee table, cut his arm up, and needed stitches.

Go-go bands also played for free at nearby Emery Heights. I fell in love with the music, which included bands like Busy Brothers and Mass Extinction. All the old heads in Palmer Park listened to Rare Essence, so they became my favorite.

I never felt like a little kid. I wonder now, so many decades later, if I missed out on childhood. Being the youngest in my family, I found myself surrounded by older influences. But I do not remember ever wanting to be a kid. I'm not sure I even knew what eight- or nine-year-olds did at that age. That's not to say I didn't ride my bike with Steve and Loopy. But all I saw were older guys doing big-boy shit; hustlers slinging drugs in the Palmer Park open market, my parents with their friends drinking and gambling at 1320. The attention of adults motivated me. Never did I really care about popularity among guys my age. Because of that, I was popular with them. But with older sisters and older role models, I easily gained the trust and friendship of guys in high school and even that of adults. I relished it at the time.

Now, I wonder if I grew up too soon.

Hustling for the Go-Go

Go-go music, familiar to anyone from Washington, DC, combines R&B, hip-hop, and funk, with live percussion instruments and constant dance beats. Go-go bands play nonstop for hours, blending one song into another, while band members step on stage. Most of the groups engage in a call-and-response with the crowd, repeating the refrain or singing the chorus. Addictive through its beats, the music creates high energy and movement. By the time I'd turned eleven, I was hooked.

Rare Essence formed three years earlier, in 1976. Led by Jas Funk, they played local area clubs. I collected Rare Essence cassette tapes and 8-tracks.

In '79 they played at Prince George's Community College, and practically the whole Palmer Park neighborhood showed up. I was the youngest in the crowd and the concert felt like a religious experience. I vividly remember the band, all wearing red-and-white tank tops and shorts with gold chains, in step with one another as they wove songs together without a break. Go-go music evolved through dance halls—its purpose to make the crowd move. Everywhere I turned I saw older neighbors in an ecstatic frenzy. And the women! I was only eleven, women still foreign to me, but I quickly realized playing in a go-go band got you attention.

Going to that concert changed me in other, subtle, ways. Other than Steve, Sean, and Loopy, I spent my time with older guys, high-school age, or even adults. My mindset did not fit a normal eleven-year-old's. I expected to be treated like an adult. In a way, I felt superior to kids my age. Not that I acted that way, but surrounding myself with older guys and doing things they did (no one else my age saw Rare Essence live, for instance) gave me a quiet, cool confidence during a period in my childhood when many boys felt awkward or unsure of themselves.

As a fan of go-go music, I got lucky. Palmer Park hosted go-go bands at both the community center and the Club LeBaron. The Club LeBaron sat in the middle of the Palmer Park Shopping Center. Basically a big warehouse, the club reeked of sweat and smoke. Warm, humid air assaulted you as soon as you entered, like a stinky sauna. The front windows fogged up during shows, allowing only the music to penetrate the night. Oddly, the LeBaron did not have a liquor license, which forced people to sneak in their own booze.

Go-go became my passion. I stayed involved in sports, but all my remaining energy went to attending shows. My parents went out every Friday and Saturday, often until two or three in the morning, leaving me in the care of my sisters. Sharon, Brenda, and Beverly, all in their teens, usually had other plans besides babysitting their brother. So almost every weekend I kicked it with my old heads, and they too loved the go-gos. We'd end up at the community center or the club dancing to Chuck Brown and the Soul Searchers, Experience Unlimited, or Trouble Funk.

The following year, Rare Essence returned to play a show at the Palmer Park Recreation Center, which sat opposite the shopping center on the other side of Barlowe Road. I could hardly wait, and on the night of the show, I dressed all fly, like a little man about to take the town in my favorite Izod shirt, shell-toe Adidas, and socks to match. A long line snaked its way around the rec center. I finally got to the door, practically hopping from foot to foot with excitement, only to be met by Ms. Mack, Rare Essence's manager.

"And what do you think you're doing, son?"

"Going to the show, Ms. Mack. I've never missed a show."

"Not tonight. You are too young. Get your little ass home."

I stared at her in disbelief. I pretended not to hear, offering up my money and my hand to be stamped.

"I'm serious. I'm not in the mood for any lip tonight. Go on now."

Anger flashed through me. "Ms. Mack, you got no idea what you did to my night!"

Ms. Mack looked like a toad. I believe she must have been bipolar because sometimes she didn't give a damn whether us younger guys came to a show and other times, like this night, she turned on us. Had the concert been another band, my young heart could have survived. But Rare Essence! In my own neighborhood! I couldn't hold back.

I started crying.

"Hey, hey, what's up Li'l Curtis?" one of my older friends called out as he stood in line.

"Ms. Mack won't let me in!"

"Ah, Mack attack," another sympathized.

Though I appreciated the sympathy—some even called Ms. Mack a few harsh names—they were going to the show, while I had been ordered out. Their compassion did not help. She was one tough lady.

I wandered aimlessly, without conscious thought, until a kind voice called out, "Hey, little man, why you so upset?"

I'd wandered around to the back of the rec center. Surprised, I looked into the face of Scotty Hazel, the organ player for Rare Essence. The band unloaded their equipment from a truck. Scotty sat on a huge black case, smoking a cigarette.

"Ms. Mack says I'm too young to get in," I explained, trying not to look pathetic in front of my heroes.

"Weren't you the young fella in the front row of our last show?" Godfather asked. He played keyboards. I'd gone to a Rare Essence show three months before. Too short to see, the old heads brought me to the front row.

"Yeah, I always come to your shows. I'm your biggest fan. It's not like I'm too young. I'm twelve."

"Come on, Shorty, we got you," Scotty said. He jumped up off the case he'd sat on and undid the clasps. The case held the large organ he played, "The Granddaddy." Twice the size of me, I easily fit into it. Friday and Burt shut the lid; I panicked for a moment. Pitch-black, hot, with an industrial plastic smell, I feared I'd suffocate. It was the greatest moment of my young life.

Then the case started moving. I spread my hands and feet, pressing them into the case's sides to keep my balance. In a few moments, I felt the case stop rolling. The case opened and I found myself backstage. I could hear a thousand voices on the other side of the curtain.

"Now, just stay out of her sight until the lights go down," Godfather said as he and Scotty headed back outside. I took their advice, watching the equipment being set up and observing Jas Funk and his band get ready to perform. Finally, the lights went out, and, in the dark, I crept from the stage to the front of the audience. I felt like I'd won the lottery. As the band started to play, I partied, dancing along step by step. The old heads around me cleared out a small space and started calling to Jas Funk and Li'l Bennie.

When Jas Funk noticed, the guys pushed me towards the stage. Li'l Bennie pulled me up, and I fell into step with the band. I really showed my ass up there. I saw older girls loving my moves.

I couldn't see Ms. Mack but knew she stood out in the dark crowd somewhere. I would've loved to see her face.

I danced on stage for a few songs and jumped back into the crowd as they transitioned into another song. The percussionist, David Green, gave me a pair of Timbale sticks, which I stuck into my back pocket. The older girls I'd spotted earlier all took turns dancing with me for the rest of the show. I loved the attention.

At the end of the night, I slipped out without seeing Ms. Mack and walked home surrounded by guys amused and happy for me, or damn jealous. I felt like the man.

Attending go-gos and buying music cost money. I've always been able to make money. I may not have been born one, but I grew up in a world of hustlers. From a very young age, I saw drugs and cash exchanged out in the open at the Palmer Park Shopping Center and in our neighborhoods. Loopy's older brothers dealt drugs. My sister Beverly dated drug dealers. Hustling would always be an option for me, but not one I particularly wanted. As a good-looking, outgoing, charismatic kid, I never had a problem charming people. But I also acted humble (usually), stayed out of trouble, and got along with mostly everyone. People liked me, and, as I grew up, guys in the hood looked out for me.

My life at that time centered around a few constants: school, where I earned good-enough grades; sports—football and, increasingly, basketball; music; and earning money by helping Uncle Monk and my grandfather, Coles Terry.

Uncle Monk worked as the building supervisor at the 1320. He wasn't actually related to me, just my dad's best friend. He hired me to help clean and maintain the place. Easy stuff, like sweeping and mopping the stairways, raking, cutting grass, scraping old paint, applying new coats. I'd work on Friday afternoon and Monk paid me twenty bucks every two weeks. I did a decent job and eventually Monk took me to a couple other buildings he maintained on 13th and 14th Streets.

I also worked with my grandfather at the National Institute of Health (NIH), where he did custodial work. I'd clean the buildings, and he would give me a few bucks. That money, combined with my wages from Monk, plus any tips I collected by being the little waiter at my grandmother's card game, earned me a good fifty to sixty dollars a month, not bad for a twelve-year-old.

I always liked having and spending money. My parents worked hard: my dad at Trailways, and my mom as a hotel maid. We were not poor. We always had food on the table, but few luxuries. Back-to-school shopping equaled about two hundred dollars for four kids. I always wanted to look sharp, a trait I inherited from both my parents. I wanted to keep up with the older guys I chilled with and tried to imitate.

Though I respected, even admired, Monk and my grandfather, I knew quickly that janitorial work would not be my future. That realization led me to ask: How can I make money without selling drugs? By the time I entered middle school, I felt ready to be an entrepreneur. I had one goal in mind: earn enough money each week to go to the go-go on Friday or Saturday while still having some pocket change. My plan, decidedly simple, involved selling candy at school. Every morning, I'd walk to the 7-Eleven across from Kenmoor Junior High and stuff my pockets with candy bars and bubble gum. I'd casually saunter out, giving my Malone smile, complete with dimples, to the half-asleep clerk. I went to school and sold the candy out of my locker all day. No expenses meant all profit, a sweet hustle. It lasted about three months but ended for a couple reasons. First, my teachers got wind of my little business. Although a few may have appreciated my ingenuity, it led to too many questions. Also, I'm a horrible thief.

I never got caught stealing candy, but two other instances made me see the writing on the wall. The first happened at the 7-Eleven. Near the front entrance, next to a cooler of juices sat an arcade game, either Pac-Man or Space Invaders. One afternoon, Loopy and I played the arcade game for hours. We stood just out of the cashier's sight, so I continuously helped myself to bottles of juice from the cooler. I must have drunk ten of them throughout the afternoon. Loopy drank his share, too. I didn't plan on paying for them, stashing each empty bottle in the trash can. Well, unknown to us, an undercover cop had parked outside, monitoring drug activity in the area. He watched us the whole time. As Loopy and I got ready to leave, a male voice asked, "You gonna pay for those, son?"

I nearly pissed myself.

"What are you talking about?" I bravely asked. He pointed to the empty bottles sitting at the top of a full trash barrel.

"Been outside watching you the whole time," he replied as he pulled his badge out.

I must have turned redder than a fire hydrant because Loopy's mouth dropped open, then he started to laugh. He quickly clasped his hand over his mouth but couldn't hold in his laughter.

"I'd really appreciate you paying for these. I'll be outside, just to make sure." He turned and walked out.

"Shut the fuck up, Loopy!" I snapped as I went to the cashier and counted out some money. A certain irony existed as I paid for my "stolen" juices with money I'd made selling stolen candy bars from the same 7-Eleven.

My second failed attempt at theft happened at the neighborhood Dart Drug. I'd walked over there on a Saturday afternoon with some friends from Palmer Park. As they went to the drink coolers and candy counter, I walked down the toy aisle. I spotted a rubber ball, red, somewhat bigger than a racquet ball but smaller than a tennis ball. I decided I wanted the ball but didn't want to waste my hard-earned candy money, so I put it in the pocket of my jeans. An obvious rubber-ball shape bulged from the side of my pants.

As I walked down the aisle and towards the exit, hoping the antics of my friends distracted the cashier, a man turned the corner and stopped short when he saw me.

Herman Malone, Senior. My dad.

We stood ten paces apart, two gunslingers about to duel.

"Now, what the hell you got in your pants?" he asked.

I had no out, no escape. I carefully pulled the ball out of my pocket, the Dart Drug price sticker, like a scarlet letter, pointedly announcing my guilt.

"You pay for that?" he asked.

I could have lied, but his sudden appearance threw me off balance. As smooth and charismatic as I could be to others, I've never charmed my dad—we are too much alike. Plus, I'd walked with my head down and didn't know how much he'd seen.

"No...."

"Boy, put that damn ball back where you got it and get your ass to the car!"

My friends stared at me as I completed my walk of shame. A solitary voice called out, "See ya, Curtis," as I left the store.

My parents grounded me for two days over a weekend, which felt like two months. After the failed Dart Drug heist, and with my teachers getting hip to what I sold, I decided to give up the candy game. I had nightmares of the undercover cop catching me stealing candy, not just juices. I wasn't ready for jail.

Though I stopped, selling candy made me realize I could make my own money. Just like the hustlers I saw everyday selling products (drugs or stolen merchandise), I, too, could take care of myself. I just needed a new idea that didn't involve stealing.

Back then, school lunch cost under one dollar. My dad left a buck for me every morning. Without my candy money coming in, I had to figure out a way to afford go-gos. I decided to save the dollar by not eating. By week's end, I had five dollars—another twenty per month. But I got hungry. We could choose from a few options in the lunch line—some were eighty, ninety, or ninety-five cents apiece—so I'd ask people for their change as they came through the line. Looking back, I suppose I panhandled, but I ate every day and it also taught me a powerful lesson. I discovered if you're nice to people, smile and laugh and act friendly, most didn't mind giving up their change or helping you out. The persona cannot be contrived or false. I genuinely was the type of kid who attracted others and who other kids wanted to befriend. As I grew up, I learned to use that to my advantage.

I think, for most people, those middle school years, at the ages of twelve, thirteen, or fourteen, represent a distinctly formative experience. What I mean is that though high school might shape the kind of adult you'll be, early adolescence molds our life outlook. If you grew up in a wealthy suburb, where every friend's father was a doctor or lawyer and your parents told you you could grow up to be anything, your outlook inspired higher expectations than someone who grew up in a different environment. By seventh grade, my association with gangstas, hustlers, and much older guys created a more limited outlook. A more negative one. Yet, as I grew up, other positive influences conflicted with the hustlers I knew. It created a scenario in which I could turn out either way: an honest, hard-working success story, or a drug dealer. My outlook became more malleable than the rich kid in the suburb. I learned there are ways to live and to make money which do not require a college degree or professional title. Yet, at the same time, I desired success, adulation, and to be seen as a leader. A college degree could provide that. Over the next few years, I just had to figure out which way to go and how to get there.

I've always enjoyed dressing well. As a kid, with my parents' limited budget, each of us only got one or two new outfits a year. This created a problem for me. Luckily, I grew up in Palmer Park. My sister Brenda always worked hard. Her boyfriend at the time, Kenny, also earned money. Together, they kept me outfitted in Polo and Izod. When they fell short, Tydie stepped in.

My sister Beverly grew up Brenda's opposite. The streets called to her at a young age. A slightly older guy named Tydie was one of her first boyfriends. Notorious as a robber, booster, and cold killer, Tydie ran with a crew of three or four others.

Early one Saturday morning, my friends and I went to the Landover Mall. We arrived before most of the stores opened. As we walked through the nearly empty mall, I spotted Tydie's crew outside the Hecht's Department Store. The store hadn't yet opened and boxes piled atop one another sat just inside the security gate, and, as the gate opened, Tydie picked them up one by one and passed them out to one of his guys. They acted in a practiced unison, like a well-trained bucket brigade, the last guy carrying boxes out to a waiting car. Intrigued, my friends and I watched. I didn't know what the boxes contained, but knew if it involved Tydie, it couldn't be good.

Later the same day, I walked to the Palmer Park Shopping Center. Tydie sat behind opened boxes full of Calvin Klein, Sergio Valente, Sasson, and Jordache clothing. I could hardly believe what I saw. Tydie smiled, a proprietor at his own flea market.

"What size you wear, Li'l Curtis?" he asked.

"You serious?" I asked.

"Go ahead, pick out whatever you want."

I rummaged through the boxes, grabbing brand new pairs of jeans, shirts, even a jacket. All around me guys ran from the street selling drugs to cars waiting in line to buy, no matter the driver's race, be it Black, white, or another; a craps game started up a few feet away; a guy who lived two streets down high on PCP started a fight. Nothing mattered to me as I outfitted myself with Tydie's boosted clothes.

This became a semi-regular occurrence, and despite Tydie's reputation as a no-good troublemaker, I began to see a certain kindness and humanity in him and guys like him. Most gangstas have a good heart, somewhere. No doubt, he contained a level of brutality; no doubt he was a criminal; yet, what I saw as generosity engendered a loyalty. Tydie kept me dressed and fly. I'd never forget that.

The open-air drug market at the shopping center became a magnet to me. After football practice, I'd wander through, observing all the illegal activities. I'd cross Barlowe Road and end up behind the rec center, where some of the biggest craps games took place. No matter how many times my parents told me to stay away from the shopping center, or how often Officer Coleman chased me off from the craps games, I always found my way back. Something about that life stood out to me: the camaraderie, the action, the fast-paced hustle.

In Palmer Park that's all we saw.

In contrast, my dad provided a role model, but at the time, I only understood he worked hard every day and didn't have much to show for it. Outside of providing what he could for our family, my father gambled every weekend. He cheated on my mom regularly. I remember their arguments, her accusations, his non-denials. So, what did he give me to run with? From him, I learned how to work in order to be a player. I never saw him open a door or hold a chair for my mother, never knew them to go out on a date. I believed him to be a good father but had no other comparison. Both my parents enjoyed partying, but we hardly ever went out as a family, never went to a movie, circus, carnival, or family vacations. Just 1320, that was it.

Honestly, I'm not sure I wanted to do something fun as a family. I was twelve, going on thirty. I had little interest in kid stuff. I didn't collect comic books or play with G.I. Joes. I hardly ever watched Saturday morning cartoons (just the Jackson Five) or played kid games with my friends. For Christmas, I asked for few toys, mostly for clothes, except one year when I wanted a set of timbales so I could be like David Green of Rare Essence.

Instead of a typical childhood, I ventured out into the streets of Palmer Park. My block offered so much activity, it seemed like a carnival itself. On any day, I might see a fistfight, a boxing match in the street, craps games on the sidewalks, and, of course, no matter whose yard you turned into, drugs for sale.

As I grew, I began spending time at Landover Mall, where the girls hung out. My detached observation of the hustle morphed into earning a few dollars by being a lookout for cops or a gofer, running errands back and forth to the Johns or liquor store in the shopping center.

The nature of the neighborhood engendered loyalty among us. Internal conflicts existed—occasionally guys from Muncy Road might beef with Normandy Road—but outside of Palmer Park, we stuck together. This devotion got tested most often at the mall, where people from all different neighborhoods congregated.

State-of-the-art at the time, the mall offered a massive food court, a movie theater, and an arcade. Someone there alone often found trouble. Anyone who waited for the bus back into the city could find himself the victim of a robbery. We didn't use guns as much back then, but knives and fists worked just as well.

One afternoon, about to head home after leaving some friends, I walked through the mall. At twelve, I weighed just under one hundred pounds, maybe five feet tall. I wore a pair of Cazal frames. As I passed a group of teens whom I recognized from the Glenarden Apartments, I caught a whisper from one named Danny.

"Hey, I want those frames."

"Let's get them," another said.

After I passed, they moved behind me, tailing me, waiting until I reached a more secluded area to pounce. No hero, especially against three older guys, I walked quickly. When I reached the exit, I bolted through the door, sprinting like Carl Lewis all the way back to my hood. Once I reached the shopping center, I stopped, doubled over with my hands on my knees, panting like a dog.

"What the fuck's up, Li'l Curtis?" my old heads asked. One we called Stickman because he always walked around with a golf club, a five iron. Another, Fat Leon, looked for fights.

"Some bitch-ass niggas from Glenarden tried to take my Cazals," I explained.

"Where they at?" Stickman asked.

"I was up at the mall. Three of them, so I just broke on those niggas."

"You hear that, Fat Leon? Some Glenarden niggas tried to take Li'l Curtis's glasses…" A small group had formed around us. About twenty older guys, hustlers and hangers-on, began asking me all sorts of questions.

"Who were they?"

"You know what they look like?"

"Who wants to put some work in?"

A smaller group, led by Stickman, broke off and pulled me aside. "We going back to the mall, Curtis, to find these suckers."

I didn't really consider consequences. Danny and his friends had scared me and feeling scared made me angry. I wanted them to see me with all these gangstas and realize you don't fuck with Curtis Malone.

I witnessed one of the worst beatings I'd ever seen. Stickman and about nine others cornered Danny and his homeboys in the parking lot at the mall. The beatdown happened swiftly and brutally. Stickman repeatedly whacked his golf club down on the Glenarden boys. The others used their fists, as if they were Sugar Ray Leonard, who came from our hood to win the Olympic boxing gold medal in '76 and had just won the welterweight world championship. Blood gushed from the heads of those chumps. I stood back, a bit in shock, a bit amazed that these older guys would stick up for me.

"You don't fuck with Palmer Park," Stickman said over and over, punctuating each word with his golf club. "Fuck. With. Palmer. Park!"

Over time, I realized they defended me for reasons other than just friendship. Yes, I felt well-liked. But the beatdown also made a statement: Don't fuck with Palmer Park. Stickman made that clear. The second reason, a more depressing one in retrospect, was that these men just had nothing productive to do with their time. Kicking three punks' asses from Glenarden served as entertainment. Afterwards, we walked back to the shopping center, and, I admit, I felt a certain pride and pleasure in being represented so well. When we got back, Stickman went right back to the craps game as if nothing had happened. The others wandered off—the whole thing just some work, nothing out of the ordinary.

By the time I reached eighth grade, sports took up much of my time. I played football for the Palmer Park Tigers, tried boxing (which my dad made me quit), and played basketball. Practices and games left little time to work at the 1320 or with my grandfather. But I'd learned how to get money with my lunch-line scheme. I soon expanded on the idea.

In my hood, older men responded to us younger guys for different reasons. A dangerous old head will identify that same potential in a kid and nurture that side of him. Conversely, if the kid is decent at heart, with a good head on his shoulders and the potential not to fall into crime, the hustlers will protect him. They'll encourage him to stay in school, to escape the neighborhood by not making the same mistakes they made. As I began to really get to know the dealers in Palmer Park, most looked out for me. They offered me money, along with the warning to stay away from the drug game.

The nickels and dimes from the cafeteria turned into twenty dollar bills from the hustlers. Whenever I planned to go somewhere, I would ask one of my old heads who'd taken a liking to me, and he made sure I had cash. In this way, in their minds, I had no reason to slip into selling drugs. A guy in his early twenties named Irvin Wallace looked out for me the most.

Wallace and Byrd

Irvin Wallace came across as one of the smoothest and most fly hustlers at the shopping center. He'd recently dropped out of Cheyney State, where he played football on scholarship. He escaped the streets, but intentionally chose to return, which added some mystery to him. Tall, handsome with light eyes (cat eyes, we called them), he kept quiet but took in everything. He could act sneaky, but everyone loved him; the ladies definitely did. Irvin garnered the respect of everyone, and he genuinely cared about younger kids in the neighborhood.

I wanted to be just like him.

He took me under his wing quickly once he returned home from Cheyney State. My athletic ability began to emerge, especially on the basketball court, and I think he saw himself in me. Though he never said so, I believe he regretted leaving school. He preached about staying focused and getting good grades.

I called Irvin my godfather because he fit well into that role, and I didn't have an actual one. He carried a pager and gave me a special code I'd add to whatever number I paged him from. No matter what, he'd call right back.

"What's wrong?" he'd ask.

"Nothing, I just need some money for the mall."

"Where you at?"

"Outside promenade three."

"Give me ten minutes."

And, sure enough, ten minutes later, he'd drive up. Small change to Irvin equaled about one hundred dollars, which seemed a small fortune to a thirteen-year-old. Irvin also schooled me on life in the streets, all the while pushing me to succeed in school and get out of Palmer Park. I think he wanted to scare me, but instead, he remained one of the most fly, smartest, smooth hustlers I knew. His tales of stickup boys, dope fiends, no snitching, and run-ins with police, intended to keep me away from the life, actually normalized the drug game for me. I saw this brilliant guy, a generous mentor, and asked myself how drug dealing could be so bad if Irvin Wallace dealt.

If these few formative years had happened a decade later, during the crack epidemic, and my role models had been crack-heads and dope fiends, my perspective of the drug game would most likely have turned out drastically different. But crack had yet to turn our neighborhood into a wasteland. Irvin glamorized drugs in a way Mario Puzo and Al Pacino glamorized the mafia in *The Godfather*. In all things, he wanted to see me succeed. He didn't wish to groom me into a dealer. But his unintended influence certainly made me take notice of the life.

My sister Beverly began dating one of the most notorious and dangerous neighborhood cats, Mike Coffer, known in Palmer Park as "Big Black." He also took me in and looked out for me. Mike's sister Sonya, whom everyone called Bones, had married Ronald Byrd. One of DC's biggest drug dealers at the time, Byrd fathered three children with Bones and as many as four more with other women. His whole family got money uptown, pushing heroin and cocaine.

My older sister, Brenda, began babysitting Byrd's youngest kids, and I met him through her. Irvin also knew him, and the two were good friends. Byrd was every hustler's role model. Once Byrd learned I was Beverly's little brother and Irvin was my "godfather," he took me under his wing.

Byrd and Bones lived in a huge house in Lanham, Maryland. He owned a sky-blue Mark V, a black-and-silver Seville, and a Corvette with removable T-tops. Walking through Byrd's front door after coming from my poorer neighborhood felt like entering a whole new world. We played pool in his billiards room and watched his huge TV. When he ordered Chinese food, which he enjoyed, he ordered the whole menu. This did not come across as a flaunting of wealth to me. Byrd did not act like some new rich man who showed off. He owned a large house and numerous cars, but I understood his lifestyle to be that of a man very comfortable, living large but not obnoxiously.

He also believed in family and easily adopted those of us he liked into his extended family of friends, inviting us over to Sunday evening dinners he prepared. I learned by watching and listening that he gave loyalty to those he loved but came down swiftly and harshly on those who betrayed his trust.

Irvin and Byrd, though much older than me, never treated me like a child. Since I always wanted to be respected as if I were older, this appealed to me, and in return, I respected them both more than other adults in my life. Many times, Byrd would pick me up and we'd drive around while he conducted his business. We had great conversations.

"Nothing I hate more than a thief or a rat, Curtis."

I stared out the window of the Seville, thinking about my candy-stealing ways the year before.

"A thief—he's another kind of addict. You can't trust addicts. That's why I don't fuck with guys who get high. You listening?"

"Yeah, I hear ya. But what's a thief addicted to?" I asked, genuinely curious, wondering if I'd been addicted to stealing.

"The thrill of it. Of not getting caught, of taking the risk, or of taking something from someone. But eventually the thief, like the dope fiend, only cares about the rush. He'll steal from his mama, his brother, his friends. He'll bite the hand that feeds him, as they say, and lie about the shit to your face."

"He's worse than a junkie?"

"A dope fiend is just pathetic. The junkie needs the high at the cost of everything else. He'll do anything: steal, rob, kill. He'll, he'll drop to his knees, well, you know…that's not a man, Curtis. Men stand up. They protect and provide for their family. They don't put a drug inside their bodies that makes them weak, pathetic. And don't get me started on rats. These muthafuckers who look you in the eye then run their mouths to the cops. I'd kill them all."

He trailed off. I saw the irony that Byrd made his money off these pathetic junkies. Yet, I wasn't supposed to know that. Though an open secret, I never saw him with drugs, never heard him speak about drugs or his operation. While driving, he told me we were checking into his legitimate businesses, of which he had several, but I didn't need a PhD to realize these legal businesses did not require multiple ten-minute stops in some of DC's seediest neighborhoods. I pretended ignorance, never bringing up or asking where his money came from. Byrd, like Irvin, encouraged me in school, rewarded good grades, came to and cheered me on during basketball games, and mentored me on how a man should act. They both became my idols.

Byrd maintained a class act. He provided generously. He chartered a private plane to fly family and friends to the Sugar Ray Leonard/Duran fight in Montreal. And, at thirteen, he took me to The Whispers concert. He brought all his kids, proclaiming we needed to hear quality music. We sat just a few rows from the stage. Thanks to him, The Whispers remain one of my favorite R&B groups.

So, intended or not, I absorbed influences and lessons from both Irvin and Byrd. Five years later, when I made a decision that set the course of my adult life, I'd reflect on what these two men taught me. First, I knew I'd never steal again. Theft did not fulfill the ideal I saw myself realizing. Who I wanted to be—a leader, not a follower—really molded my behavior. I also knew I wanted to make my own money. Self-dependency came with risks, but my entrepreneurial spirit just remained too strong.

I truly believed having class and respect acted as two of the most important characteristics a person could display. All the sharp cats I knew growing up bonded and clicked with one another. A major difference existed between drug runners on the street and the guys like Byrd who employed them. I didn't want to be a street hustler. If you showed everyone respect, respect came back to you. Loyalty earned through generosity remained stronger than being feared. I knew I'd never use hard drugs or be an addict. Big-time hustlers didn't use. But these reflections and decisions came a few years later. As I left junior high and prepared for my freshman year at Parkdale High School, I still thought of myself as just a short, skinny, curly-haired kid trying to get by.

Ken Freeman's Guide to Success

"You're gonna be a freshman, Curtis. Everyone gets high in high school," explained Loopy, laughing. "Get it? High in high school!"

"No man, that shit's corny. Got-damn, how many papers you gonna waste?"

"I think I figured it out." He wasted about twenty papers trying to roll a joint.

"Give me that, you sorry-rolling motherfucker. I've seen Bev do this enough," I said as he ripped yet another. I packed the rolling paper with the weed Loopy had stolen from his older brother. I deftly rolled the joint, spilling some weed on the floor of the shed we hid in. I licked one end to seal it, then held it up in the faint light. "See, I'm a bad motherfucker. Here. You go first."

Loopy produced a lighter and took a deep hit. With his eyes bulging out, his face turned blacker than he already was.

"Gotta…hold…it…" he stammered but couldn't handle it. Smoke poured out of his mouth in an explosion of coughing.

I grabbed the joint as he rolled on his side, trying to catch his breath. "I'm good. Hit it before it burns out."

I took a pull, hesitant at first, then sucked smoke in deeper. I held my breath, silently counting out the seconds, trying to hold the smoke in longer than Loopy had. I couldn't. Loopy giggled as I choked.

"Damn, you look sick, Li'l Curtis!" He took another hit off the joint, almost killing it. "Here, last hit."

Still coughing, I took another hit and did my best to hold the smoke in. I felt a hot wave pass through my body. I felt light and embraced in a comfort, a relaxation, previously unknown to me. Then I fell into another coughing fit.

For the next hour we coughed and laughed. Having no other high to compare, I bullshitted to Loopy how this was an easy high, like the gentle caress of a known lover. I talked out my ass.

For a couple months, I smoked almost daily. Every time I ran into Loopy's brother, Stink, I'd bum a hit off the joint he smoked. The smoking only lasted the summer, a phase, but I felt older, cooler, and a part of my environment. I thought I had grown up.

As summer passed into fall, my excitement for high school grew. Thanks to my older sisters, I already knew many people at Parkdale. I had attended high school football and basketball games for a while. So, I did not feel intimidated going to school with older guys and girls.

I wanted to look fly. My mother took me out on our annual back-to-school shopping trip. But I had money from Byrd, Irvin, and my other old heads, so I made sure my wardrobe included the best brands. I planned on trying out for football in the fall and basketball in the winter. I stood fivefoot-two, maybe a hundred pounds. I showed up to football tryouts in late August, took one look at the size of the guys out on the field, and left. I wasn't crazy. My dad hoped I'd play high school football because he'd played growing up, and he'd been the one who signed me up originally to keep me out of trouble. But I did not wish to get killed or simply ride the bench.

So, basketball became my focus. Still small, I'd developed my game to use my size as an advantage. Quick, with terrific dribbling and passing skills, I made myself into a great assist man. Realistic about my shooting ability, I found a joy in helping others score. I played unselfishly by necessity, which led my teammates to trust me. If they passed me the ball, they knew they'd get it back.

Despite my lack of height, I felt confident I'd make varsity as a freshman. That summer I'd played Summer League for Parkdale and had done well. At tryouts for the high school season, I moved the ball around, never dreaming to score, but relishing in making the older guys look good. I always have been the kind of guy who gets a high by making other people happy, and I think a large part of why I'm like that stems from knowing my own limitations, both in sports and in life. So, when I played football early on and only came in on special teams, I found solidarity with my teammates whenever one of them made a play or scored a touchdown. In basketball, because I was so short, all my shots could be blocked. That led me to understand the mechanics of the game. I saw the cuts before my teammates made them and realized how moving the ball around opened gaps in the defense I could exploit. Never a scorer, I always led on the court.

I made the junior varsity team.

At first, I felt disappointed at being cut from the varsity roster. However, I soon realized only one other freshman had made the JV team. Everyone else was a sophomore or junior, and I started at point guard. We had a decent season, and I started almost every game. The varsity team, meanwhile, stunk.

Parkdale differed from junior high in many ways. Larger, the school was also predominantly white, a change from my mainly Black neighborhood. At that time, I still felt uncertain about who I wanted to be. My long drives with Byrd continued. Irvin kept schooling me, but I also had to figure things out for myself. I enjoyed attention. I liked being a leader, but I had not learned how to garner positive attention and lead from a position of strength. I continued as I always had, acting like the class clown.

This led to consequences. Nearly once a week I ended up in Vice Principal McAlpine's office. A short, balding white guy and a strict stickler for the rules, he roamed the hallways looking for troublemakers. We developed a relationship, which straddled the divide between respect and hate. I believe he knew I was a decent kid, but he more than likely felt deeply frustrated and disappointed in how I acted. I chafed under his authority. He represented the opposite of everyone else in my life whom I respected.

Ken Freeman, who, prior to desegregation, had been our area's winningest basketball coach, served as another vice principal at the school. He posted up outside the building as the buses loaded and unloaded. With an eye for anything improper, Freeman could verbally cut down anyone who stepped out of line. He had one of the filthiest mouths I've ever heard. The way he verbally spit on kids would probably never stand today. But Freeman came from another age and experienced the loss of the Black middle class after desegregation. In hindsight, I suppose he'd be labeled a racist, as he favored Black students over white. Yet, nothing bothered him more than seeing Black kids making the same mistakes over and over again, or worse, not giving a damn.

"The Black man continues to fucking denigrate himself," he explained to me. "Hey! Asshole! No fucking play-fighting. What? Let me find out who your daddy is!" He yelled at two kids fooling around about twenty feet away. "See, Curtis. Those two dumbasses prove my point. They see me here, know I'm watching, but are too stupid not to piss me off."

I looked up at him. Tall, dark-skinned, and bald, Freeman radiated authority and intimidation. He took pride in knowing all of Parkdale's students and had taken a liking to me. I often found myself in conversation with him before school each morning. By the end of my freshman year, I may have had more in-depth conversations with Mr. Freeman than I'd had with my dad my entire young life. Although we spoke regularly, Freeman hadn't taken any special interest in me until one day early in the school year.

"And that's what pisses me off the most," Freeman finished.

Out of the corner of my eye, I saw McAlpine power walking toward us. McAlpine kind of strutted, a man always on a mission. I held my breath, hoping he wouldn't stop. He did.

"Ah, Mr. Freeman, I see you know Mr. Malone."

"Yes, sir. Seems like a good kid to me."

"Oh, perhaps you don't know him so well, then."

"What do you mean?"

"Mr. Malone makes weekly trips to my office. He likes the attention he gets from disrupting class, I think."

"Is that true, Curtis?"

Unsure whether he meant the weekly trips to McAlpine's office or that I enjoyed the attention (both were true), I simply looked at the ground.

"I think I'll help Mr. Malone out, Mr. McAlpine. From now on, every time he's sent to your office, send him down to me."

That pissed me off. I'd developed a good relationship with Freeman, but I knew how he treated kids who messed up. I didn't want his eye constantly on me.

"Now, a woman should be treated like a queen, Mr. Malone," Freeman preached. "They are not walking baby factories or meant to just please the male. The woman should be flattered, placed upon a pedestal, honored, cherished. Now, all these walking hormonal time bombs around here are humping with no knowledge of how to treat the girl. Watch him, right there," he pointed to an upperclassman walking with a girl. "Bet he doesn't get the door for her. Five bucks, bet?"

"Bet."

"Well, got dammit, fuck me twice. He actually held the door...." Freeman always acted surprised when wrong.

"Pay up," I said.

He placed a five-dollar bill in my hand. "Whatcha got for classes today?" he asked.

"Movie in social studies."

"Wanna pass?"

"Absolutely."

"Treat her good," he advised me as he wrote out a pass for me to miss my social studies class. I'd learned, since McAlpine ratted me out, that Freeman was tough but fair. I'd redoubled my efforts in class, making sure to behave as best I could. I did not wish to receive a verbal dressing-down by Freeman, nor did I want to disappoint him. If I did well, kept my grades up, and didn't cause problems, he'd reward me with passes out of class. Sometimes I would go to his office and chill; other times I'd just walk the hallways and avoid McAlpine. And sometimes I would meet a girl in some quiet, deserted stairwell....

I landed my first serious girlfriend, Darlene Hamilton, in ninth grade. She lived in the Village in The Woods apartments and attended DuVal High School. We met at one of our shows at the Glenarden Rec Center when I'd played for a go-go band called The Young Groovers. I saw her in the crowd and couldn't take my eyes off her. Loopy, who went to DuVal, had a huge crush on Darlene. At the show, I sent a few friends to hook me up, then talked to her after our set. The Young Groovers didn't last long, but Darlene and I would be together for the next twelve years.

However, since my girlfriend attended a different school, opportunities emerged for light-skinned, curly-haired Curtis to play the field at Parkdale. I was, after all, my father's son. Staying on Freeman's good side and getting those passes out of class really helped.

Every Friday I'd catch the bus or hop on the Metro to the 1320 and my grandma's place. Still the party building, the card games lasted all night. Most weekends my friends and I found the party. We'd catch the bus down to the Howard Theatre or walk to the Colony Theatre for a go-go. Heading back, we'd stop at Holly Farms on Georgia Avenue for potato wedges, the only thing we could afford. So, my freshman year passed by. Thanks to my fear of pissing Freeman off, I passed all my classes. I knew I'd play Summer League for Parkdale once school ended and would work my ass off to play varsity as a sophomore. I felt popular, had a smoking hot girlfriend, spent my weekends partying...what more could I need?

Maybe another old head to look out for me.

Twin

I first met Harold Jones at George and Ruby Rustin's house. The Rustins had three sons, all older than me: Peanut, Kevin, and Sweetpea. Peanut stayed in and out of jail, where he'd eventually die. Kevin and Sweetpea trained in boxing. All were decent guys who made sure my friends and I made it home from school without trouble when we were younger. Mr. Rustin, George, always stopped me in the street and shared some wisdom. They were all good people to me.

Harold Jones, whom we called Twin on account of his having a twin brother, wasn't known as a good person. At twenty-five, he'd just returned home from prison. Twin and Peanut grew up together as friends and the two were celebrating Twin's return when I happened to stop by.

"Yo, Li'l Curtis, meet my OG, Twin," Peanut said as soon as I walked in the door. OG meant "Original Gangsta," a designation we gave to good men who'd done prison bids or had killed someone.

"Wut up, little man?" Twin showed me some love and we started talking.

"Curtis is Irvin's li'l man," Peanut said.

"Yeah? I know Irvin. How is Slim?"

"He's good, doing well," I answered.

"He still getting money?"

"The man doing his thing, ain't he, Shawty?" Peanut added.

"He looks out for sure," I said.

Some of the older folks in the neighborhood raised their eyebrows when I began spending time with Twin. They considered him a bad influence on an otherwise good kid. I showed some promise, both in school and on the basketball court. I had good manners and an easygoing, gentle manner—at least publicly. They thought I might escape the slow decay that took over Palmer Park in the '80s. I was fifteen. At twenty-five, Twin represented everything wrong with our community.

But as I got to know him better, I saw a much different person. Twin epitomized a drug dealer. But he also worked hard, valued honesty and loyalty, and took care of those he liked. He had plans, which he explained to me the first time I met him.

"I'm gonna start a moving company. Got a truck. Know a guy from jail whose uncle can get me work."

"Moving what?"

"Anything. Houses, furniture…shit, my man's uncle got some pull at the Pentagon."

"The Pentagon?" I asked.

"They move stuff all the time."

As I began tenth grade, I turned my attention back to basketball. Freeman stopped me on the first day of school.

"You work your ass off this summer?"

I hadn't, not really, but didn't think admitting it would be a good idea.

"Sure did. I'm going to make varsity this year."

"With the lack of depth, they're going to need whoever they can get."

"I hope Coach Davis does a better job," I added, but Freeman ignored me. He wouldn't bad-mouth the coach, even to me.

"Listen, Curtis, there's no shortcuts in life. If you put in 40 percent, you'll get 40 percent back. You want to play varsity? Then put the work in so when tryouts come around, you'll be ready."

Sound advice, but at fifteen difficult to follow through on. I didn't see a clear path to my future. It seemed I'd be the first awake on my block and the last asleep. I wanted to be a basketball player, around the ballers, a ladies' man and go to any go-go any night of the week. Go-gos in the city were often hard to get to unless I jumped into a stolen car—hardly anyone owned their own—but I never would do it. Irvin always told me that if I broke the law, make sure the crime was worth it. I couldn't justify going to jail just to get to a go-go.

So, I filed Freeman's admonition into the back of my brain, where I kept all the other teenage junk. I did train for the season. I practiced every day after school at the Palmer Park Rec and outdoor courts and made sure I stayed in shape. Given how many guys graduated the year before, I figured Coach Davis already knew who'd be on the team.

I made varsity and thought we had a good squad.

It ended up being the worst season I ever had, for any sport, in my entire life, including as a coach myself.

We went 0-22. Coach Davis constantly changed the lineup, hoping to find some combination that worked, but it prevented us from developing any chemistry. In my opinion, he had no idea how to coach.

"I remember when my sister's boyfriend played," I bitched to Freeman. "His father used to curse Coach Davis out back then, too."

"You gotta stay focused. You're dwelling on the negative. It's a young team."

"He's awful. We've won more fights this year than games!"

"Well, that's gotta change."

I hadn't exaggerated. Our frustration would boil over, and by the end of the game, fists flew. I complained, but nothing improved. In the last game of the season, a road game against Friendly High School, we competed for three quarters, but lost. Exiting the gym to load onto the bus, we heard some of their fans talking shit.

"Parkdale pussies."

"Our JV team would beat them."

"Play like a bunch of bitches."

Coach Davis loaded us onto the bus, demanding no one get off as he went to double-check our locker room.

"Yo, we should show these motherfuckers who they're fucking with," one of my teammates shouted.

"You wanna hit the back door?" I asked.

"I'm in," another replied.

"If you do it, Curtis, we're right behind you."

"Alright, let's whip these niggas' asses for running their mouths," I said as I popped the emergency door at the rear of the bus. We swarmed out like a bunch of bees. They had no chance. We were on their asses like flies on shit. It turned into an ass-whipping, which reminded me of Stickman's work on the Glenarden boys. The Friendly High School principal tried to break it up. One moment I saw him pulling two guys off one another; the next he disappeared, knocked down and swallowed up by the melee.

Two weeks later a Prince George County sheriff knocked on our door. My dad answered.

"Are you the parent or guardian of Herman Curtis Malone, Junior?"

"Yes?" my dad answered.

"You've officially been served." The sheriff handed my father an envelope and walked away.

"What the hell is this?" my dad asked me. I just shrugged. I honestly didn't know. "It's a subpoena to show up to court!" He sat down in a kitchen chair, staring at the paper, looking pissed.

I got off the sofa and read over his shoulder. Evidently, the principal at Friendly had pressed charges. The subpoena listed all of our names and ordered us to appear in court the following week.

At the hearing, the principal sat in the witness stand and pointed to our team manager, Kevin Keys, as the one who'd hit and kicked him. All of us were warned about our behavior, but the police arrested Kevin and charged him with first-degree assault.

With basketball season over, I only had to work hard enough in school to pass my classes. My approach to school: just do enough to get by, free up time to enjoy myself. More and more often, Twin and I spent time together.

"Twin, can I get fifty bucks?" I asked.

"What you need fifty for?" he asked, already reaching into his pocket.

"Gotta hit up the go-go this weekend." I stared at the cash, about five hundred in his hand. "Actually, a hundred would be better."

"Nah, li'l homie. In this life you only get what you ask for. Shoulda asked for a hundred the first time." He handed me two twenties and a ten. "You wanna catch a fight next weekend?"

"Skinny fightin'?" Twin managed a pro fighter named Skinny.

"He's fighting some dude from Dover. Fight's over in Crystal City."

"Can we go to Cavalier's first?" Cavalier's was a clothing store at the Landover Mall that carried the silk shirts that all the old heads rocked.

"Of course, I want my li'l partner representing." Twin would take me shopping before we'd go to the fight, which took place at a hotel. I'd buy some slacks and a silk shirt, and new shoes at Hahn's. Twin wore a fly suit and always looked slick. We'd go to Club Utopia after the fight. I could never have gotten in, at fifteen, but Twin would bribe the doorman.

"I'm definitely in," I said. I wouldn't miss one of Skinny's fights since Twin would have me looking sharp.

"I'll pick you up." Back then Twin drove a Cressida. We often drove around to his various job sites. He started his moving company, but I knew he got money on the side. He dealt coke, PCP, and weed, but I never witnessed it directly, not back then. Twin often tested me. He'd leave me alone with his piles of cash. I probably could have taken a few bucks without him really knowing, but I truly respected him and valued his friendship. Twin, even more than Byrd or Irvin, made me feel like an equal. I wouldn't have violated his trust for anything.

"I don't like thieves or liars," Twin explained to me one day as we drove to DC. His main man Rocky rode shotgun while I sat in the back. "If you can't trust a guy, you can't ride with him. Right, Rocky?"

"You know it."

All my old heads I knew growing up followed the same code: They considered a thief to be a piece of shit, and honesty meant everything. Byrd didn't like addicts who let their addiction take them down and made them lose everything. I suspected Twin got high, though he never used in front of me.

We often drove to a spot up near North Capital and New York Avenue. Twin and Rocky would hop out and walk a couple blocks away while I waited in the car. I found out later they went to Hanover Place, one of the biggest cocaine strips in DC. Some days we made the same trip seven or eight times. I might have been young, but not so naive that I couldn't figure out what went on.

I internalized these lessons from my three old heads until each became a rule of life. While I watched, silently learning, I saw real players playing the game. Byrd, Irvin and Twin were some of the best mentors I could've had.

By the end of my tenth-grade year, the members of the varsity basketball team heard Coach Davis would not return. I was one happy guy since I thought we could have won some close games had Davis made better decisions. Of course, we all wondered who would replace him. Freeman broke the news.

"The Colonel," he announced.

"The Colonel? You mean the ROTC teacher?"

"Yep. Colonel Thompson."

"Man, no more behind-the-back passes or dunks off the backboard."

"Why you think that?" Freeman asked.

"He seems so…strict. Or, square?"

"Ask me who the assistant coach's gonna be?"

"Alright, who?"

"You're looking at him."

"What! For real? You're coaching?!" This was great news. Freeman knew the game better than anyone.

"Colonel asked, and when a high-ranking military officer asks you to serve, you gotta say yes. So, you better work your ass off this summer, Malone. Don't think we won't cut you."

I ended up failing my tenth grade English class taught by Ms. Markie. In order to remain academically eligible, I'd have to take it over in summer school. Other than that inconvenience, I planned to attend Five-Star Basketball Camp in Pennsylvania and Blue-Chip/Cage Scope Basketball Camp in Kentucky that summer. But I always thought adult opponents were my best teachers. We called Adult Night at the Palmer Park Rec Center *good bump*. I'd go to different recs on different nights: Peppermill, Columbia Park, Glenarden, Seat Pleasant. Plus, I'd jump into pickup games at outdoor courts wherever I could find that *good bump*.

The old-timers taught me the game's fundamentals: passing, ball handling, movement off the ball. Spread the floor and make cuts into the open lanes. Their approach developed my philosophy, which I in turn drilled into my players years later. Because I lacked height, I developed a basketball IQ, which improved my teammates. In today's game the emphasis often falls on dunks or threes. Golden State brought fast, beautiful ball movement back in vogue, yet their "shoot from anywhere" style breaks with the fundamentals I love. Sacrificing defense in order to just outscore the other team eliminates 50 percent of basketball's beauty. Though basketball has always showcased individual talent, modern teams obsess over a franchise player, rather than building a team organically.

In addition to playing in adult leagues and attending camps, I also tried out for my first AAU team that summer. My friends Mike Sumner and Steve Hood encouraged me to join them at tryouts for the Prince George All-Stars. I'd known Steve for years and played intramural basketball with him in junior high. Steve stood at an awkward six-foot-five. Back at the end of eighth grade he tried to get me to go to DeMatha High School, a national basketball powerhouse. But DeMatha, a private Catholic high school, wasn't coed and its whole vibe turned me off.

I went to the tryouts, and as soon as I walked into the gym, I knew I'd made a mistake. It appeared the PG All-Stars would be filled with Catholic school players. I already resented the buddy system among private school guys who acted superior to us public school kids. The situation only got worse when I met the coach, Mr. Holmes. His son Rodney played on the team and Mrs. Holmes was the team mom.

"I don't think I'll come back tomorrow," I told Steve and Mike after the first night of tryouts.

"What are you talking about?" Steve asked.

"I don't have a chance of making this team. Y'all are big; I'm five-seven! Plus, you know one another from fucking DeMatha and the private schools."

"Man, you know your game's strong," Mike said.

"Yeah. I got some skill. But you know Holmes's got Rodney on the team and his little butt-boyfriend Kevin will make it too.

That's two roster spots gone." To be fair, both Rodney Holmes and his best friend, Kevin White, went on to play Division I ball. But it felt like Mr. Holmes started an AAU team so his son would have a team. Over the years I've seen so many parent-coaches hurt player development in order to cater to their kids. I made a rule with DC Assault: No parent-coaches. Too many conflicts.

"Just stick it out, man."

"We'll see, Steve."

"We want you on the team," Mike added. Both he and Steve knew my game. As a pass-first point guard, both would benefit from my unselfish style of play. I also know they genuinely liked me and wanted me on the team.

I went to all three tryout nights, but my prediction came true. I got cut, which really hurt since I'd not been cut since my freshman year at Parkdale. Yet, I also realized the teams I'd face next season would put plenty of big, athletic players on the court. To have a winning season, I'd need to step up my game. Though I ultimately felt the Catholic buddy system hurt me more than my lack of height or skill, I tried to use the feeling of getting cut to redouble my training efforts that summer.

My first AAU experience left a lasting impression More of one than I realized at the time. When I started DC Assault, I'd remember the pampered, smug private school players who came to that PG All-Stars tryout already knowing they had a leg up. When it came to finding top players for our Assault teams, I never just looked to the private schools but hung out at the street courts in the underprivileged neighborhoods.

Ken Freeman's Guide to Success, Part 2

Freeman and I stood outside Parkdale on the first day of my junior year. I scoped out the new freshmen and transfer students. One freshman, Henry Hall, knew me from Columbia Park Rec, where we played pickup together. He had tremendous talent. After he stopped and introduced himself to Freeman, I talked him up.

"Henry should make varsity," I said.

"We'll see. He's fucking big for a freshman."

"His game is the truth. Great shooter."

"No one's spot is a sure thing this season. Gotta motivate your punk asses, maybe win a fucking game."

As we spoke I saw my English teacher, Ms. Markie, walking towards us, carrying a box full of papers.

"Well, hello there, Ms. Markie," Freeman said. She stopped to talk. I tried to disappear but couldn't pull it off.

"Do you know Mr. Malone?" Freeman asked.

"Yes, Mr. Freeman. Curtis took my class last year."

"How'd he do?"

"Not so good, had to fail him," she replied.

"Well, I hope you know, Ms. Markie, that Mr. Malone went to summer school and passed." Freeman had already known about the damn class.

I became extremely nervous. This light bullshit between the two of them couldn't lead to anything good.

"Did he now? Well, I hope he cut out some of his silly antics in order to pass."

"Guess what, Ms. Markie?" Freeman continued.

"Oh, I don't like guessing games. Just tell me."

"Mr. Malone is gonna sign up for another class with you this year!"

I almost died. Ms. Markie, a mean, old-school teacher, tolerated no bullshit. One of the best parts of my junior year would be avoiding her. I trusted Freeman, but this felt like being thrown to the wolves.

"That should be interesting, Mr. Freeman. I look forward to it."

"One last thing, Ms. Markie: That box looks heavy. You carry it into the building every day?"

"Yes, it's all my papers."

"Well, starting today, Mr. Malone will carry that box from your car to your class. Every morning." Freeman broke into a wide grin, white teeth gleaming. He put his arm around my shoulder.

"You don't mind helping, right, Curtis?"

Of course, I did! What a way to start my junior year. But as Freeman squeezed my shoulder, only one answer was possible.

"Of course not. Anything to help."

"Thank you, Curtis," Ms. Markie replied as she handed me the box. "And thanks, Ken."

The next morning, I confronted him. "She's one of the toughest, meanest bitches in this school, and you're making me take one of her classes?!"

"Gonna check with your guidance counselor to make sure you signed up."

"You realize she could fail me just out of spite. I might have to go to summer school all over again!"

"I was under the impression she failed you last year because you didn't do the work and acted like a fucking fool."

"You have any idea how boring her class is? And now I'm lugging her heavy-ass box around."

"Listen here, Curtis. It's time you decide who you're gonna be. You like being a leader, I can tell. You get attention and guys look up to you. Well, there's two ways to lead: You can act a fool and get a laugh and people will like you 'cause they can laugh at you, or you can actually be a leader, earn their fucking respect, and take charge. You hearing me?"

"Yes…."

"Well, last year, from what I've learned, you decided to be a class clown and disrupt her class, didn't do the work, and ended up failing her class. This year you'll be a leader and pass the class. And you'll carry that damn box." He pointed out to the road where Ms. Markie had just gotten out of her car. "Go," he told me.

So, I did. That day and every morning for half the year I worked on my leadership by carrying that box. Guys laughed at me. Girls giggled and whispered, "teacher's pet" behind my back. Several crude jokes about Curtis Malone getting into Ms. Markie's box were scribbled on the bathroom stalls. But I persevered, and over time her rough facade softened a bit. Some mornings I was greeted with a smile; others she brought me coffee. She heard the whispers and how I got teased. Another student might have stopped showing up each morning, but I respected Freeman—feared him a little, too—and did my duty.

I also enrolled in her English class. I still struggled with the material. My older sister Brenda, who always acted like a mother and checked over my homework (and made me actually do it), had moved out the year before. So, I had little to no supervision at home. My parents never questioned me about school unless I got into trouble and the school contacted them. So, it became easy for me to avoid doing homework.

But the Curtis Malone who attended Ms. Markie's class acted much differently the second time around. My behavior improved, though I certainly didn't transform into a model student. I think my attitude—in addition to all those mornings carrying that damn box—improved enough to help Ms. Markie overlook incorrect answers or unfinished homework. I passed.

On the final day of class that year she pulled me aside, thanked me for my help, and offered one word of advice.

"Succeed."

While my relationship with Ms. Markie raged, more important things also occurred: basketball. We quickly realized that Colonel Thompson had no coaching experience and most of us believed he had never played basketball, either. Luckily, Freeman handled the Xs and Os. The season felt full of potential, especially when the varsity roster went up and I saw Henry Hall's name on the list. As we all congratulated ourselves, I saw Henry talking to the Colonel and Freeman. The three parted ways and Freeman walked up to me.

"Your superstar friend quit."

"He what?"

"Would rather play JV. Wants more playing time."

"He what?!" I asked again, not sure I heard right.

"He asked us if we thought he'd start. I told him he'd probably come off the bench, but the tougher competition would be good for him."

"So, he wants to play JV?"

"Yep. Asshole. A freshman gets an offer to play varsity and says no. What the fuck is this generation coming to?"

I felt equally surprised. Henry played JV and averaged fifty points a game. When the JV season ended a few weeks prior to our own, he got moved up and contributed about thirty points a game. We ended up winning fourteen games. A huge turnaround from our 0-22 season. Henry was such a special player I felt we could have done better and made the playoffs had he played all season on varsity, but his skill gave me huge hopes for my senior year.

After the season, Freeman called me into his office.

"Shut the door, Curtis," he told me. I wasn't sure what to expect.

"Senior year is coming up."

"Yep. I think we're gonna be strong with Henry next season."

"Whatcha gonna do after high school?"

I hesitated. Honestly, I had no idea. "Um, haven't really thought about it."

"It's time to start. Now, let's be honest. Even if you grow a few more inches, top out at five-nine or -ten, D-Is are probably not gonna bite. But your game is strong. And you really emerged as a leader this year. You thinking about college?"

No. I hadn't at all. I didn't know any college grads and my parents barely mentioned it. Freeman could tell by the look on my face that I hadn't.

"Well, you should be. I got some contacts at Division II schools who'd be interested. If you actually can focus on school now that the season's over, and if you keep working hard on your game, we might be able to land you a scholarship. Get you out of Palmer Park."

"You really believe that, or you just blowing smoke?"

"You think I'd lie? I'm serious, but you need to put both school and improving your game first. All the other bullshit comes second."

He spoke true. During basketball season, I focused on my schoolwork more, making sure I stayed eligible to play. The strategy my father had implemented, back when he signed me up for football as an incentive to behave in school, held. After basketball ended, I stopped caring as much. Now Freeman told me I'd have a new reason to stay focused and do well: college. The idea appealed to me.

I especially felt obligated to try because all my other mentors—Byrd, Irvin, and Twin—all told me to get out of Palmer Park and not repeat their mistakes. Irvin, who had received a college football scholarship, really pushed me to excel at basketball as a way of improving my entire situation. So, the idea Freeman proposed, novel to me, aligned itself with the advice I'd been hearing for a few years. Yet, until that conversation with Freeman, I'd never really believed the chance truly existed.

"You think my game's strong enough?"

"You're a phenomenal ball handler. Great vision and a huge basketball IQ. That's what separates really good high school players from college players. Physical skill tops out, but if your basketball intelligence continues to grow, you'll continue to improve players. College coaches fall in love with high IQ players."

"So don't fail any classes, get better on the court." I trailed off.

"You got it. Now get the hell out of my office and handle your business."

"Man, I don't know how I'm gonna improve if I can't get to camps," I complained to Twin and Irvin.

"What camp?" Irvin asked.

"Five-Star Basketball Camp. One of the best around. But my folks been complaining about money."

"You really think this one camp make that much difference?" asked Twin.

"Gotta play against top players to improve, right, Twin? I mean, I think I got game, but college would be a whole other level."

"So, you gonna play college now?"

"Freeman thinks I could. I've kept my grades up. Now I just need to continue to work on my game this summer."

"College women, man, best time of my life. It's something you really wanna do?" Irvin pressed.

"I think so…I mean, no one else has gone past high school in my family. If basketball can get me out of Palmer Park, I don't know, it feels like something someone else would get to do, not me."

"But?"

"But Freeman's really motivating me to try. My folks don't know shit about going to school. I doubt they could afford it without a basketball scholarship. I haven't even bothered to tell them Freeman suggested it."

"How much is the camp?" Twin asked.

The sun scorched down on us, one of those hot, early June days, the weather awkward for being too warm, too soon. Twin, Irvin, and I leaned against Twin's car; Rocky sat in the passenger seat, listening to Chuck Brown.

"About four hundred."

"That's it? You sweating four hundred, Shawty?"

"Parents can't afford it."

Twin took out a wad of cash and began counting off bills. "Here, give this to them. Make sure you're signed up."

"You know I appreciate this, right?" I said.

"And I know how many times you could've disrespected me by taking cash when I wasn't around. You never dishonored our friendship. You my little brother. If four hundred can help make something of you, then I got you."

Twin's generosity and loyalty became the standard I'd live the rest of my life by. Loyalty among friends, looking out for them and for younger guys who just needed advice and help, served as guiding principles for me.

I attended the camp that summer, which I felt really helped my game, and when I returned to Parkdale in the fall, Freeman and the Colonel announced I'd be senior captain. I ran preseason practices during open gym after school and evaluated who I thought should make the team. I knew we would be much better than the previous year, mostly because of Henry Hall and a fellow senior, Eric Sanders, who played center.

The Colonel allowed Freeman to run the team, even though he held the title of head coach. We didn't run many set plays on offense—our style was more anything goes—but Freeman sure knew how to curse us out if we fucked up. A few weeks into the season, we ranked among the top in the county. I began to see myself graduating Parkdale, leaving Palmer Park, and playing Division II ball. The thought excited me. I always saw myself as different, someone set apart. Maybe that was arrogance, but the men I looked up to carried themselves with a level of class I admired and tried to emulate. My neighbors, my old heads, and hustlers all told me of my potential. I was the good kid who had a chance, they said. By the midpoint of my senior season, I believed them.

Then everything fucked up.

My bad luck began at practice. Eric Sanders threw a long outlet pass off a rebound. The pass went over my head, and I tried to chase it down. I glanced up as I neared the opposite baseline and saw our team managers sitting under the window to the coach's office. My momentum carried me out of bounds, and, to avoid a collision, I leaped over them, trying to kick off the wall and miss the window.

Unfortunately, I went feet first through the glass, which shattered. The glass had wire mesh within it, which caused more damage.

I found myself in the coach's office with one leg up on the desk. I had just hobbled to my feet when Freeman and the Colonel rushed over. Freeman bent down and placed my arm over his shoulders, practically pulling me out of the office. I didn't feel much pain until I caught a glimpse of the facial expressions of our managers and my teammates. Then my left leg started screaming.

"Don't look, Curtis," Freeman warned as I started to glance at my leg. "Let's just sit you down on the bench here."

I could feel the blood running down, soaking through my sock. The Colonel started taking his belt off, while at the same time, I began to feel cold all over.

"Wrap this around his knee, Ken, try to stop the bleeding. You boys head to the locker room," he told everyone else.

"Wow, Ken, I hope he didn't nick an artery. Here, let me do this. Go call an ambulance." The Colonel tightened the belt and held a shirt to my lower thigh and knee. I noticed my blood on Freeman's hands as he rushed back into the office.

Freeman followed the ambulance to the hospital and called my parents. He also sat with me as a doctor put sixty-five stitches into my leg.

"What about colleges?" I asked as the doctor stitched me up. I feared my leg wouldn't be the same and I'd lose any chance of getting a scholarship.

"Doc here said nothing too important got cut. Just some meat that needs mending. Don't worry about that right now."

"How the hell I end up in the office?"

"You jumped over the managers. Practically karate-kicked the damn office window. Better your leg than your face."

My parents arrived and Freeman explained what happened to my dad.

"Why the fuck is there a window just a few feet from the baseline?" my dad asked.

"I don't know, Herman. Seems stupid now that something like this happened."

"Shouldn't it have been plexiglass or safety glass?" he asked.

Freeman just held his hands up, helpless.

My prognosis turned out better than I feared. I ended up missing nine games, just over eight weeks, but made it back before the season ended. I'd felt miserable letting my team down. While I recovered, I spent time at the rec center. I was talking to my man named Curtis Richardson who worked there. He was older and taller, so we called him Big Curtis while I answered to Li'l Curtis. Big Curtis and his brother, Vick, were big-time gamblers and also in the drug game. The two of us began to get even closer over my weeks of recovery.

"You should hire a lawyer," he told me.

"What for?"

"Yo, your leg fucked up. Can't play. Maybe can't get a scholarship. Who puts a fucking glass window next to a basketball court? The school should pay. Plus, your parents got bills now, right?"

"Well, yeah...."

"Way I figure, if you got compensatory damages for those medical bills, plus all the emotional stress and turmoil, et cetera, et cetera...."

"You're right. I should sue the fuck out of them."

"I got a good lawyer. He's helped me and my bro outta some shit. Name's John C. Williams. You should tell your parents to call him."

I told my parents, who, coincidentally, knew John C. Williams. He told us the school should have placed safety glass in the window and advised us to sue for damages. We filed a suit in early 1986.

Meanwhile, a few Division II schools had called Freeman, inquiring about me. Coach Ford from Hampton University in Virginia showed strong interest before my injury. I just needed to get back on the court.

I fought hard and followed my doctor's orders and soon enough returned. I'd missed nine games but the team had played strong, led by Sanders and Henry Hall, who may have been the best sophomore in the area. He led the team in scoring even though he didn't start. When I returned, I regained my place as the starting point guard. Towards the end of the season, I had twenty-five assists in a double-overtime loss against Crossland High School.

After away games, Freeman drove me home. My dad, always a jokester, got along with Freeman real well. He found out Freeman loved vodka and ginger ale, so soon he started having Smirnoff and a lime waiting. For Freeman, I think my dad represented something he felt he'd lost: an honest, working Black man who tried his hardest to provide. Freeman knew making money was tough for our community, especially as the Black middle and professional classes began to shrink and then flee the city. He gloried in the days when segregation provided an opportunity for Blacks to support Blacks within our own neighborhoods. He felt we had turned on one another, fighting for whatever scraps were left over, selling drugs in search of material gain instead of learning the values his generation held.

So, a certain kinship existed. My dad knew Freeman truly cared about me, proven by the visits a number of college coaches made to my house. Freeman, my parents, and I would sit with coaches from Belmont Abby, Campbell, and others as they pitched their schools and their programs.

Coach Ford at Hampton University pursued me aggressively for a time, including a recruiting visit. But Freeman, who'd been designated my unofficial college coordinator, kept putting him off.

"What's wrong with Hampton?" I asked him.

"Trying for something better," he answered.

"You're the one who told me I'm a D-II guy. I don't get it," I said exasperated.

"It's complicated."

"Coach Ford told us he had scholarship money for me months ago. You know my parents can't afford school without a scholarship!" I felt pretty anxious. Ford had given his pitch, but Freeman's attitude seemed dismissive of Hampton. I worried Ford would lose interest and my opportunity would pass.

"I have a plan," Freeman replied; then, seeing my look, continued. "Eric is getting pretty strong interest from some big schools." He meant our center, Eric Sanders. "I'm trying to package the two of you."

"What does that mean?"

"Trying to send you both to where Eric ends up."

"Wait, like, if you want Sanders you gotta take Malone?"

"That's how this shit works, Curtis. You gotta make the best fucking deal you can. Sanders is an asset to us. If I can get you a scholarship to a D-I school on his back, then I've just helped you tremendously."

"And if you can't?"

"We'll worry about that if it happens."

For the first time in a decade, the Parkdale High School boys' varsity basketball team headed to the playoffs. We faced Kennedy High from Montgomery County. They had a kid named Curtis Pride who was death to opposing teams, and we had no answer for him. My dad came to the game—his first and only time watching me play high school ball. He paced the sideline yelling at the refs and our players whenever we made a poor play. He became so loud and obnoxious, the refs stopped the game, threatened us with a technical foul, and refused to restart the game until my dad left the gym. I was so embarrassed. The Montgomery County Police Department ended up escorting him out. Curtis Pride schooled us that night. He went on to play basketball and baseball at William & Mary, then on to a career in Major League Baseball.

Though we lost in the playoff game, I felt proud about the team's turnaround and my part in it. I played in the Prince George County All-Star game and continued training in preparation for college.

Once the season ended, I focused on passing my classes and taking the SATs. I took the test a couple times, and I'm not too proud to admit they weren't the easiest tests I'd ever taken. My scores were too low to be NCAA eligible, so I knew I'd have to take some college prep classes to gain eligibility. If I got an offer, of course.

I took my longtime girlfriend, Darlene, to the senior prom and prepared to graduate. Time was running out on my college hopes.

"Eric declared today, Curtis," Freeman said.

"I heard. Virginia Tech, huh?"

"Yeah. Good for him. The Hokies get a 6'9" center."

"They don't need a five-nine point guard, do they?"

Freeman looked wistful. "They landed Bimbo Coles." Bimbo was drafted by the Miami Heat and went on to play in the NBA for over ten years, but at that point I still felt jaded. "I'm gonna contact some of the other schools who came to visit. I'll figure something out."

"I hope so."

I honestly did not know what to think. I trusted Freeman. I even loved Freeman a bit. I knew he wanted the best for me. But if he hadn't tried to get fancy and bundle a Sanders-Malone deal, like he was some general manager trading a top prospect and dead weight, I could've committed to Hampton University before my season ended. Now, with just weeks left until graduation, I felt my chances at college slipping away.

"Hey, whose car is that?"

Twin and I were walking down Muncy Road, and a car sat in front of the house.

"Huh? Oh, Mr. Freeman's. Come on. Let's see what's up."

Twin and I walked in to find my mom, dad, and Freeman in the living room.

"What's going on?" I asked.

"Hey, Harold," my mom said, smiling at Twin. "Ken called and asked to meet us. Said he had big news." I could tell she felt excited. If Freeman had news, it could only mean one of the schools he'd talked to wanted me to play.

"Mr. Freeman, this is Twin," I said, trying to be polite. Freeman gave Twin an odd look and only nodded. Twin looked uncomfortable, but before I could figure out why, Freeman spoke up.

"Well, I have good news and bad news."

We all sat silent, expectant. Freeman, realizing no one else would speak, finally began.

"Well, good news first. Talked to Coach Ford at Hampton and he'd love to see you there."

My mom clapped her hands together in excitement. I felt excited, too. Out of all the schools who'd expressed interest I liked Hampton the best.

"But there's bad news. He doesn't have any scholarships left."

An audible silence descended upon us. Everyone in the room knew my chances of going to college depended largely on getting a scholarship.

"So…" I finally said.

"He suggests you come down, walk on, and next year he'll have scholarship money available. He'll even arrange for you to live in the dorms with other players on the team."

"Wait," my mother said. "What does 'walk on' mean?"

"Means I need to try out," I answered.

"But the coach made it very clear he wants Curtis on the team," added Freeman.

"Yeah, but the money." I felt pretty let down and pissed. I blamed Freeman for playing too many games, causing me to lose the scholarship money.

"We'll make it work, Curtis," my mother suddenly said. "I don't care about the cost. We'll get some financial aid, and your father and I—" here she gave my dad a fierce look—"will figure something out. You're going to college. "

"Mom, I—"

"Don't say another word. You're gonna get out of Palmer Park and get a college education." She gave Twin a defiant look this time.

"Then I'll call Ford, tell him you're in," Freeman said.

"Thanks, Ken." My mother stood up and gave him a brief hug.

I realized, at that moment, just how important college was to her. My acceptance represented an achievement not just for myself, but for our family.

I shook Freeman's hand as he reminded me to enroll in the pre-college courses I had to pass. He left and it suddenly felt awkward being there with my parents.

"Come on, college boy, let's go," Twin suggested. We left and walked the neighborhood, Twin stopping everyone we knew to tell them the good news.

The next morning at school, Freeman stood practically in front of the bus. I figured he'd spoken to Coach Ford and had more news.

"Why in the holy hell are you hanging out with Harold Jones?" he began right away.

"You know him? He's an OG from the neighborhood that looks out for me."

Freeman brought his right hand to his face, rubbing his chin. He actually began to pace.

"You need to watch your fucking company. You're going to let Mr. Jones fuck your life up."

His tone caught me off guard. He was really pissed. "Why do you say that? He's not a bad guy."

"Those twins were some of the worst kids I've ever had to deal with in over thirty years working in this school system. They're no good. Nothing worthwhile will ever come from them."

I should have known Freeman knew Twin and his brother, Harry. But his attitude pissed me off. Twin had been nothing but good to me. I counted him among my closest friends. Freeman served as a mentor, a role model, but he was closer to sixty years old than seventeen. He might have cared for me like I was his son, but Twin was my brother.

"This is a moment of choosing, Curtis. You're either going to get the hell out and make something of yourself, or you're gonna fuck up and turn out like those brothers and the rest of those nothing-ass hoodlums out of Palmer Park. This is your opportunity. You've worked hard and you deserve it. Don't fuck it up."

"I'm going to Hampton, aren't I?" I fired back.

"Yeah, you're going."

And right then I realized something: I really was going to college. I thought about Byrd and Irvin and Twin. I thought of all the other hustlers and good men in my neighborhood. Then I thought about Freeman and my mom. My dad fell in there, too. I thought about all the lessons and guidance each of the people in my life had provided. What did it all mean? I faced that metaphorical fork in the road of my life. A choice of consequence. Do I go left or right? I made my decision.

And I hoped I didn't fuck up.

Part 2

Ballin'

1986–1991

Residential Life

Where I'm from, surviving just means living. Pensions, 401Ks, and golden parachutes don't exist in the hood. You are what you make yourself. You become the person you project onto the world. I was going to be someone. Freeman told me there were no shortcuts in life, that a shortcut would always catch up to you. Maybe. But there was also a fucking lot of money to be made, and I was going to make it.

* * *

Hampton University, 140 years old, sits on 314 beautiful acres in Hampton, Virginia. The campus overlooks Hampton Roads Harbor. Founded by the American Missionary Association to teach freed slaves, this historical Black college now annually matriculates more than four thousand students and boasts an endowment of over $260 million.

Until I arrived at Hampton, I'd only ever traveled out of Maryland to attend a few basketball camps and to Atlanta to my mom's church convention. I never spent significant time away from home. I'd met a few people during the prep classes I took over the summer, and I knew I could make friends easily. However, the campus, so different than my old neighborhood, with its mature, academically-focused students, felt like a whole new world. As my mother and I walked the grounds, I distinctly missed my friends back home.

"I'm proud of you, Curtis," my mother said as we waited in line outside the dorm Freeman told me I'd live in. All around us parents helped unload carloads of clothing, bedding, futons, TVs, and stereos. Voices with the twang of the Deep South mingled with New Yorkers' heavy accents. Student volunteers helped carry luggage into the building. Eric B. & Rakim blared out from a window. Black faces surrounded us, and I felt overcome with sudden pride that I was attending the alma mater of Booker T. Washington.

We finally got to the table set up near the entrance, where a brown-skinned upperclassman with a huge afro asked my name.

"Malone, Herman," I told her.

She flipped through a list a few times, then moved her finger down a long column of names. "That's M-A, right?"

"Yeah."

"Hmmm. You sure you're assigned to this dorm?"

My stomach lurched. "What is going on?" my mom asked from behind me. I waved her off.

"I'm supposed to play basketball," I explained. The day was pleasant but sweat trickled down my back. "Coach Ford told me I'd be with some of the other guys on the team. In the dorm," I added.

"Well, I know a few players here, but you're not on the list. Hold on." She called an older woman over and quietly explained the situation. The new woman, given how nicely she dressed, obviously worked for the school.

"Have you seen the registrar yet?" she asked.

"Yes, and I've already gotten my schedule for classes, too."

"Hmmm." She double-checked the list then looked up, giving us a professional smile that screamed, *Don't blame me, but....*

"I'm sorry. You don't appear on the list. You'll need to go to Residential Life and get this sorted out." She handed me a printed map of the campus and circled a building.

"Sorry."

So, Mom and I walked back through campus to the residential life department, where a dark-skinned woman with gray hair, tortoiseshell glasses, and a puckered mouth explained we'd never sent in my dorm deposit and therefore had not secured a place to live on campus, and *unfortunately, young man, no dorms were available, but if you wished, I could put your name on a waiting list...if something came available...these things happen, people drop out, so sorry and have a wonderful year...*

"But the basketball coach told my high school coach he'd take care of the dorm..." I tried to explain.

"Well, we certainly have nothing here to that affect. I suppose one positive is you won't have to pay dorm fees."

"So, what is my son supposed to do?" my mom asked.

The old prune pointed to a bulletin board where apartment listings, layered atop one another, competed for space. "There's also a Motel Six in Hampton Roads."

My mom and I stood outside Residential Life looking dumbfounded. We felt in over our heads. My mom had done her best with applications, FAFSA forms, and all the paperwork, but Freeman had told us Coach Ford had assured him the living arrangements were set.

As we contemplated what to do, George Hughes and Skip Walker, two friends I'd met in summer school, walked over.

"Curtis!" Skip yelled.

"Yo, bro, you got yourself settled in?" George asked. His head, covered in nappy hair, looked too big for his body. He came from North Carolina and spoke with a thick accent.

Skip was a light-skinned pretty boy who thought he was the coolest cat on Earth.

I introduced them to my mother, then explained the situation.

"Hey, why not crash with me in the dorm?" George suggested.

Skip said, "My cousin Eric and I are waiting to move into an apartment off campus. You can move in with me and him once we get the keys."

I looked at my mother, who shrugged. It seemed the only option. "If you guys don't mind. It shouldn't be too long. I put my name on a waiting list." The last thing I wanted to do was go back to Palmer Park and face the hood. I would've been embarrassed.

Thanks to George, Eric Cooper, and Skip, I had a place to stay. We took some of my stuff to George's dorm, and Skip took the rest to his aunt's house in Hampton until the apartment was ready.

Attending Hampton opened my eyes and made me realize people could succeed without selling drugs. I met so many new brothers and sisters from all walks of life, expanding my vision of what life could be. But I never really felt comfortable at Hampton, either. The way Freeman handled my recruitment cost me my scholarship. The fiasco with the dorm made me question how serious Coach Ford felt about my value to his team. I knew I must try, however, because my mom had put so much into it for me. Without the scholarship, the tuition would be hard to manage. Since we applied late, we received less financial aid than we could have. My mom's high hopes propelled me forward, awkwardly.

I never forgot the experience of losing the scholarship money. Once I launched DC Assault, I always advised players to take scholarships and not play games during the recruitment process: to find a coach and program they felt comfortable with, and to be straightforward with their intentions.

Coach Ford certainly did not act in a straightforward way. Several weeks passed, and though we told him what had happened, he either could not or did not want to resolve my dorm issue. I spent those weeks crashing on George's floor. Classes started and I felt really ignored. I knew if Coach Ford believed me to be a great player or program changer he'd have fixed the problem. Now, I knew I had a solid game. I never considered myself great, but I also knew playing college ball would get me a college degree. I needed the game for that reason alone. However, I also needed to feel part of a team.

"I think Coach Ford is full of shit," I told my mom one day several weeks into the school year. I sat in a chair at the pay phone on the wall in the dorm hallway.

"I'm really pissed at him for doing this," she said.

"I can't keep sleeping on the floor here in George's room. He has been so supportive, and I don't want to wear out my welcome."

"What can we do?"

"Eric and Skip's apartment should be ready next week. They asked me to split the rent three ways."

She didn't respond right away. I almost jumped in, but she began talking slowly, as if trying to find the right words. "I'm not sure, Curtis…I mean, it's probably expensive and…what I mean is, we're kinda strapped as it is."

"If I end up in a dorm, they'll add the dorm fees to the tuition we owe. We're fucked either way."

"Boy, you better watch your damn mouth. Who the hell you think you talking to, Curtis…is the place nice?

"Very nice, mom. It's a brand-new complex. They don't have much furniture, but yeah, it's nice."

"Why don't I come down next week? I'll come by and we can talk about it then?"

She visited the following weekend, and I showed her the apartment. The place, located in a complex called the Wyndham, really looked nice. After some discussion, she agreed to pay my share of the rent. I felt bad for my mom, who had just launched her own cleaning company after working housekeeping in a hotel for years. She did everything in her power to ensure I made it in school. She hustled and grinded to afford it.

Eric and Skip welcomed me, adding a bed in Skip's room. I transitioned from dorm floor to a real apartment with a roommate.

At times I had a helluva lot of fun my first semester in college. Maybe too much fun. I'd never been much of a drinker. In fact, I didn't have my first real drink until my high school graduation party when my father poured me a Christian Brothers brandy and Coke. I discovered Bacardi at Hampton. The parties were off the chain, the girls incredible. I tried to maintain my relationship with Darlene, but, well, I was in college.

The semester passed, and soon I began attending preseason workouts with the basketball team. I felt out of place. The situation reminded me of trying out for the AAU team, the PG All

Stars, with Steve Hood and Mike Sumner. For most of my life I've always felt like I belonged, or, more so, that others desired my company. I never got such a feeling from the Hampton basketball team, from Coach Ford to the damn student managers.

"Foul, man!" I yelled. We played full court at an unofficial practice one Wednesday. I'd driven to my right, using a pick one of our forwards had set, and the defender reached in and slapped my arm.

"Bullshit. Didn't even touch you!"

"We heard you slap my arm. It's a foul."

Technically the team's captains ran these pickup games, but some assistant coaches always hung around to watch.

"Man, just play," another teammate said.

"No," I answered. "It's a foul. I'm taking the ball up top." I grabbed the ball and moved just beyond the three-point line, waiting for the defender to check the ball.

"Malone!" one of the assistant coaches called out. I looked over to the bleachers where he sat with another coach and an athletic trainer.

"Blue's ball. That was no foul. You just turned it over."

"What!"

"Malone. Blue's ball."

"That's bullshit." I tossed the ball to a player on the other side and switched to defense. They ran a play and I found myself caught in the paint as their center drove the lane. I had clear positioning and held my ground, expecting to take a charge.

The whistle blew. "Blocking foul," the same assistant called out. A few of my teammates smirked. My face turned deep red. I knew these guys had decided to haze me a bit, the walk-on. Had I felt more welcomed, had I believed that Hampton's team held some talent, I might have sucked it up, stepped up my game, and earned a spot. But I already felt unwanted, not important, and even neglected. I knew my mom struggled to pay tuition. I believed Ford could've helped my living situation if he'd wanted to. At that point, I felt frustrated and pissed off.

I didn't bother to try out.

All Freeman's efforts—for better or worse—went for nothing. I put my goal of playing college basketball on hold. I almost gave up on college right then and there. I told Freeman first.

"It just doesn't feel right. Ford has hardly spoken to me."

"You're not the senior captain anymore, Curtis," Freeman tried to explain. "You earned your spot on the Parkdale team. Gotta earn the muthafucker at Hampton, too."

"I know that. You know I've never thought I was a superstar. I know what my role is. But I honestly don't think I have a role here."

"You still want to play college ball?"

I thought about it for a second. "Of course."

"I'll make some calls, try to find you a school."

"I don't think I even want to stay here, coach."

"That's between you and your folks, Curtis. Don't disappoint your mom, man. And I'd hate to see you be even more of a fucking quitter."

"Yeah, you're right. Thanks, man!" I said with a smile on my face.

Next, I told my mom. I took Trailways back home and sat down with her.

"I don't see the point. If I don't play basketball, there's no chance at a scholarship, and I know you and dad can't afford the tuition." I thought rationalizing the financial constraints would help my argument with her.

"No. You earned the chance. You've never been in serious trouble. You worked hard in school. You can make something of yourself if you just want it bad enough."

"But Mom—"

"I want you to stick it out. At least finish your first year. I know I can afford that. If you miss being home, then grab a bus every weekend. It's free."

Her words didn't move me. Neither did her point about coming home (since Dad worked for the bus company, I got free fare). No, her face prevented further objection. I realized she'd put an awful lot of hope into my success. My sisters would get married. They'd have husbands responsible for providing for them. Beverly, my mother knew, would always struggle with addiction. But I, unlike my sisters, needed to stand on my own two feet. The potential existed; I had all the charisma in the world. I just lacked the education (in her opinion) college provided.

But I knew I'd received a different kind of education growing up in Palmer Park. Unlike my mom, I never thought a college degree was my only option or path to success. Still, I couldn't hurt her.

"Freeman's going to try to find me another school for next year. He's gonna call around to some coaches,"

"See? Ken Freeman looks out for you. I'm sure he'll find something." Her hopes revived, a huge smile spread across her face.

"Alright. I'll try to stick it out for the year," I finally said.

Attending college is not the same as trying in college. Classes got boring without basketball to motivate me. As had been my pattern throughout high school, I slacked off when I didn't worry about eligibility. I felt dispirited without the game, and I truly only stayed because my mom asked me to.

There was another reason for my apathy, and it had nothing to do with basketball.

I was broke.

For the first time in years, I had no money. I'd grown accustomed to just asking an old head for cash whenever I needed it. Now, three hours away from Palmer Park, I couldn't just page Irvin or Byrd and have them show up ten minutes later. When I went home on the weekends, I'd get some money, but living with Eric and Skip could get expensive. Since we lived off campus, I wasn't on any kind of meal plan. I paid for almost all my food, and we loved to eat out. When I couldn't pay, my friends picked up the tab. I hated that. We also partied. Clubs and liquor added up. And I dressed fly but was as broke as a bag of glass.

I befriended an upperclassman named Wanda Tidline, who would pick me up at the apartment and drop me off so I could get to class. I couldn't even afford to help her with gas.

A story George told me after I'd left Hampton reinforced that even though I was truly broke, people thought I has money. "Curtis, Skip, and I thought you were loaded. Seriously, you dressed up all the time. You'd go home for the weekend and come back with cash." He shook his head back and forth in disbelief. "Here we were, hustling all summer to pay for the apartment and food and all this shit…then we drove you home one time. I think we went to your dad's house. And, bro, there was this tiny-ass house with aluminum siding and a rusty fence. We dropped you off, and I turned to Skip, and I say, 'Curtis just as poor as we are!'"

His anecdote provided some real insight into how I lived and would live all my life. Despite being broke and hating it, I never considered getting a real job. I never, ever, wanted to look poor. And I believed that if I couldn't do, or buy, whatever I wanted or needed whenever I wanted to, then I was poor. So I believed if I left school and returned home, I'd at least have more money in my pocket. But I also knew what happened to guys who didn't get out. Did I really want to deal drugs?

No money, no basketball, and no interest in classes took its toll. My first semester at Hampton sucked. Something had to give.

New York C

"She says you disrespected her, muthafucker," he yelled in my face as he shoved me back. I held my ground, but two more Hampton University football players stepped up to me. I didn't like my odds: three against me.

The night started well enough. I found myself at an off-campus party in February of 1987. I saw a girl I'd gone to Parkdale with, and we began to talk. The more she drank, the more shit she talked. I'm not one who claims to be a perfect gentleman, but she knew that I had a girlfriend since high school. She was drunk and claimed I was messing with other women at Hampton.

Now I had three huge muthafuckers looking at me crazy.

"She said that you're disrespecting her. Don't make me fuck you up, little man," the biggest one said.

"Gentlemen, my niggas, what's the problem?" asked a brown-skinned guy with close-cropped hair. He wore jeans and a silk button-down shirt. A huge gold chain hung from his neck. The football players immediately deferred to him.

"No problem, New York C. Just a misunderstanding."

The new guy looked from them to me.

"Seems maybe a big misunderstanding if all three of you need to step to him." He caught my eye. "What's the problem, Shawty?" he asked me.

"They think I disrespected they sister that I've been fucking with since the eleventh grade, 'cept she's drunk, and I told her I have a girl, and she and I can only continue to be friends."

"Think she playing games? Sure sounds like," he said to the biggest player.

"Could be," he answered. "Come on, let's go."

The three walked off, leaving me and the other guy standing in a corner of the room.

"What's your name?" he asked me.

"Curtis."

"That's my name too, but here they just call me New York C."

"New York C?"

"Born and raised in Hollis, Queens. You don't look stupid. So whatcha doing almost getting your little ass kicked?"

"Not gonna back down when I'm right. I didn't disrespect the bitch. If I got my ass kicked, I promise you, half of DC/Maryland would've been down here and shut this muthafucker down. She know the repercussions that come with fucking with me."

"Well, right is right. Wanna drink?"

I spent the rest of the party getting to know New York C. At twenty-four, he had left the city for Hampton in order to "find his future." The way he spoke and carried himself made me suspect he came from the street, but at that point I assumed he had decided to go straight and get a college degree. We instantly hit it off. I'd drunk enough to open up to him about my lack of enthusiasm for school, my homesickness, and the frustration and anger I felt over the basketball situation.

For the rest of the semester, New York C adopted me as if I were his little brother. He'd pick me up at my apartment in his BMW 528i and we'd get something to eat, then go to class or play ball or just cruise around. He lived in a nice place off campus in Newport News and clearly had bread.

The first time he asked me to ride with him to Richmond, Virginia, he told me he needed to return some clothes to a homeboy. We drove up, and he ran a duffle bag into the Hillside projects. We repeated this trip a couple more times, and it became pretty obvious what was really going down. The whole thing reminded me too much of Byrd and Irvin. I suspected New York C had never left the streets.

Other things made me suspicious. First, New York C blew through money like he printed it. He drove the Beamer, rented a nice apartment, dressed fly, ate out every meal, and often used Western Union to send money home. Eric, Skip, and I often talked about needing cash from our parents. Curt never did. I knew he hid something from me. I assumed he dealt, but so what? Questioning him wasn't my place. If I earned his trust, he'd tell me.

I've always gravitated towards older guys who respected me like an equal. New York C acted no differently. He took care of me when I needed his help and treated me like a real brother, always.

Meanwhile, I'd hop on a Trailways bus every other weekend to kick it with my old heads back in Palmer Park. In hindsight, so many people my own age made me feel uncomfortable at Hampton. I'd grown up hanging with guys ten to fifteen years older than me. Was I more mature than my peers? Probably not. Did I think I was? Definitely.

Not to say I didn't enjoy Hampton. I did. The atmosphere was just so different, like I was on another planet. No drug activity. Not a lot of fights. No robbing and killing. I met some of my closest friends there—New York C, Eric Cooper, George, Malik, and Skip—just five examples. And I loved the parties and social scene. But playing basketball served as my whole reason for going to college. Without it, I had no interest.

Whenever I went home, I'd move some PCP with Curtis Richardson in order to earn some bread. Nothing big. I mainly just got it from Big Curtis and gave to a few friends who would move it. I didn't enjoy dealing, but I needed money. During that time, I began hearing more and more about crack cocaine. Most guys still used PCP or powder cocaine (if they could afford it). If they wanted the rock, they'd have to cook it themselves. I'd seen crack, but never smoked it and never cooked it.

"So yeah, you wouldn't believe how quickly the shit's taking off," I explained to New York C as we ate at Quincy's Steak House.

"Shit's been around for a few years now. I'm surprised it's just coming into your town," he said.

"Nobody's selling rock. It's all powder or Love Boat. Cats making more money selling PCP than crack..."

"You know guys connected to the coke game?"

"Of course. My old head like my uncle, and my godfather Irvin some of the biggest coke dealers in DC."

New York C rubbed his hand through his goatee. "What you think I do for money, Curtis?"

I gave him my Malone smile. "Well, I don't think you're bringing back clothes from Richmond."

"Understand something here: I trust you and I like you. Think you got a good fucking head on your shoulders," New York C said. He very deliberately placed his knife and fork across his plate and folded his hands together. "It's about supply and demand. Back home, crack on every corner. You got brothers killing brothers over turf, spies killing everyone. Shit's crazy. The demand's high, but so is the supply. Means prices are low." He paused and sipped on his Arnold Palmer. "You come down South and you Southern niggas like a bunch of virgins just waiting for your cherry to get popped. Demand's high, but supply's low. Means higher prices. Now, you sittin' here telling me the rock's starting to take off in your hood, but no one's there supplying?"

The waitress collected our plates and left a dessert menu.

"Honestly, guys gotta cook it themselves. But none of the coke dealers smart or rich enough to buy weight and start supplying the hood," I said.

"But you're smart enough."

"Not rich enough."

"You got a connect. Byrd. He could front you the powder."

"He wanted better for me...I'm afraid to ask him to supply me with drugs."

"What's the difference? I took Intro to Business 101 last semester. I took Economics. I took Minority Entrepreneurship in the Twenty-fucking-First Century. He wanted better for you, but it's all the same thing: crack, PCP, or car parts. All need a supplier, a manufacturer, a distributor. All got profit margins and market consideration, competitive pressures. All are products the customer wants, and they all got a fucking brand name..." He trailed off and picked up the dessert menu.

I sat there thinking. Being the college boy hadn't panned out. But I didn't want to give up on it, either. I needed money. My mom did her best, but I knew she was strapped. I could've gotten a real job and slaved away like my father. If I could manage to make bread in the drug game but still go to college and play basketball, I'd live in both worlds—the best of both.

"Yo, Earth to Curtis." New York C snapped his fingers to get my attention. "Here's a lesson from that Intro to Business class: You've got access to a product whose popularity is exploding. You have access to an underserved market. You've got brains and street smarts." He looked up at me expectantly.

"I don't know how to cook it." My last feeble excuse fell from my lips.

"You can learn." He leaned in close to me, lowered his voice. "Plus, you're sitting across from a nigga who can get all the rock you need."

I just nodded my head up and down.

"You want dessert?" New York C asked, sitting back, smiling. "I'm in the mood for some cake. You want cake?"

"Yeah," I said. "Cake sounds good."

"Well, let's get some cake and bake some cakes, little nigga."

Drug Dealing 101: Introduction to Crack Cocaine

"Bro, there's a fucking lot of titties in this room. Let's get some pussy now, conversate later."

Curtis Richardson looked at me over the shoulder of a redbone broad who ground her crotch against his. Naked women moved around his living room. Others bent over chairs or laid atop tables, our friends pounding them out. I sat on his sofa, legs spread, naked from the waist down, getting head. I felt a nice buzz in my brain from the liquor I'd drunk. The brown-skinned beauty who buried her face in my lap wore extensions in her hair, which kept tickling my thigh. It was fucking distracting.

A large box of condoms and a pile of crack sat on a plate on the coffee table.

This was Big Curtis's introduction to my new meal ticket.

I'd tried to explain the appeal of crack to him: how we would cut the coke to double or even triple our quantities; how, at a lower price, everyone in our hood could afford the drug, unlike pure powder; how easy we could hide and transport it.

But Big Curtis held a loyalty to PCP, and, at first, I couldn't convince him of crack's potential. So, we planned this party to show him crack's popularity.

I wanted Big Curtis involved. I needed someone who lived the life, unlike myself, who knew the players but never truly hustled. Big Curtis had the connects, knew the turf, and I trusted him enough to operate when I couldn't be there. I didn't want to turn to Twin or Irvin because I thought they'd be disappointed in me.

For now, I wore two faces: the innocent college kid the neighborhood could hold as a positive example and the crack dealer with the best product in Palmer Park.

New York C gave me about 200 capsules of crack that night as he dropped me off at Trailways. I'd taken a bus home for the weekend and by Saturday night had sold all 200. New York C fronted me at twenty dollars per capsule. I turned each capsule into three or four rocks of crack. After paying workers and crackheads, I made fifty dollars off each capsule—or around $4,000 in just over twenty-four hours. I'd never be the same. After that first weekend, demand just increased. After a month, I brought in about $7,000-$8,000 for two days of work. My money problems ended.

I decided to enter the drug game for a few different reasons. First, it was in me. I grew up with hustlers and ballers as role models. Second, my mom had spent a ton of money for college, and I got sick of freeloading off her. If I found a way to pay for my lifestyle without needing her, so much the better. Finally, the basketball dream barely existed. I knew I would never be an NBA player. Coach Ford beat that notion from my mind. I'm not sure whether he intentionally spited me for not accepting his recruitment offer right away, or if I'd just failed some test, but basketball drifted away from me. Since I'd only ever focused on academics as a means to remain eligible to play ball, I knew I needed to find a way to make money without a college degree.

To be fair, the idea of college and college ball had not entirely died. Freeman had a strong contact at a small community college in West Virginia. But making the kind of cash crack brought in, in such a short time, at eighteen years old, I found it hard to see other possibilities.

I began making trips home every weekend. I told my family I felt homesick, that Hampton got boring. Instead, I posted up outside Palmer's Liquor Store. Other dealers sold powder cocaine there, and I saw them get paid. But I realized for every customer who bought coke, three others couldn't afford it. So, I showed up peddling twenty-dollar rocks of crack, and suddenly, I was moving product quickly. I explained my plan to Big Curtis, and we began to expand our crack game and expanded our customer base. Once a junkie got a taste of crack, it was over. He or she would do anything for the high. The traffic was unreal once the word got out.

At that point, I operated alone, but I envisioned what my operation (and my profit) could be if I jumped into the game full-time. I never wanted to be a corner hustler. I always saw myself as someone bigger, heavier. I wanted to deal weight, but in order to get there, I needed help.

I needed Big Curtis, mostly because he had a connect that could get us more cocaine outside of New York.

"Imagine how much money we could make if I wasn't just hustling on weekends," I said to Big Curtis as we walked down Muncy Road.

"You dropping out?" he asked.

"Gonna try to play at Potomac State in the fall."

"Where the fuck's that?"

"West Virginia."

"Honky central."

"Probably, but if I'm in West Virginia, I can't be here all the time. I need you to incorporate the crack in with the Love Boat game when I'm away."

"Why not Twin or Irvin?"

I hesitated. "It's just…I don't want them knowing what I'm doing. Not yet, anyway. Twin, he'd be cool with it. But Irvin, what I'm doing's just too close to what he did."

"You mean drop out to sell dope?"

"I'm not quitting. I want to play college ball. I need to find my groove."

We stopped in front of my house. Dusk settled over us, a late spring evening.

"So, can I count on you?" I finally asked.

"This crack shit, it's pumping right now, but I don't want to give up on the PCP."

"So, don't. My connect will give me enough rock to last the week, I'll re-up every weekend. I really just need you to collect from my team. You in or what?"

He shrugged, then met my eye. "I'm in."

Crack does some crazy shit to people. I've seen married women suck and fuck their dealer for a rock. I've known people who've stolen from their mother—their children—to get high. I've seen grown men rob their kids' Christmas presents. Crack took men we considered true gangsters and reduced them to weak, pathetic junkies who'd drop to their knees and suck another man's dick. Crack destroyed Palmer Park and my city. It took over my neighborhood, and I hate what crack did to the people I knew and loved.

Still, I dealt.

Big Curtis, New York C, and I stood in Darlene's kitchen. New York C prepared to show us how to cook crack.

"This is about an ounce," he said, as he dumped pure cocaine into a glass jar. "So, an ounce is twenty-eight grams. We want to cut it with baking soda."

"Why? Just to get more?" Big Curtis asked.

"You'll see. So, measure out about eight grams of baking soda." He spooned the baking soda onto a triple beam scale, then dumped it into the jar with the coke.

"Now, we add a little water. Not too much. We just moisten it. Then it goes into the microwave."

"Thought niggas used a stove."

"Yeah. Back in the old days. Gas stove best 'cause you can control the heat. But this works, too. You want the water to start boiling."

Once the water reached a boil, he took the jar out. The solid powder had turned into a liquid. New York C shook the jar in circles.

"Why you doing that?" I asked.

"Gotta mix the oils, get the oils to form together. When we boiled the water, all the powder turned to oils. We want the oils to come together. That's also why we need the baking soda."

"That's the tricky part?" Big Curtis asked.

"Yeah. Now, once we shake it, and it starts to come together, we sprinkle cold water into it." He went to the sink and began flicking cold water off his fingers into the jar. "This hardens the oils."

"So, it's crack now?" I asked.

"You got it." He dumped the jar's contents onto the counter. A hardened rock fell out. "Now you break or cut it into those rocks your customers fiend for." New York C used a butter knife to break off small sections of the hardened cocaine. He held up a piece of crack that I'd probably sell for fifty bucks: Working Fifties, we called them.

"You always use the same amounts?" I asked.

"You can get away with making sixty-two grams of cocaine into eighty-five grams of crack. The more you cut it, the weaker it's gonna be." He pulled out another ounce of cocaine. "Here, you do it now. This time, add some food coloring to the powder before you boil it."

"Why?"

"Branding, Curtis. It's all about branding."

I repeated the process he'd shown me, eventually breaking off pieces with a blue hue from the dye I'd added. Cooking crack was easy.

"Since Li'l Curtis here won't be back to Hampton in the fall, and since he's told me he plans on expanding the operation this summer, you need to cook your own shit. I'll prolly hook you up twice a month. Some months might be less often. Depends on supply back home."

"What if it's not enough?" Big Curtis asked. New York C just shrugged.

"Don't worry about it," I told him. I already knew what we'd do, something the business majors at Hampton would call "supply chain diversification," but I didn't want to discuss it with New York C there.

At about this time, I met a girl my age at a go-go named Tawanna. We would dance together, and I got the word that she was attracted to me. I don't remember exactly why I slept with her. She was attractive, but most likely I'd been fighting with Darlene. Tawanna and I saw one another on the side for several months.

"Curtis, I'm pregnant," Tawanna told me in September of '87.

"You're lying and it's not mine."

"I'm not. It's yours, Curtis."

"How the hell you know that?"

"Curtis, it's your fucking baby."

"You're gonna keep it?"

Tawanna, thankfully, did keep the baby: my first daughter, Tanay. But I didn't feel ready to be a father and for a time didn't acknowledge Tanay or support Tawanna. Eventually, word got back to my father. He lectured me on responsibility. From then on, I made sure Tanay lacked for nothing, but for most of my daughter's early childhood, I was an absent father. I definitely didn't tell Darlene.

I really loved Darlene, who stayed by my side no matter what, and I didn't want to hurt her by admitting I had cheated and now had a kid. I also acted like a coward who didn't want to deal with Darlene's probable reaction or face losing her because I couldn't keep my dick in my pants.

As I prepared to put my drug crew together, I reflected on some rules I'd learned from my old heads:

Rule 1: Death before dishonor.

Rule 2: Money and materialistic things don't make a man. Character says it all.

Rule 3: Build a strong crew of money-getters and keep stand-up men around you at all times.

Rule 4: Abide by the street codes at all times.

Rule 5: Never keep drugs where you or your family lay their heads.

I really focused on rules one and two. As word spread, big-time dealers and suppliers from Palmer Park approached me. Did I want to work for (or with) them? But I always did things differently. I could have sourced my cocaine from a local supplier, but I always went outside of Palmer Park for my drugs. And I believed in loyalty, so I stayed close to the people who I felt played big brother roles in my life. They mentored me and I accepted their help.

"You're in that crack game now, huh?" Twin asked.

"Come on, bro, you asking me questions you already know the answers to," I said.

"From what I hear, you're blowing up."

"Let's just say there's a very good opportunity for us to make some bread."

"Us?"

"I want you in and need you, but only if you promise me to stay clean. It's summer, so I don't need to be at school. We're gonna turn it up."

"Who else?"

"Big Curtis, EW, C Ricks, Reese, and Jay. Keeping it small, tight. For now."

"What about school?"

"Transferring this fall. Gonna make money now. You guys can keep it going while I'm away."

"This ain't you."

"This is me. Always been me."

"What about basketball playing, go-go loving, smiling, innocent Little Curtis?"

"He's still here. Two sides to a coin, ya know?"

"Not that simple, this game. Guys coming up with this crack. Gonna be turf battles. There's a War on Drugs now. Little Nancy in the White House saying 'Just Say No.' You up for this?"

"You gonna help me?"

"Figure someone's gotta watch your back."

"Good. You're my enforcer."

"Like I said, someone's gotta be."

Loyal crew and niggas that could think. I needed the right mix. Some guys, like Twin, would not hesitate to kill a guy and never question the murder's necessity. Others, like EW, could handle the money side of the business with no problem. Like New York C explained, this hustle operated the same as any legit business. We had to monitor cashflow, payroll, profit margin, pricing strategies. But unlike opening up some retail storefront on Wisconsin Avenue, sometimes you had to tough up your competition or shoot one of your customers. That side of the drug business never appealed to me. I'm not quick to get angry or be violent. Yet, I needed enforcers who could be.

Jabouri McClamb would be another one of my soldiers. I'd met him my senior year at Parkdale. A few years younger than me, Jay, as we called him, acted stubborn and hotheaded, but would smile with his chipped front tooth and get his way. My mother called it his "Sneaky Innocent Smile." My whole family loved Jay, and I'd serve as godfather to his only child. He acted wild and unpredictable and always willing to fight.

With Jay and Twin as muscle, and Big Curtis and EW as the more rational half, I thought I had a strong crew to expand our operation over the summer. Now, I just needed to diversify that supply chain.

New York C's supply of cocaine came and went inconsistently. One month he'd make two runs, another month he might only make one. Big Curtis had access to PCP, but coke wasn't his connect's thing. I felt I needed another supplier to keep things growing. Enter Butch Byrd, my old head's brother.

"Pull up over here," I told Big Curtis. He parked his car on the side of Sherman Avenue.

"Alright. Go down to the next block. The guy's on the corner wearing a big chain around his neck, black leather shirling."

"Again, why am I doing this?"

"Bro, I told you. I don't want Byrd knowing I'm in the game. His brother knows me. If they see me, Byrd will hear about it."

"Fine. I'm going." He left the car and headed down the block. We'd buy about twenty to thirty fifties and take it back to Palmer Park where we'd cook it up. By the height of the summer, we'd make the trip five times a day.

I felt intrigued by Butch's operation, which I'd never seen close up on all those car rides I'd taken. People lined up, and one of Butch's guys on the left side of the street collected the cash. Then the buyer crossed to the right to pick up the product. I watched Big Curtis pay, then cross over and grab a small bag from one of the workers. The operation ran smoothly. By never having the cash and drugs on the same guy, he cut his risk.

I sat there watching buyer after buyer crossing the street and realized I could replicate this in my neighborhood. I'd grown tired of corner hustling and wanted to move into a bigger role. Let Jay and C Ricks run the street crew, while I handled the suppliers and dealt with more weight.

But for the time being, crack was booming. We'd cook a batch and immediately sell out and have to drive uptown to buy more cocaine.

"Vick can get us more powder at a better price," Big Curtis told me, referring to his brother.

"Is the shit good?"

"Does it even matter at this point? We need to do something. Running uptown all day sucks."

"And Butch Byrd's prices are steep," I added. "How much?"

"Coke?"

"Yeah."

"Two hundred fifty grams. When's New York C coming back around?"

"Supposed to been last week. Now he's telling me it'll be next."

"Let's check the numbers from Vick's people."

"Alright. Let's do it, but I want to meet him."

"Fine. I'll make the call."

Vick and Big Curtis called the connect, and soon we started snatching. We'd get the cocaine in powder, rock it up, and it would only last one or two days. Crack brought a lot of bullshit with it. Palmer Liquors got hot, with police constantly coming through. All levels of fiends showed up to buy, including heroin addicts. Most heroin addicts who shot dope did so in the morning. Then they smoked crack at night. The dope dealers at Palmer's cleared out by midday, but the junkies could get crack all day long. Heroin users were notorious criminals. Once their dope-high faded, they wanted to smoke to get high again. But they had already spent their money earlier in the day. This led to guys getting robbed and killed so the junkies could buy crack. It fucked the game up because the crime rate spiked, and the police had to step up patrols. Some days they'd come through Palmer's with ten or more cars and just line us all up for pat searches. They'd go into the store and search people shopping.

"Our spot's hot," I told Twin.

"The liquor store? No shit. Every hustler in the hood posted up all day."

"Gotta roll out, find somewhere else."

"Try Capitol Hill East."

"Thought the Jacs ran that area?"

"Yeah right, they don't run shit. You know there's two ways into the apartment complex, right?"

"No shit. So what?"

"The Jamaicans all post up near the front or in the damn buildings. We go around the backside and catch all the fiends before they even make it into CHE."

"They're gonna get pissed the fuck off."

"Who the fuck cares about the Jamaicans?" Twin asked.

"Alright, but you're coming with me."

So, we began selling at the Capitol Hill East apartment complex. I started my mornings down bottom at the backside entrance, catching all the sales before they went to the Jamaicans and easily made six grand in a few hours. Then I'd go shoot hoops for the afternoon.

"We need more powder," I complained to my crew. "Big Curt, tell the connect we gotta get more cocaine. We run out too quick; even buying off Byrd's crew and what New York C supplies is not enough. It's like a got-damn twenty-four-hour grocery store out there."

"I'll take care of it," Big Curtis said.

"And, I got some bad news," I continued. "Police are trying to close down Capitol Hill East. We need another spot."

"Glenarden," said Jay.

"I've heard it's money there," added Twin.

"We gotta be more consistent with product," EW began. "We go up to Glenarden, and shit starts poppin', and then we hit a drought..." He referred to when we ran out of powder to cook into crack. "It'll kill our game. Someone else'll move in while we wait to get more."

"Big Curt, tell Vick to get no less than a kilo."

"He might not front us that much."

"We've been showing this nigga love for two months now. He sees how fast the money coming in. You and Vick get him to give us a key."

A few days later I got the call from Big Curtis to come by his house. I walked into his kitchen and saw the kilo on the table. We immediately broke it down, cooked and bagged the crack.

"Alright, I'm gone," I said.

"Where you headed?" Vick asked.

"Got Twin meeting me at Glenarden."

"I'm coming with you," Big Curtis added.

I'd decided to operate at Glenarden late at night, near midnight. When going to a new spot, you had to rely on the crackheads who lived there. They knew everything about the complex: who did what, where; who sold the best crack; whether the police rolled up in cars or on foot and from which direction. You also had to thoroughly know the crackhead. He needed to be a stand-up guy who wouldn't snitch if he got busted. I always made sure any user who worked for me knew I'd bail him out and pay for a lawyer. I engendered loyalty that way and treated everyone the same no matter their personal situation or addiction.

I'd done well when I posted up at Palmer's or at Capitol Hill East, but I killed it that first night at Glenarden. We made five trips back to Palmer Park to re-up and brought in almost twenty grand. No wonder I'd heard so many good things about the development. Eventually, the crackheads got to know us and ran up like eager pets as soon as we pulled in. I brought at least three guys with me and posted two crackheads as lookouts. My men back at Palmer Park who cooked up the crack couldn't believe how fast the work came in. The kilo didn't last long.

"I can't get in touch with him," Big Curtis explained.

"What the fuck you mean?"

"You know how he is," Big Curtis spoke of his cocaine connection. "The nigga disappears for weeks."

After working with this supplier, we'd realized he ran one of the smoothest, safest operations. He kept no active lines of communication and constantly switched vehicles. He'd tell us he'd be out of town for a few days, but usually the days turned to weeks. He made his money but never became greedy. Staying out of jail remained his focus. Unfortunately, that didn't help us.

"We started working with this guy to avoid these droughts!" I ranted. The money had begun working on me. Like a drug itself, I couldn't get enough. Going a couple weeks without the hustle killed me. By this time I made enough money to live fast: I went to go-gos five nights a week; I ate at expensive restaurants every meal; and, of course, I dressed to impress, always. I also put a little money up, knowing a time would come when I needed cash. Still, the lifestyle called to me. I needed the money coming in.

"Curtis, did you forget we still have access to PCP?" Big Curtis asked. The Love Boat (street slang for PCP) had always been how he and his brother Vick made their money. I'd sold small amounts, but never in any weight. "You know I got a mean plug," he continued.

"It's not worth it to me to sell 102 vanilla abstract bottles," I said.

"Trust me, it's worth it. His prices are great."

"How much?"

"Prolly get a gallon for seven grand."

Just to provide context, in 1988 a gallon of PCP could produce enough sacs to bring in a hundred grand or more, street value, but I didn't want to peddle sacs. I wanted lower risk, quicker turnaround if I played the Love Boat game.

"What you think we could move it for?" I asked.

"Shit, Landover lovin' the juice…prolly get twenty to twenty-four grand for it."

"Three times what we pay? That's a nice profit. I don't want our crew involved, though."

"Why?"

"Just the risk. Guys head into Landover and get popped, screws up the crack game here. You got a crew?"

"I can put something together. But how much you want to buy?"

"You sure the profit's there?"

"Yeah. Definitely."

"Get three gallons, and we'll turn them into four or five gallons. Let's see how we do…."

Big Curtis grabbed a handful of guys, and we began moving PCP out at Kings Square, Dodge View, and Stratford Woods, as well as at the twenty-four-hour convenience store in Landover. We sold gallons, quarts, liters, and ounces. Within a couple weeks, we started buying six gallons for seven grand each and moving it quick at twenty-four grand a piece. The run with

PCP was steady with good profits. I quickly realized why the Richardson brothers hyped it.

"You see, now that's product diversification," explained New York C late that summer when he finally made a run through Palmer Park.

"Well, something had to give…you're inconsistent," I said.

"Give me some time, Li'l Curtis. I'm thinking of relocating."

"When?"

"I'll let you know, bro. What you doing this fall?"

"Getting ready to go back to school, Potomac State."

"You see? I knew you was smart. Little tip: major in business."

College Redux

My mom finally began to suspect I dealt drugs as I prepared to leave for Potomac State. She saw all types of new, expensive clothing and shoes and knew I stayed out with the wrong crowd. I couldn't hide my affiliation with the streets, though I wanted to. No matter how hard I tried, drugs attracted attention like a magnet. Attention I didn't want. I told people, "Don't talk about this in front of my family," but I spoke to brick walls. The crackheads don't care when they need a fix.

My mother got fed up. Frustrated over my failure at Hampton and heartbroken that I'd resorted to the street life, she threw her hands up. We loved one another; she's my mom, but during those years, she wore disappointment on her face, always.

I didn't make the decision to leave for Potomac State easily. A part of me wanted to stay in the streets. Early on I knew only two things came from drugs: death or jail. Going to college not only provided an alternative ending for me, it represented a come-up for my family and neighborhood. I could count on one hand how many people on my block attended college at any level. It meant a lot to me to do the neighborhood proud. I also wanted to try to play college ball again. But the money!

Making what someone may earn in one year in just a few months appealed to me. How could it not? I didn't care that dealing was illegal, and I definitely did not think about how crack affected our community.

A two-year college in Keyser, West Virginia, Potomac State lies three hours from Palmer Park. The college competed in a pretty competitive athletic conference against other junior colleges, such as Hagerstown Community College, Essex, and Allegheny. The campus could not compare to Hampton. First, Hampton is a historically Black college, and African-Americans made up almost the entire student body there. Potomac, in the heart of West Virginia, had almost no Blacks, and those of us who attended played sports. We definitely had to watch out where we went in town, especially where we ate or went to gas up our cars. This culture change shocked me when I first arrived. I'd never been to many places before. I promised myself I'd make the best of it. I established some strong relationships with white students and teammates. Though I'd played with white guys at Parkdale, outside of basketball we lived separate lives. At Potomac, we all lived in the same dorm with plenty of opportunity to interact and get to know one another. This changed my perceptions. Growing up, I'd learned to think all whites were racist, which proved very wrong. Yes, we did experience racism every day, but not everyone held racist views. If college provided me with only one lesson, I learned I held some biases. Had I not left Palmer Park to attend school, I might have held on to my incorrect perceptions all my life.

I felt the need to prove myself on the basketball court considering I hadn't played real competitive ball since my senior year at Parkdale. So, I played in a few summer leagues and a lot of adult pickup games throughout town. I'd almost forgotten what it felt like to play under the lights.

Neither the team nor the competition equaled Hampton, but the Potomac State coaching staff welcomed me with open arms. That in itself improved my confidence. Due to my transfer, I sat out a few games early on, but once officially eligible, I became the starting point guard. A few fellow Parkdale alums also played at Potomac, which further helped my transition. Over the season, I averaged around sixteen points and eight assists a game. I was an All-Region selection.

Then the season ended.

Once again, I went into the classroom without basketball to anchor my focus. Once more, college lost its appeal. Big Curtis had run the operations while I attended school, though he usually picked me up on weekends when I didn't have a game. If we had work, he'd come get me on a Friday night, then drive me back to school Sunday afternoon. We continued to exploit Glenarden, and I'd never head back to Potomac without at least five grand in my pocket. The money just grew and grew. But Glenarden also began attracting heavy police attention. More than once, I got put on the ground and searched. If the cops found money on you, they'd take it, so we developed a system: every thirty to forty minutes, I'd hand off about a grand. Once we got to five grand, my guy would head back to Palmer Park to drop off the cash and re-up with more crack.

We made money so easily, we never learned to cherish it. I'd blow a thousand bucks on clothes and sneakers, returning to school and making sure I outfitted all my teammates with anything they needed. In this way, I began modeling my behavior after New York C, Irvin, and Byrd.

In the spring of '88, my family and I finally reached a settlement with the Prince George County School Board for my accident at basketball practice. After legal bills, we received almost twenty grand. I gave my mom some money for all she did while I attended Hampton, which left about fifteen grand for me. I decided I needed a car. Having Big Curtis drive me back and forth had become impractical. So, I used the money to make a down payment on a red Alfa Romeo Milano. I'd always loved Alfa Romeo, and when they released the Milano, I knew I needed one. My dad put the car in his name (the authorities cannot confiscate something you don't own) and knew I made plenty of cash to cover monthly payments and insurance.

Once basketball season ended, I made trips home every weekend. I really had no interest in school. My grades suffered. Eventually I withdrew from Potomac State, deciding my future lie in the hustle game. If I was meant to be a baller, I'd be a certified street baller.

Drug Dealing 201: The Perils of the Game

One day in early '89, I went to the Trailways station to drop some money off with my dad. When I found him, he stood in conversation with a guy a few years older than me who could have passed for my father's little brother. I couldn't believe my eyes, so I took off my shades, cleaned them, and looked again. The guy definitely resembled my father. I thought maybe he was my father's brother.

"Oh, hey, Curtis," my father said as I approached them. He acted a bit surprised. I gave him a look, as if to ask, *Who's he?* "Curtis, this is your brother, Andre."

I looked closely at Andre. He had darker skin than me. He was probably twenty-six or seven. Around five-foot-one, wavy hair, and, like a miniature Herman, a slick dresser. I put my hand out to shake.

"Andre, this is your little brother, Curtis," my dad continued. "Actually, this is good you two can meet."

"Nice to know you," Andre said as he shook my hand and hugged me. The moment felt a bit awkward, to say the least, but Andre ended up being a great guy who took to me and my sisters immediately. Once he got to know us, and we him, he acted like the big brother and always tried to protect us. He was great fun and always in a good mood and loved to party, just like our father.

A few days after meeting him, we chilled together in Palmer Park. We drank some Heinekens while we watched a guy clean my car.

"You know we got another sister?" he asked.

"Lola up in Detroit," I answered.

"Who?"

"Lola lives with her mother in Detroit. She's older than us or around your age. Dad told us about her a long time ago."

"Nah, I'm talking about Marie, right here in DC."

"That muthafucker," I exclaimed, but not in anger. "How many damn kids he got?"

"Yo, our pop's a playa for real."

Once I left Potomac State, the drug game became my life. Hustling crack and PCP brought in more cash than I knew what to do with. The crackheads knew I sold good rock. No matter how many times I told them not to come by my house, they wouldn't listen. They'd come begging at all hours asking for the "Red" or the "Green" or whatever shade of food coloring I'd added to the batch that day. I'd party at go-gos almost every night. I spent money like it meant nothing, because it didn't, but I also kept putting money aside—a part of me knowing the good times might not last forever.

One reason for my anxiety lie in the increased police activity as the "War on Drugs" took off. Eventually, Glenarden became too hot, and my crew hunted for new turf. Then, two things happened almost simultaneously which changed the game for me.

"Got busted with seventy-five gallons!" Big Curtis raged.

"He's fucked," I replied, calmly.

"We're fucked, too."

"We can find a new supply."

"He was the supply!"

Our PCP supplier had been arrested after a raid on his apartment, killing our access to the drug which represented a steady source of income—a large income. As a result, my business suffered over the next few weeks.

Then New York C finally decided Palmer Park seemed worth his effort and began making regular runs of cocaine. This secured my supply chain, with quantities in the kilos, not ounces. Because Glenarden dried up, I needed a new spot. I decided to do something I'd avoided until that point.

"We're gonna open up on Muncy," I told my crew. "We'll run my block sunup 'til sundown."

"Po-po," Jay chimed in.

"We're gonna run it like Butch. No product and cash on the same guy. We'll set up a crack house, trade a little rock to rent stash houses, and cook the crack."

"Enough demand?" asked EW, trying to sound smart.

"Look around," I said, dead serious. "Only a couple ways onto the street, plus the alley. Easy to control."

"What about my crew?" Big Curtis asked, referring to the guys who peddled our PCP out in Landover.

"We'll run them out to southeast and northwest," I answered.

"The city?"

I pulled a kilo from a backpack on the floor, slammed it down onto the table. "We'll have the supply. It's time to turn up."

Muncy Road became a twenty-four-hour crack strip. As soon as New York C brought the cocaine, we cooked and bagged. Within a couple days, he headed back north with money, returning by week's end with coke. His quantities increased practically with every run. First a kilo, then a kilo and a half, then two keys. Crackheads came begging all hours. Demand soared. Business boomed.

I began to fade into the background, allowing others to oversee more and more of the operation. I dealt with New York C and helped cook but otherwise just managed money and personnel—and problems; there were always problems.

The drug business is inherently dangerous. Other industries have risks, of course, but most legal businesses don't have to deal with employees getting robbed and shot. As Muncy took off, stickup boys from other neighborhoods would drive through (or park on another street and move on foot) and rob my guys. I always told my corner men that their lives held more value than the drugs and to hand the crack over. Still, sometimes a guy got shot. If a stickup boy drove through, my guys would open fire on the car if he tried to rob one of our crew. We traded product for access to a house, for runners and lookouts. But a junkie would jump in bed with another dealer if he needed a fix.

And speaking of other dealers, once Muncy turned up, it attracted guys from Normandy and other streets who used the back alley to catch the junkies on their way onto my road, much like how I used the back entrance of Capitol Hill East the year before. We would run those suckers out, but everyone wanted to be where the action happened—which leads me to the Jamaicans.

When the Prince George County police shut down Capitol Hill East, the Jamaicans fled like rats on a sinking ship to new spots. Of course, they heard my block was popping, so they tried to move in. I won't exaggerate the details. No real turf war occurred. We outnumbered the Jamaicans. But it still took work.

As crack took off in the south, DC Jamaicans told relatives up north, in New York and Boston, of how much money could be made. Soon those northern relatives headed south. A lot ended up at Capitol Hill East. When that development got too hot with police, they migrated to other parts of DC and Prince George County looking for opportunities. In my neighborhood, a handful of Jamaicans began to use some crackhead's place as a stash house and cook house.

When I first heard of it, I didn't immediately react. But when it soon became obvious they intended to stay and sell on Muncy, we had to do something. Initially, I told both my crew and all the old gangstas on the block to rob the Jamaicans the minute they hit the street to sell. Keep the product to do with as you please, I said. My crew would protect them if the Jamaicans tried to start shit.

This began to have an effect. Imagine how long a business would last if it lost a grand every day. But they continued to try to operate on the street. Eventually, I had my guys shoot the house up every day. The crackheads stopped going to the house because they didn't want to get shot. No one got hurt. The last thing I wanted was to go to jail for something stupid. I intended to shoot up the house to send a message. I certainly didn't want bombs thrown or anyone killed, though we had the artillery (grenades and AK-47s).

This wasn't personal. It was street business. The Jamaicans only did what I had done when I went to Capitol Hill East. The difference resided in proximity. At CHE, I set up near the back entrance, intercepting the drug traffic that would have otherwise bought from them, but also respecting their territory enough that I avoided selling in their buildings. They, on the other hand, tried operating in the middle of my neighborhood.

Within a couple weeks, the Jamaicans packed up and headed out. With Muncy under control, I relaxed a bit. The loss of the PCP money had hurt at first, but our volume in crack now made up for it and more.

One day in early summer, my dad asked me to take a ride with him. This seemed strange to me. Since I'd become an adult, I'm not sure we'd ever just taken a ride together. I gamely climbed into his white Grand Prix, wondering what he had planned.

For the first few minutes, we rode without speaking, listening to the radio. My curiosity got the better of me, and I finally asked what was going on.

"Your mother's leaving," he said without any warning.

"What do you mean?"

"She's moving out, gonna rent a place across town."

"What are you talking about? You two getting divorced?"

He stared out the windshield. He drove without a destination, just moving. "I don't think so. She says she still loves me, just can't sleep under the same roof anymore."

"Then I don't get it. What's her problem?"

"Us."

"What does that mean?"

"Calm down. I don't mean to act mysterious, I'm just collecting my thoughts.... Mostly, she's sick of me cheating, staying out, running the streets. She's put up with my shit all these years, but things have changed to the point where she's tired of all the bullshit."

"What's changed?" I asked, expecting him to tell me I had yet another brother or sister.

"Muncy's changed," he said instead. "And that's on you. Your mom dealt with my shit because we had a safe place to live, a little extra money now and then. She never had to worry about getting shot when she stepped out of the house. And she knew, even with all the hustling over at the shopping center and rec, that you kids would be okay. But you're all grown up and the hood's changed."

"And that's on me." It wasn't a question.

"Hmmm, yeah, Curtis, it is. She doesn't want to bury you. She definitely doesn't want to be there if you get killed. These crackheads always hanging around, knocking on the door, the windows, all hours. It's freaked her out."

I looked out the passenger window. Despite the rules of the game, I had gotten sloppy. We never dealt directly from my dad's house, but we cooked there sometimes. And I did keep drugs in the house occasionally, when business got too crazy or hectic to run to one of my stash houses.

"She's also disappointed. Probably heartbroken. She really thought you'd avoid this life."

"It's too deep inside me," I whispered.

"Is it? Or is that just an excuse?"

"I tried!" My anger flared. "Once basketball season ends, I'm just not focused. School bores me. I only wanted to go to college to be a basketball player. Besides, do you realize how much money I make?"

"Oh, no question there. I see the clothes, the shoes, how often you're out all night. Yeah, you're making money, son. But it's fast money."

"What does a man do when what he really hopes for doesn't happen? I can make money without some paper degree. You two couldn't afford it anyway...."

"You had talent. A little more effort off the court—"

"How'd you know I was good? You came to one game!"

He looked away and I regretted my tone.

"I'm sorry about that, Curtis," he said. "I should have been there more, but that doesn't mean I wasn't proud of you."

We rode on in silence, wandering both the streets of DC and the depths of our relationship. I could have said plenty of hurtful things but held back. Eventually he spoke up.

"The point is that your mom no longer wants to live with me or in Palmer Park, but she still loves both of us.

"As for the drugs: What you're doing isn't right, Curtis. Just look at what our neighborhood's become. The consequences of this shit is real. Any day, you could end up in jail, or dead. That's the only two ways out of the game you're playing. Any day I could get a call at work with bad news. That's part of why your mom is moving out.

"But I can't leave," he continued. "And you're my son, and I love you. Because you're my son, I also know nothing I say will change your mind about this. You're not gonna give up the game any more than I'd give up living my life. So, I got your back on whatever you choose to do. I understand your reasons. I wish I'd given a better example, something for you to follow, but if this is how it's gonna be, then I'm with you no matter.

But boy, you better know what the fuck you're doing and the consequences that come with the life you're choosing."

He drove back towards his house, made more spacious now with him living alone. I was living full-time at Darlene's mom's house. I thought a lot about what he'd said. I really saw no other option for my life. It had always been either college and basketball or hustling. I'd tried to make it out. Yes, I could've tried harder, but the benefits of the drug game fit so well with my need for material gain and respect that no other option could fulfill those needs. At twenty-one years old, I could make as much money in a month as my dad made in a year. He had provided an example. But I couldn't accept the lessons of his example under any circumstance. My greed never allowed it.

After that car ride, our relationship changed. We became closer; friends, even. He may not have liked my lifestyle, but he'd accepted it and me. I no longer needed to display any pretext of going to college or hide who I was.

Not so with Ken Freeman. During the high school season, I attended Parkdale games to cheer on Henry Hall, who continued to dominate his opponents. Freeman and I always spoke at these games. Though he felt disappointed when I dropped out of Potomac State, I'd reasoned being so far away from home combined with the area's cultural differences made me uncomfortable. He never actively pushed going back to college, but Freeman never gave up the hope.

Whenever he had a problem with a player, he'd call me and ask that I speak with the kid. Most of the guys on the basketball team either knew me or knew of me. They knew me better than Freeman did at that time. Ken would ask me to set a kid straight, offer some motivation: Work hard, go to class, don't disrespect your mama, that kind of thing. I felt like the biggest hypocrite whenever he promoted me as a guy who'd worked hard and made it to college. But I actually enjoyed the brief moments of mentorship. I ended up in a similar position as Irvin: the college athlete back in the streets, pushing a younger guy to avoid my mistakes. Except Irvin meant what he said, while I just played a role. In fact, I enjoyed running Muncy Road and had reconciled my decision to leave college without many regrets. Still, whenever Freeman called, I dutifully ran through my tough-love pep talk.

Years later, these initial opportunities to mentor proved great experience for me. As I rose as a coach and then consultant, too many young men needed a real adult to lean on them and push them in the right direction. I think Freeman always saw an ability within me to encourage and motivate. Once I aimed towards positive things, I could honestly give that guidance. I believe Freeman saw more in me than I saw in myself, and I wish I'd listened to him more.

The drug game continued. Crack spread through Palmer Park like wildfire, leaving char and destruction in its path. Guys I'd grown up with died or went to prison, yet my crew survived.

But the neighborhood became so crime-ridden and dangerous, the Prince George County police moved their precinct into the neighborhood.

In the summer of 1991, I stood outside my dad's house with my sister, Beverly. We planned on going to Georgetown to buy outfits to wear at my friend Kevin Rustin's wedding that weekend. My dad fussed around in the house. As I climbed into my Alfa Romeo, police cruisers screeched to a stop around us, and officers with guns drawn swarmed us.

"Down! Down! Get on the ground—"

"Hands! Let us see your hands!"

They threw Beverly and me onto the ground. A cop slammed a knee into my lower back, twisting my arms behind me. I could hear Beverly screaming as they handled her the same way. Police stormed my house, dragging my father into the yard and tossing him onto the ground.

"How ya doing, Curtis?" a plainclothes cop said as he squatted in front of me. "Got a warrant for your arrest."

I looked up. My friends and neighbors all stood out on the road and sidewalk, watching.

"Seems like you're the top dog in this neighborhood," the cop continued. "Our sources tell us you're responsible for all the crack running through here." He exaggerated, but I got the point.

"Now, you'll get to play basketball in Hagerstown prison. Bet you'll make the all-star team," he taunted.

Another cop approached. He held up a clear plastic bag with about fifteen to twenty grams of crack in it and, in his other hand, a gun. The police found the crack in a stereo speaker. I'd forgotten about the shit. Fucking rule number five.

"Herman Malone, you are under arrest."

"Beverly Malone, you also are under arrest."

"Herman Curtis Malone, you, especially, are under arrest."

They saved me for last. Sat me up on the curb with my hands cuffed behind my back and let me watch as my sister and father were shoved into a van.

Part 3

The Rise of DC Assault

1992–2000

College. Convict. Crack.

"The way I see it, there's no reason a hardworking, clean-cut brother like you should sacrifice your college education. So, I plan on trying to get a suspended sentence, some probation," my lawyer explained as I sat in his office. My dad was released on personal recognizance awaiting trial. Because of her criminal history, Beverly was held with no bond. She had offered to claim the crack belonged to her, which meant a lot to me, but I'd refused.

"Wait," I interrupted. "What are you talking about? I don't have a job, and I'm not in college."

"By the time we're ready to plea out, I suggest you have a job. And if I can present you as the Palmer Park success story—college student, not crack dealer—I'll be able to help you a lot more. So, what do you think? Can you get a job, go back to school?"

The strategy made sense. The police labeled me as the guy flooding most of Palmer Park with cocaine. They had only found fifteen grams and a gun, which I'm sure disappointed them. Still, they wanted me off the streets, and the county prosecutor would paint a picture depicting me as a dangerous drug dealer. Combating that depiction, my lawyer claimed, hinged on showing I really was a college student just trying to get by in a bad environment.

"I mean, I'll try," I answered, not knowing exactly how I'd pull it all off.

The job ended up being easy. My father worked as a supervisor at Greyhound, so he hired me to work at the station in the baggage claim area. As for going back to college, I got lucky.

I'd known Harold Bates my whole life. He ran the Executive III AAU basketball team and always attended local games to scout talent. He had helped numerous guys get into college across the country, but Freeman disliked him because he thought Bates took bribes to direct players to certain programs.

"Harold Bates sells players," he'd told me. But with my arrest, I needed help. As it happened, I ran into Bates at a game, and he coincidentally asked me if I wanted to go back to school.

"Well, yeah. Definitely," I answered.

"I might have an opportunity for you. Junior college in Alvin, Texas, needs a point guard."

"Texas?"

"Yeah, town about thirty miles from Houston. Nolan Ryan grew up there. They're losing the kid, Curt Smith. You've heard of him, right? The coach contacted me asking if I knew anyone."

"Yeah, I've seen Curt play. But damn, Texas is far away."

"Curtis, if you're interested, let me know, and I'll put a word in, help you out. I've always liked your game. You're a good kid. I hated to hear you dropped out."

No matter Freeman's opinion of Bates, or his reputation, his offer seemed like a gift from heaven. I obviously couldn't say no.

"I'm definitely interested, Mr. Bates. I'd appreciate it."

"Your Honor, the plea agreement stipulates my client will begin his sentence after the current semester ends. We feel this agreement is in the best interest of both my client and the state of Maryland," my lawyer concluded.

"Mr. Malone, you've entered into this plea of your own accord?"

I glanced at my lawyer, who nodded his head.

"Yes, Your Honor."

"Then I accept the plea and sentence you to five years. I'll suspend all but six months of that sentence, per your agreement with the state. I also sentence you to three years of probation. You will surrender in June, after your current semester of college concludes. Do you understand this sentence?"

"Yes, sir."

In retrospect, I wish I'd fought the case rather than plea out. But by taking responsibility, the state dropped charges against both my sister and my father. Now, I just had to get to school.

I flew to Houston on a Tuesday in January of 1992. I needed to take and pass a few courses during the spring semester if I wanted to be eligible to play that fall. Bates came through and secured me some grants to make Alvin affordable.

Alvin Community College sits just outside Houston, and I quickly fell in love with the city. Houston remains one of my favorite places to this day. On weekends my teammates and I would party downtown. Friends who owned cars always complained about paying for gas. I made a deal: If you had a ride, I bought the gas, drinks, and paid the cover charges at the club. I always kept a few thousand on me. I may have gotten busted and fled to Texas, but Big Curtis and the crew still ran the show back home. I'd have money wired to me every week.

The younger brother of Hakeem Olajuwon, Afis, played on my team. He'd take us to Houston Rockets games to cheer on his brother. We always tried to get Afis to party with us in the city, but he complained about money and gas all the time. I couldn't understand how the little brother of one of the NBA's top players could complain about being broke, but I later learned Hakeem only provided Afis with a fifty-dollar allowance each week. At the time, I thought such a small allowance selfish or stingy on Hakeem's part. I mean, the man made millions every year. I had no concept of the value of money. Now, I realize what I considered stingy behavior actually provided Afis with a strong lesson in working hard and budgeting his money. Hakeem, unlike so many young, Black athletes, probably saved his earnings from his NBA days. A lesson I tried to instill in my players.

My few months in Houston flew by too quickly. In June, I self-surrendered to Upper Marlboro, the Prince George County detention center. I immediately went to the work detail unit, assigned to kitchen duty. I had to serve about three months of the six months that hadn't been suspended. My sister, Beverly, came and went from Upper Marlboro so often, both the inmates and staff already knew of me. So, my whole little bid went smoothly. When I decided to get into the drug game, I knew jail could happen. I felt prepared for it.

By the beginning of September, I'd done my time and returned home to Palmer Park. I needed to make a decision regarding college. My coach and my parents kept asking when I would head back to school. Both my mom and dad urged me to return, but the older street guys really pushed me, too.

"Don't make the same damn mistake I did, Curtis," Irvin urged me. We sat on my dad's front porch. "You've got an out. The chance is right there in front of you. Turn your back on this, and you won't get another. I know it in my gut. Don't waste this."

Even members of my own crew pushed me to go back. Twin and I stood in the cook-house kitchen, pure powder on the counter.

"It's a free education, Li'l Curtis. You should take advantage of it."

"We've got a damn nice run going here, Twin. I don't think I want to be sitting in a classroom in Texas studying art history."

"Every run ends sooner or later, bro."

"I got a feeling our run's just beginning."

I informed my family and coach I wouldn't be returning to Alvin. I called Mr. Bates and explained I wanted to stay home. He offered to help me if I ever decided to go back, and I thanked him for his support.

Once I made the decision not to go back to school, I moved quickly to up my drug business. My days consisted of returning calls and pages from my crew. I kept track of who had finished up and who needed more work. Once I knew how fast the product moved, I'd meet to collect money or drop off more coke. This lasted all day and into the night. I hated working late because I considered that party time for myself. My friends and I would hit a go-go club every night of the week. By the beginning of '93, my arrest had faded to a temporary bump in the road.

"The plug's named Pedro. He and his bro out of New York," Twin's uncle, C Ricks, explained. "He's willing to supply 'cause I talked you up, put in a word, but there's an issue."

"What?"

"He don't wanna deal with Twin."

"What the fuck I do?" Twin asked.

"It's your reputation. He doesn't trust you."

"This was my damn idea. I'm trying to make the muthafucker money and he's disrespecting me!" Twin was pissed. He started pacing around the kitchen table where I sat with his uncle.

"See how you are? Pedro's family. He knows you."

"Tell him that I said, 'Fuck him,' Uncle C Ricks. We don't need his shit!"

"Now hold on," I said. "What are we talking about here?"

C Ricks looked at me. "Steady runs. Good powder. A connect like this isn't easy to find. Reasonable-enough prices."

"I like to cook my own…"

"So do they."

"Yeah, but tough to guarantee quality. Think it's negotiable?"

"Once you build the relationship, probably. But," he glanced at his nephew, "dumbass here trying to fuck it up."

"Ask him to meet me. Let me talk to him. Maybe if I'm handling the relationship, we can make something work."

"Thanks, son. Throwing me under the bus?" Twin asked me.

"We're a team, man. I'm not throwing you anywhere. I'll make it clear you're part of my crew, but I'll deal with them directly."

I met Pedro for the first time a few weeks later. We made a deal on price and quantity. Just like Twin's uncle C Ricks expected, Pedro sold me soft powder cocaine and "hard," already-cooked crack. I didn't like his cooked coke and didn't want it but accepted it at first to gain his trust in order to build the relationship.

About a month later, I arrived at C Ricks's place to meet Pedro to pick up more cocaine. Several other guys also sat around waiting for him to arrive. I realized Pedro must be a major player because the other dealers moved a lot of crack in the DC area. I recognized a childhood friend, whom I called my cousin, Cat Eyes. He'd lived in Palmer Park back in the day. I hadn't seen Cat Eyes in years, so we got to talking.

"Yo, man, I'm so glad to see you," I told him and meant it. "Cuz, you here getting work?"

"Waiting for the man.... You too?"

"I'm eating with these guys."

"I don't like this rock shit he's giving me," I said. "Would rather cook it myself."

"Man, someday I gotta cook your shit for you. I could teach you something."

"What do you mean?" I asked, but before he answered, Pedro walked in.

We each met with him privately. As I stood in the bedroom, he'd have a guy count out the kilos.

"Pedro, my man, I need the soft powder. My guys don't like the hard shit."

"You got to take what we got. I got some soft and some hard. I got others I have to hit with work. You telling me you can't move the product, I'll find someone who can. Lotsa guys out there waiting."

I had to impress upon him that my crew and I could move product, so I didn't press the point. But man, it pissed me off. Pedro's supply kept us in business, and we made great money, but I strongly believed in cooking my own crack and controlling the quality. New York C would've called it "Managing Brand Reputation."

Pedro continued supplying both soft powder and hard rock for a while, and it felt like pulling teeth to get him to budge. Finally, I came up with a plan. He'd fronted us ten kilos, six hard plus four soft. I explained my idea to Twin.

"We're gonna sit on these hard ones for like a month, until his next run. Then I'm just gonna give 'em back and tell him our people couldn't move it."

"Just give it back? Fuck that. Sell that shit and don't pay."

"Twin, that's why I'm dealing with him and not you. You gonna fuck the plug and live every day looking over your shoulder? Come on, man, smarten up."

The following month, I met with Pedro and his brother Mario and returned the six kilos of rock.

"You serious, Curtis? I'm fronting you this crack and you're bringing it back to me?"

"Listen, Pedro. I can move good product. I want powder. If you don't want to supply, then I'm good. I'm thinking about going back to school anyway."

"You gonna be a college boy again?" Pedro asked sarcastically. He knew about my history with college.

"Trying to make moms proud," I answered truthfully. Over the year I'd dealt with Pedro, I'd gotten my money back up. I had the itch to try again with school.

"Alright, smart guy. Mario, give him some more powder."

From then on Pedro treated me better. I still had to deal with his already-cooked, hard crack, but if the quality was good enough, I'd recook it and add to the batch (including my food coloring). If he gave me shit product, I'd bring it back to him.

If I hadn't partied five or six nights a week, I really could have saved a ton of money. I lived an expensive lifestyle. We partied at night, shopped during the day. I always kept my crew around me because you never knew when someone might try you. My motto was, *Don't look for trouble, but be ready if it finds you.* I had some great guys working for me during this time. An awful lot died young and really never got to live life. But we chose the lifestyle knowing the risk and what came with it. We all saw the stickups, the drive-bys, and the murders. We all knew friends or had family in prison. Death or jail became an accepted part of our reality, an aspect of our identity.

We created titles like "OG" to honor those who'd survived. We idolized hardcore gangstas who represented the epitome of our image of the Black male: strong, feared, respected. We made our money on the backs of junkies and fiends, enslaving them with the product we peddled and enslaving ourselves in the process. And we didn't realize our actions just perpetuated a cycle of poverty and dependency because we loved dropping two grand at a club every night.

My indecision regarding college seems comical now, as I look back on it. Honestly, I wanted to make my parents proud. My actions, specifically turning Muncy Road into a crack strip, had helped to push my mom away. I really needed to please her. To take the little spark of hope left inside her and stoke it into a blaze. I didn't want to be just another "Almost Made It," the subject of a story for some old head: *Curtis Malone almost made it outta Palmer Park but....*

So, I called Harold Bates and told him I wanted to go back to school. He found a school in Panama City, Florida, Gulf Coast Community College, that needed a point guard. I was getting a bit old to keep trying, but I decided I'd make one more effort. Just like at Alvin, I had to pass my classes during the spring semester to gain eligibility to play that fall. I left for Florida in January.

Before leaving, I told my crew of my plans. Most knew this routine by now. I would've rather had Big Curtis run the show, but because of Pedro's connection to Twin's family, Twin would have to take the lead with the plug. Pedro didn't want to deal with him until C Ricks stepped in. I begged Twin not to fuck our situation up. I explained I'd fly home at least once a month. The money might slow down until May, when the semester ended, but less work could also help get some heat off us with the police, who constantly patrolled our turf. Though the crew griped, I felt comfortable with my decision to go back to school. I promised myself I'd do better.

I expected Panama City to be fun and exciting. Boy, was I wrong. By the end of my first week, I knew the place didn't offer enough to keep me focused or happy. I immediately made plans to fly back and forth between school and Maryland more frequently.

I returned to Florida from my first trip home when, due to bad weather, my plane was diverted to Atlanta. It was Sunday and the airline put us in a hotel overnight. Since I had time to kill, I called New York C, who had moved to the city the year before.

"My man, what's going on in the A-T-L on a Sunday night?" I asked.

"You ever heard of Magic City?"

"It's a club—"

"Only the best strip club on the East Coast. Don't matter if it's Sunday, it'll be popping."

"Come pick me up," I said eagerly.

I had brought about four grand back with me, enough to keep me full for the month. When I woke up Monday morning, too late to catch my flight, I'd burned through more than a thousand dollars. I figured I might as well chill with New York C one more night considering I hadn't seen him for a while, so we hit Magic City again. Then again on Tuesday.

Drunk, at about two on Wednesday morning, I realized I'd already royally fucked up on this latest college try. I asked Twin to go to Western Union and wire another four thousand dollars to me: some to cover my college expenses, some to pay for my hotel and plane ticket, most to blow at clubs for one more night. I made it back to Florida late Thursday.

Several weeks later, I saw a news story on TV about Boston Celtics guard Charles Smith. He'd been arrested for a DUI hit-and-run vehicular homicide. I'd known Smith for years from youth basketball in DC, and we'd become very close. His arrest really affected me, so I asked my coach for permission to return home. He was completely supportive, and I flew back to Maryland.

But I knew I didn't want to return. This one foot in, one foot out of college just couldn't work. Yet, dealing drugs doesn't provide a long career. So, over the next several weeks, I contemplated what kind of business I could launch to make money the legal way.

Where guys like me come from, it's so common to see people shot or murdered or arrested and sent away for ten, twenty, thirty years or longer. It's the same news every day. What happens in the hood now is the same as what happened twenty years ago. We've become numb to bad news.

I decided not to be bad news. I'd already been arrested once, and I promised myself it would never happen again. The problem lies in our level of knowledge. A drug dealer could have a million dollars, but it wouldn't be enough. Most dope dealers didn't grow up in educated households. Money managers, investment portfolios, stocks, bonds, mutual funds—all a foreign language. We get rich but not wealthy. We drop fifty grand on a watch, a hundred thousand on a car, then get busted and the Feds take it all. We leave our families with nothing.

And when the dope dealer gets killed? We don't write wills. We don't leave estates. Our descendants and relatives squabble over a crappy house or worn-down furniture. Table scraps serve as your legacy. I've seen relatives boycott a funeral because they're fighting over the furniture or car. But that dead dealer probably wasted hundreds of thousands of dollars—maybe millions—on material possessions or nightclubs or women. It's sad.

I've known drug dealers with the ability to run successful companies, if not for their lack of vocabulary and presentation. They could have become a CEO, but all they knew were other hustlers and dealers growing up. I saw how easy the money came in through drugs, and I saw how hard my father worked to earn his little salary. Should I be blamed for choosing the easy path? At that point in my life, I felt torn between two roads. Freeman tried leading me down one. Byrd, Irvin, and Twin unintentionally showed me another. I'd been trying to blaze a third trail: the drug dealing college boy. It didn't work.

Yet, I couldn't just give into the drug game completely. I knew it would swallow me up. I needed the rush and the adrenaline of the game. I loved the money. But dealing drugs made me feel like a typical failure. I may have run a great operation, but it was so...expected of someone my age, my race, and from where I came.

I left Gulf Coast Community College at the end of the semester, and I also rededicated myself to become good news in my neighborhood. I did not exactly know how, but I decided to start a legitimate business.

Legit. Kind of...

After thinking on it for a few weeks, I realized one of the people who influenced my idolization of drugs also knew a thing or two about starting a real business. Twin founded a moving company at about the same age. Why not learn from him?

"A moving company?" Twin asked.

"You did alright with it for a while." Twin had let the company lapse once crack began making us serious money.

"Why you want to do this?"

"I'm hoping to do something real. Plus, I'm making all this money from the drug game, and all I do is run through it. Putting it into starting a business makes more sense to me, right now, than blowing it on a club or materialistic shit. You think you could show me the ropes?"

"Yeah, if that's what you want."

Twin put the paperwork together. We named the company Premier Movers.

"Hey, I found a few trucks for sale we should check out," Twin told me one day.

"Under thirty feet, right?" I asked. Trucks over thirty feet required a CDL license.

"Yeah. One's listed for seventeen grand, the other thirteen."

I knew my parents felt disappointed that, once again, I'd left school. But by starting my own business, I thought I might appease them. I named my friend Mike Sumner as vice president. I'd known Mike from the basketball court, since before my failed tryout for the PG All-Stars. He was a sharp guy who had just graduated from American University and was eager to help launch the business.

Twin and I went to see the trucks. I didn't know shit about cars, so we asked C Ricks to come. I thought both looked good, but C Ricks thought the cheaper truck needed some minor work. The seller agreed to get the repairs done, and I paid him thirty thousand for both. We drove the decent truck home and had Premier Mover's logo painted on the side. We had both titles, our articles of incorporation and the company's EIN. Now we just needed some clients.

"We could post some flyers. Do an ad in the yellow pages," Twin said.

"Yeah. Do that. Maybe run some ads in the local newspapers or in those little advertisement books with apartment and house listings."

"Alright. I'll put something together."

Twin did great. I needed someone laser-focused because I decided to open a second company promoting parties.

I'd read somewhere that the best way to succeed in business is to work in a field you know. Well, I definitely knew how to party.

Curtis Malone Entertainment booked small venues that always sold out. I realized early that lines outside and a reputation of being difficult to get into drove more demand. These parties never earned me the kind of money drugs did, but they attracted drug dealers, many of whom became customers of my crew.

As the popularity of my parties picked up, I began booking fire stations, a fashionable venue for these types of privately hosted events back then. I had to pay to have police present, and some of my guys acted as bouncers and security. I held the first fire station party at the Addison Road station. The event sold out with a line snaking around the building.

Inside, people crowded one another shoulder to shoulder. Out of the corner of my eye, I saw my cousin Cat Eyes and some of his friends in a heated argument with a few other people I knew. I walked over to find out what was wrong.

"What's up, Cuz?" Cat Eyes looked pissed but seemed to settle down once I showed up. The argument, he explained, stemmed from some past disrespect done to a member of Cat Eyes's crew.

"Just dealing with some suckas, Cuz. No problem though," he told me.

I looked at the other group.

"Everybody cool here? I don't want any problems at my party."

"We cool," one answered. We spoke a few more minutes, until I felt the situation had settled down. I eventually walked away and rejoined the partying crowd.

As the party ended, gunshots rang out in the parking lot. The couple of police on duty tried to control the situation, but people ran everywhere. I couldn't tell what had happened or if anyone had been shot. The county decided there wouldn't be any more fire station parties after that.

The next day, I learned that Cat Eyes had been hit by a bullet in the neck. He'd jumped into his car and drove himself to the hospital, where they kept him a few days. I went to visit him to make sure he was okay.

Twin and Mike Sumner did a fantastic job getting Premier Movers up and running. We received our business license and got bonded. Twin had a business phone line set up and Mike Sumner began advertising. We lined up some estimates. I felt proud to be a real business owner. We experienced one hitch: the second truck. The seller had promised to get the repairs done but kept bullshitting us. We stopped by twice and finally just told him to refund our thirteen grand. He couldn't produce that much all at once, so he agreed to pay a little each week until he fully refunded us. We had to make do with one truck, but at the time, the volume of business didn't force us to buy a second vehicle.

Of course, I couldn't completely leave the drug game. I began hanging out with Cuz since we hadn't seen one another in over twenty years. He'd moved from Palmer Park to Clay Terrace in Northeast DC back when we were kids. Cat Eyes had been in and out of jail a lot growing up. We both used Pedro as a connect now, but I quickly realized Cat Eyes made a lot of paper.

"Cuz, we getting almost the same amount of powder, the same lame-ass rock, but you're making way more than me. What the fuck are you doing so different from me?"

"Yo, I told you, I'm the best chef in town. Come on, let's take a ride. I want to show you something."

We drove to Oakcrest Towers, a high-rise apartment complex, and we went up to an empty unit. In the kitchen, I saw nothing but Visions cookware, stainless steel pots, industrial cake blenders, and boxes upon boxes of baking soda.

"Got-damn, Cuz, what you got, a bakery in this muthafucker?" Cat Eyes took a kilo of cocaine from his backpack, unwrapped it, and poured it onto a scale. He weighed it and put it in the big pot after breaking it all up into sand. Then he dumped about 1,000 grams of baking soda onto the scale and mixed it into the pot holding the cocaine.

"There's no way that's all gonna fit."

"Just observe, Cuz. You wanted to know how I'm eating so good."

He then moistened it and put it on the stove to cook. He'd almost melted down the combined 2,000 grams of powder when he told me to plug in one of the big blenders.

"Now, when the powder's almost done cookin', we mix it." He started blending the powder like a real cake mix. After a few minutes, the whole batch began to harden like any of mine would. He dumped it onto the counter.

"That's literally the biggest crack rock I've ever seen," I practically whispered in awe. Cat Eyes had to hit it with a hammer to break it apart in order to weigh it.

"This shit's so diluted you might as well call me Garbage Man," he said, "but we just doubled our quantity."

"Fuck it, call me Garbage Man, too."

"Just don't tell anyone, ya know? The crackheads don't seem to care so long as they getting a high."

"I can't fucking wait to get back," I exclaimed as we drove off.

By nearly doubling the quantity, I could take ten kilos and turn it into nineteen—easy money. My crew worked on consignment, so without any more work on my part, and my only expense baking soda, my profit margin soared. I'd cook batches for a select few dealers in the neighborhood but would never let them into the kitchen in order to protect Cat Eyes's formula. If I heard too much bad talk about quality, I'd drop the price and wouldn't put as much baking soda in it. Now, even when Pedro forced me to take already-cooked rock, I could double-down on the powder he gave me.

I'd been with Darlene since age thirteen. We'd had our ups and downs, but she'd faithfully stuck by me. In 1994—I still hadn't told her about Tawanna and Tanay—she announced she was pregnant. For a long time, I believed Darlene and I would get married, even as I cheated on her with many other women. My lifestyle also presented obstacles: Rival dealers often kidnapped a girl and demanded a ransom. So, whenever Darlene and I went to a club, I'd have my guys with us to watch our backs. She hated this and, more often than not, stayed home when I went out. I'd take her to dinner, but again, we'd always have someone else around. If she went out—shopping, to a club, wherever—I made sure Twin, Jay, or Uncle Rick got her home safely, even as it put stress on us. It made for a complex relationship, but Darlene loved me. My lifestyle ensured she never went without. I'd lived with her and her mom since Palmer Park had become too busy, and I didn't feel safe laying my head there. We had a good, if not perfect, situation.

I felt excited to be a father again, even if, in hindsight, our relationship never matured. By constantly leaving for school, spending four to five months away, and with the danger of my lifestyle always present, we never formed a serious adult-level bond. A more consistent and safer environment may have made a difference. Still, in '94, we both believed that we loved one another and that the pregnancy was a blessing.

My moving company had jobs lined up and needed employees. I tried to hire young guys from the neighborhood, especially anyone trying to get clean. Our biggest concern and problem: finding workers who wouldn't steal our clients' shit. Twin always threatened to break anyone's hands if they got caught stealing on a job. It wasn't an idle threat. Though the company landed jobs and brought in money, I realized just breaking even would take longer than I'd expected.

Curtis Malone Entertainment threw a bash at St. Luke's, a well-known church in Southeast Washington a few months after Cat Eyes showed me how he cooked. I oversold the venue that night. About 600 people crowded into the church while another 300 lined up outside. Even those in line with a ticket had to be turned away. Suddenly, the crowd outside began surging towards the entrance, trying to get inside. They knocked down and nearly trampled a couple of police officers near the door. More police showed up and tried to restore order. The crowd was pissed they couldn't get in, but we'd reached capacity according to the fire code. Once everyone rushed the building, the police ended the party, pissing off all the people inside.

Each event made me between ten and fifteen grand. The damage to my reputation and negative attention from the police made the parties not worth the trouble, especially when crack brought in so much. I stopped hosting them.

College basketball hadn't worked out and neither had college in general. I learned being a legitimate businessman took more effort than I'd thought. In reality, at that point in my life, I'd only succeeded at dealing drugs. But I really didn't want to do that forever. In order to get away from the crack game, I needed to find something else to do with my life. Luckily, I still had one option left.

Coach Malone

"He's too talented."

"Don't tamper, Curtis. He's on my roster."

"He's what, twelve? He's schooling kids two, three years older. Let me get him."

"No."

"He should decide. Hey, Hill, come over here!" The kid jogged over, said hello to Troy, gave me a shy smile.

"Do you know who I am?" I asked.

"No, not really. . . ."

"I'm Coach Malone, and I coach the Columbia Park fifteen-and-unders. Coach Weaver and I both want you on our teams," I explained. "But we decided to let you make the decision." As I spoke, I pulled out a wad of bills, twenties mostly, and began counting them. The kid's eyes bulged out. I smiled at him.

"So, Dalonte, you wanna play up on my team with the older guys, or you happy beating down on little kids?"

He looked at Troy briefly, then met my eye. "I think I want to play up."

Around the same time I started Premier Mover, I also thought about how I might help my neighborhood. Basketball had always been my first love, so I decided to try and coach. I thought I could help these kids and steer them clear of the drug life I couldn't seem to get away from.

Mr. Barksdale ran the Palmer Park Rec Center and didn't care too much for me. The police held neighborhood meetings at the rec center regularly and Barksdale knew everything going on in our hood. Though people liked and respected me, there's no doubt Barksdale heard that I played a major role in the drug trade in Palmer Park. He forbade his daughter, Hillary, from speaking to me, even though we were friends. Whenever he thought she was out front talking to me, he would make her come inside the rec. So I honestly expected him to say no when I asked if I could coach a team.

"You're serious?" he asked.

"Yes. Absolutely," I answered.

"You want to coach a rec team? You realize it's a commitment? You gotta be on time, hold practices, games...."

"Yeah. I know. I want to coach."

"Alright. Season starts in a couple months. I'll let you know."

As the season approached, I felt excited. I really looked forward to coaching. Part of it came from working with the kids, but I also wanted to have the game of basketball back in my life. I always felt better about myself and my life when out on the court. Barksdale assigned me a team. I had a mixed reputation among the parents, at least among those who cared. I tried to reassure them I took the job of coach seriously, but my age worked against me.

A week into the season, I rushed back from DC, trying to make practice without being too late. I didn't bother to call ahead, thinking I'd only arrive fifteen minutes after our scheduled start time. When I got to the rec, I walked into the gym and saw some other guy running my team's practice.

"Hey, what's going on?" I asked Barksdale, who had emerged from his office as soon as I I'd come in.

"You're an hour late!"

I glanced at my watch. "Thirty minutes, Mr. Barksdale. Traffic leaving the city was awful."

"I don't think you're ready to be a coach, Curtis. I'm giving your team to someone more responsible."

"That's crazy! I really want to coach this team!"

"I've made my decision, Curtis."

Barksdale's decision hurt me more than when I got cut from the PG All-Stars AAU team years before. I'd already formed bonds with my players. All the kids in the neighborhood knew I coached and would come up to me and brag about being on my team. Barksdale deflated my enthusiasm.

But one thing about me, I don't take no for an answer. Challenge me, doubt me, or patronize me, and I'll come back even harder. Barksdale might not have thought me good enough to coach his rec team or allow his daughter to talk to me, but he only pushed me to prove him wrong.

With a chip on my shoulder, I decided to go to our rival neighborhood, Columbia Park. I'd spent a lot of time there, playing at their rec in pickup games and attending go-gos. Mr. Mackins ran the Columbia Park Rec Center, and he and I had always had a great relationship. He genuinely liked me. I also didn't carry any of the same negative baggage in Columbia Park.

As I entered the rec, I ran into a good friend named Troy Weaver whom I'd gotten to know growing up through basketball. Troy worked at the rec center part-time and taught at a local elementary school. Troy also coached Columbia Park's thirteen-and-under team. He hoped to one day start a personal training company that prepared guys for the NBA draft—like private coaching between the time they declared for the draft and actually got picked—as well as off-season training for pros. I thought it a cool idea. We got to talking, and I explained what had happened with Barksdale.

"So, you think Mackins will hire me?"

"He needs a fifteen-and-under coach right now. You want me to talk to him?"

"Yeah. Put in a good word for me. I'm serious about coaching, and now I want to beat Barksdale's Palmer Park team."

Mackins was out of the office, but a couple of days later, Troy called me and told me Mackins said yes. I drove back to Columbia Park to meet with him in person.

"So, Barksdale sent you packing, huh?" he teased.

"Guy's never liked me."

"Still, I know from experience, we don't get a lot of volunteers knocking our doors down. He really must not like you to fire you."

"His daughter and I like one another, and he knows it. That might'a had something to do with it," I joked.

"Well, I want you to watch a few of Troy's practices since this is your first gig. Fourteen- and fifteen-year-olds are a tough age to coach, especially your first time."

"Wasn't too long ago I was their age."

"That isn't always good."

"Mac, I got some kids from Palmer Park who want to come over and play here. That okay?"

"Sure. Long as they aren't troublemakers, I don't mind."

I followed Mackins's instruction and attended a few of Troy's practices. I could tell he had experience gaining kids' respect and trust. He was also great with tactics and drawing up plays. I believed my strength lay in identifying talent. I could watch a kid play and see beyond any temporary, age-induced awkwardness to the real skill hidden underneath. I believe my basketball IQ, which Freeman had praised, helped. I knew the game so well, I could anticipate movement on the court. When I watched a young player, I looked to see if he, too, had that intelligence, but I also realized I could learn from Troy. I immediately incorporated things he did into my coaching.

"I think I want to play up."

"The kid has made his choice," I said to Troy. "Go on back to the game, Dalonte, Coach Weaver and I will take care of it."

As Dalonte ran back to the practice, I turned to Troy. "No hard feelings?"

"You know he's my best player?"

"But he's—"

"It's alright. You're right. He needs to be playing up. It'll be good for him. Just make sure playing against older kids doesn't kill his confidence."

Dalonte Hill, at twelve years old, competed just fine on my fifteen-and-under team. He became my first special player, and our Columbia Park team went undefeated that season, including a beatdown on Barksdale's Palmer Park team. I felt bad beating up on kids I knew from my hood, but I also enjoyed the look on Barksdale's face.

Within the first week of that first season at Columbia Park, I realized just how tough some of these kids had it. Some talented kids would show up to practice with holes in their sneakers. Others walked home on winter nights with no coat to keep them warm. I had players who arrived with black eyes given to them by abusive brothers or fathers. Others shared one bedroom with five or six siblings. Basketball served as a means to escape their lives, if only for a few hours. A period of time relatively safe and fun when each of them could just be a goofy fourteen- or fifteen-year-old. Their fears and concerns dropped away during our practices and games. Not to say we entered into some kind of wonderland; the hood still surrounded us. Trouble still hovered nearby. Players still returned to homes bare of food or to crackaddicted mothers and absent fathers.

I realized how lucky I'd been to grow up in the family I had. And I became determined to help as many of these kids as I could. I felt little self-interest in doing so. I became a coach, mentor, father figure, and friend to my players because I'd been raised by my mom and dad, and Byrd, Irvin, Twin, and Freeman. Coaching represented the culmination of all the lessons I'd learned growing up. Barksdale could judge me for my hustle, but my dedication to those kids was legitimate.

Dalonte Hill really blossomed under my laid-back style. My Columbia Park team went undefeated and won the league championship two years in a row. A lot of parents wanted to bring their kids over to my team. The buzz also drew the attention of high school coaches who recruited my top players. This made me realize I could provide these kids a vehicle to improve their lives. If I ran strong teams and helped to develop top players, they literally could escape their violent DC schools and be educated at a private school like DeMatha or Gonzaga, both of which sent athletes to Division I colleges all the time. Suddenly, my role felt a lot bigger than just that of a coach. I believed I could truly make a difference.

Troy's thirteen-and-under team also dominated, and soon AAU teams began to ask us to leave Columbia Park and work with them. The Amateur Athletic Union, or AAU, formed in January of 1888 to organize amateur sports around some basic standards. Since then, it's expanded into over thirty sports and 670,000 participants. AAU basketball features tournaments across the country. Top prospects typically play for high-profile AAU programs sponsored by the big athletic apparel companies such as Nike, Adidas, and Under Armour.

Ms. Joyce Tillman, who ran the Prince George Jaguars, an AAU program, through the local Boys & Girls Club, wanted to recruit us. Growing up playing basketball in the area allowed me to know a lot of different people, and I'd known Ms. Tillman practically my whole life. I felt comfortable working with her but wanted Troy on board. Mike Sumner had been my assistant coach, and I needed them both to support the decision to leave Columbia Park. I still hustled drugs, so having Troy and Mike's commitment felt crucial to me because they were clean. They both did things right, and I knew I could count on both to cover a practice or game if I got caught up.

Troy and Mike agreed, and on pretty short notice. We rushed to put a team together for the Jaguars. With the three of us coaching, the team did pretty well our first season, and we knew we could recruit top players citywide.

At this point in my life, the moving company, the drug game, and coaching took up most of my time. Darlene was pregnant; my parents, though separated, remained friendly. My business and personal lives were going well, and I didn't regret my decision to forgo college.

One night, Twin and I drove around, taking care of business, picking up money and dropping off work, when Twin got a call from a friend of his who owned an ice cream parlor. The guy asked Twin to come by. Since we were only about ten minutes away, I said no problem.

"Curtis, you got a gun on you?" Twin asked.

"Yeah, but what the fuck you need a gun for? I thought you two were cool?"

"Just to be on the safe side," he answered mysteriously.

I handed him the gun, which he put in his front jacket pocket. I pulled up to the shop and Twin hopped out. I drove around the side of the building to park, grabbed my phone, and made some calls. While on the phone, I heard arguing and looked up to see Twin pull the pistol out and start shooting at the guy he'd been arguing with. Twin ran and ducked while dodging return fire from another guy who emerged from the shop. I started the engine and Twin literally dove into the car. We took off.

"What the fuck was that about?" I yelled.

"Just some bullshit I didn't want to deal with."

"I thought you were cool with them?"

"Just drive, Curtis."

Troy and I knew our second season coaching with the PG Jaguars would be our last. We had talked about the situation and agreed we could start our own AAU program. Our team that season lost in regionals but impressed a lot of people. Ms. Tillman wanted several of our top players to combine with a few from another Jaguars team to make a strong roster for the AAU nationals. Troy and I let some of our players go, knowing it was our last year and wanting them to have fun.

To pay for the trip to nationals, Ms. Tillman had every Jaguar player participate in fundraisers. As she sat in the shade on the side of the road, players asked for donations. They ran from car to car as drivers waited for the streetlight to change. Each kid then delivered their money to Tillman and ran back out there.

"This is crazy," Troy said as we stood watching the scene.

"It's too hot and kinda dangerous for these kids," I replied.

"And how do they know how much money they're making? Ms. Tillman could be pocketing most of it."

"Or the kids could be. That's what I'd do," I said. The system did seem crazy. Having young players begging for spare change didn't seem right to me. "I've got an idea."

"What?"

"You'll see. Hey, Frank, get everyone from our team and come over here!"

The kids who played for us gathered around.

"Guys, listen up. I don't mind if you keep some of that money. Give Ms. Tillman some, but keep a little for yourselves."

"What about nationals?" one asked.

"How we gonna pay to go?"

"You guys who played for Coach Weaver and me who are going to nationals, don't worry. I'm gonna pay for your trip."

This caused a bunch of smiles, and the kids ran back out to beg for money.

"Why'd you tell them to keep some money? It's kinda like stealing."

"Troy, these kids got nothing. She's got them sweating bullets running around, and most of them aren't even going to nationals. If they leave ten or twenty dollars in their pockets and can eat tonight, I'm good with that. Right?"

"Yeah. You're right."

"Besides, I'll cover their trip."

I hadn't exaggerated. Most of the kids didn't have anything but their skills on the basketball court. I wanted to help them get the most out of the game. If my players felt hungry, I fed them. If I got to know their family, I'd feed the whole household. When I came to pick up their son, parents knew for a short time their kid would get out of the hood and be safe and knew he'd come home with a full stomach. For years, I'd wasted money I made from drugs on clubs, clothes, and parties. Now, I invested that money back into young guys in the community, hoping if I provided a pathway to success through basketball, they could escape the life I'd embraced.

Working with those kids forced me to question my lifestyle. The drug hustle put me in danger. Having kids around put them in danger, too. After Twin's shootout, I had my crew on point. My guys would go outside the gym and check the parking lot after practice to make sure no one could get a jump on us.

One day, I drove some players to practice in my Cressida station wagon with tinted windows. A police cruiser pulled behind me and flashed his blues. I didn't pull over immediately, and three more police cars joined the first, as if they'd been waiting for me. Eventually, I stopped and handed over my license and registration. One cop asked me to step out of the car.

"I've got kids in the car, so let's be cool, alright?" I said to the cop. I wanted to avoid a scene where these kids would end up face down on the ground. The cop who held my arm looked at the players and couldn't believe they were minors.

"It's just 'cause of their height. They're all teenagers. We're on our way to basketball practice," I tried to explain.

The police didn't seem to care. They pat-searched us and had us sitting on the curb while they searched the car. This definitely wasn't something I wanted the kids to experience and associate with their coach, even if this kind of thing happened to Black people all the time.

The police finished their search and began driving off. One cop lingered behind, and I recognized him as Joey McCann, whom I'd gone to elementary school with. Joey's father was a DC detective, and I always knew he'd be a cop.

"How you doing, Curtis?"

"Been better, Joey. You?"

"Just doing my job, ya know?"

"Went into the family business, I see."

"Listen, Curtis." He lowered his voice. "Just watch yourself, okay? Some of these guys have a hard-on for you, if you catch my meaning?" He'd given friendly advice, and I took it seriously.

"Thanks, Joey," I said, and he drove off.

A few weeks later we ended practice, but Troy and I stayed behind to talk.

"Can we have the keys, Curtis?" one of the kids I drove home asked. I shuttled three players to and from practice, and they liked to race to see who got the front seat. I tossed the keys and they took off.

When I came out of the gym to the car, the three kids sat holding a bunch of money. I'd forgotten I'd put cash in the glove compartment and armrest. I stashed cash in certain places in the car to remind me of who I'd collected money from that day. The kids were all excited.

"Coach, how much money is this?"

"What the hell y'all doing going through my stuff?" But I couldn't be angry with them. They simply acted like typical, curious fourteen- and fifteen-year-olds. I'd left the damn money there.

Incidents like these made me further question the drug hustle. Ever since my cousin, Cat Eyes, showed me how to double my quantity, I had saved more money. I could live off it and fall back significantly if I wanted to. The question was, did I want to?

A good run in the drug game doesn't last forever. Top hustlers know this and thank God every day the work comes in. One Saturday over the summer of '95, my cousin Cat Eyes, some other friends, and I played basketball at the Lee District gymnasium in Virginia. After the game, we checked our phones. Cat Eyes and I had a bunch of missed calls, and Twin had left me an urgent message to call him. I tried to reach him and got no answer. Eventually, we got word from a mutual friend that there had been a shooting at C Ricks's house. I immediately worried that Twin's beef from the ice cream parlor had caught up to him, so we drove straight to the house.

The police had cordoned off the area, with cruisers blocking C Ricks's street. Cat Eyes, myself, and a few others decided to go our own way to shower and change and meet up later. Before I left, I heard from a neighbor that the police were questioning Twin, C Ricks, and some other family members inside the house. Knowing Twin was okay put my mind at ease but left me wondering who'd been killed.

Two hours later, Twin called me to meet up with him. I immediately asked who got shot.

"Fucking Pedro," Twin said.

"You're kidding me!"

"Found his ass dead in the basement. None of us were home."

"So who the fuck killed him?"

"People on the block saying your cuz seen hanging around."

"Well got-damn, he must have a twin 'cause we were in Lee District playing ball all day. Typical bullshit streets trying to put a bad bone on a nigga."

C Ricks, Twin, and his family had solid alibis. So did Cat Eyes. The case remains unsolved.

Pedro's murder caused his brother Mario to pull out of DC. Not knowing who killed Pedro, or why, eroded any remaining trust Mario had in us for the time being. Pedro never liked Twin, and our relationship existed only because C Ricks had vouched for me, and Pedro had come to like me.

Without Pedro's cocaine, our supply dried up. I knew I could eat for a while off the money I'd put aside. I also knew I could pick up some work from Byrd if needed. Getting out of the drug game appeared to make more sense at the time.

Then Twin's shootout at the shop caught up with him. The police arrested him and charged him with assault with intent to kill. I hired him a lawyer, but with his priors, the judge denied bail. I suddenly lost not just one of my bruisers and best friend, but also Premier Movers's general manager.

Troy and I felt ready to launch our own AAU team. Mike Sumner would also coach, and we brought in A. Brown, who was into the sports management business, to oversee the program. Troy also recruited a friend he knew, a fellow teacher in the Prince George County school system, Damon Handon. He was named an assistant coach. The five of us set our sights on finding the best players throughout the city, no matter what neighborhoods or backgrounds they came from.

With my drug business hurting, and my moving company missing its general manager, I turned my full attention to basketball.

"Let's do something big," I told Troy.

Suffering Losses

The first half of the '90s were an exciting, successful period for me. The drug business always has ups and downs, but from the time I returned home from jail in the fall of '92 until Pedro's murder three years later, crack made me enough money to live very well and put up for my retirement from the game. Premier Movers gave me a taste of legitimacy, and by the time the crack game slowed, basketball became both my focus and how I planned to give back to my community.

Though those five years helped define who I'd be. They also came with challenges and sorrows. I lost some of the people closest to me. Death wasn't new. You couldn't grow up in a place like Palmer Park during the crack explosion of the eighties without experiencing loss. But such frequent exposure didn't mean the deaths of friends and family hurt less.

I pulled up to Palmer's Liquor Store with Randy Sutton, a childhood friend, who had recently buried his brother. Randy's mom had just buried one son, and Randy wanted to get some perspective on his life. The drug game took more than it gave, and Randy was thinking of getting out. We knew the risk and toll the hustle put on us all, and if Randy wanted to go legit, I supported him.

People crowded into Palmer's Liquors, as usual, with all the regular hustlers out front making sales. We hopped out of the Milano. Randy got called over by a guy we knew from the neighborhood while I went inside. I grabbed a twelve-pack of Lowenbrau and stood in line when a mutual friend ran in.

"Curtis, Randy's been stabbed up real bad," he told me.

"What the fuck?" I ran outside. People yelled and screamed, all bunched up. I couldn't see Randy. "Where is he?" I yelled.

"Dude stabbed him, and he ran across the street," someone said, pointing. "People saying his throat slashed." I looked and saw Randy lying in the grass. I ran across the road to my friend. Blood covered his shirt. In that moment, I thought Randy was dead.

I learned later this all came from a misunderstanding. When we pulled into the liquor store, Randy approached a group of people. One guy in the group thought Randy had been given some stolen drugs, which had belonged to him. When confronted, Randy, not realizing the danger of the situation, played along and jokingly claimed he had them. The guy didn't bother with conversation. Instead, he stabbed Randy in the torso. Randy ran across the road and collapsed. The guy then followed him and sliced his throat.

Dread filled me as I knocked on the door of Randy's mother's house. They'd just lost his brother, Jeff, and now I had to deliver this awful news. Randy had wanted out. We'd just spoken about it. That quick—a snap of fingers—and he was dead in the streets. Drug dealers often romanticize the game, but there's nothing romantic about dancing with death every day. There's nothing romantic about knocking on the door of a mother who just lost one son to tell her another had died. One of Randy's twin sisters opened the door.

"Twin, I've got some bad news."

"Curtis, what is it?"

"Randy's been stabbed up real bad. He should be on his way to the hospital." I didn't really want to admit he'd looked dead, but I also couldn't mislead her. "Listen, you guys need to be prepared. It's real bad."

"No. No. No."

"I'm sorry. We were at Palmer's. Just stopped in for a quick minute. I'm sorry."

I left as they rushed to the hospital. I didn't need to follow.

Ella C. passed away in March of 1991 after suffering a stroke and then a heart attack. My grandmother lived like a firecracker, quick to jump on someone's ass if you bothered her or her loved ones. She loved her family and friends unconditionally. I'll never forget weekends at 1320 and the group of family and friends she collected. I'll always remember her generosity towards me and the love she bestowed, no matter what I did or didn't do in my life. She passed before I got arrested, for which I feel fortunate, and though I know she watches over me still, I would've hated her to be there while I served my sentence.

Though I didn't know him long, my half-brother Andre lived a life of fun. He died of an overdose in August of 1992, while I did my jail time at Upper Marlboro. I feel blessed to have known him and glad to be in my nephew Mann's life, who does his father proud.

Ken Freeman died of cancer in 1993. Towards the end of his life, I avoided him. I felt embarrassed about my arrest and believed I'd disappointed him by selling drugs. Too immature to deal with seeing him sick, I stayed away. Young men dislike acknowledging their own mortality. To watch strong, determined Ken Freeman succumb would've reminded me of my own mortal weakness during a time when I believed I had to appear tough. I regret it now, of course. I realize Freeman impacted my life more than I knew. Had there been no Freeman, the whole concept of college never could have blossomed in my mind. But, more than that, he saw a potential inside of me I did not see. Freeman set me straight my freshman year. Freeman made me carry those boxes for Ms. Markie. Freeman named me senior captain, nurturing my leadership ability, and Freeman asked me to speak to younger players: to encourage, to motivate, and, most importantly, to guide them.

I feel, all these years since, that my good qualities reflect Ken Freeman. I knew many strong-willed Black men growing up, but Ken lived with the strength of a man who knew himself, knew what he valued, and knew his purpose. He lived to help uplift young Black men. So many of my other mentors, though I love them, worked only for the dollar, bringing us down. Who would I be without Freeman? I fear the answer.

A year later, I lost Jabouri McClamb. Jay was one of my young muscles, but I also considered him my little brother. We met in the late eighties and bonded instantly. He could be stubborn and hotheaded, but also loyal and loving. My family loved Jay and his chipped-tooth smile.

One night, Jay and I chilled at a cookout over at a friend's house in College Park when my phone rang.

"Yo, Curtis, some muthafucker just pulled a gun on your dad," a member of my crew told me.

"What? What the fuck is you talking 'bout?" I asked.

"I don't know. The dude pointed a gun in Pop's face and pulled the trigger, empty chamber."

"Okay. I'm on my way," I said as I hung up.

"What's going on?" Jay asked.

"Some nigga pointed a pistol in my dad's face."

We drove back to Palmer Park to check on my dad. He was fine and explained what had happened and who did it. Jay demanded we respond. When Jay got something in his head, you couldn't change his mind. My crew had gathered, and we decided to head to the house the guy stayed at and pull him out or just bust in and get him. I'm not sure we knew what we'd actually do to him once we got our hands on him. I grabbed my gun. Jay and the rest of the crew were already strapped up.

We all met at my dad's and walked down the street to the house we heard he was at. We decided to send some of my guys to the front door while a few waited outside. Jay and a couple others busted in the door, and I heard shots fired. They came back out a second later.

"Nigga ran out the back door," Jay told me.

"Son of a bitch." I was pissed, but we knew the guy, so I knew we would eventually run him down. "Let's go back to the house, so I can put my pistol up."

"I'm keeping mine," Jay said, which was normal because he didn't leave home without it.

"I don't think that's a good idea, Jay." By then the police had rolled in due to the gunshots, but I also knew Jay never put his pistol away, and we were stuck with it.

Once I dropped my gun off, we decided to drive to the store. We both still felt hyped with adrenaline. In hindsight, we should have just laid low at my dad's place. But I doubt we could've sat still after knowing what had happened to my dad.

Police cruised the streets. As I turned the corner, two cars pulled behind me. After a few minutes, another three joined them, and all five put their lights on.

"Aw, fuck," Jay said.

"Well, I'm not pulling over." The police had to have been told of shots fired, and Jay had his pistol on him. Who knew who they'd suspect?

The line of police cruisers grew to about fifteen as I desperately tried to lose them. After five minutes, I knew I couldn't get away.

"Loop back around to the alley and I'll hit it," Jay said.

The alley ran through our entire neighborhood, connecting all the streets. If he could get away, there would be plenty of places to ditch the gun. As I turned back down my block, we had to drive through a crowd. Whenever police activity got hot in the hood, the neighbors came out to rubberneck and gossip.

I pulled over as close to the alley as I could get, and Jay jumped out and ran. One cop tried to catch him, but I knew once he got into the alley, he'd get away. The rest of the cops, including Joey McCann, drew their guns and pulled me from the car. I let them fuck me up a little bit, hoping to buy Jay some time.

They put me in cuffs and arrested me. I sat at the station until almost four in the morning and never saw Jay there. I assumed he got away. Once released, I went to my dad's house to see if he'd heard from Jay. He hadn't, but he'd found a gun out behind his house. I checked it out, and it was Jay's gun. I also called his mom and girlfriend, who was pregnant with Jay's son, and no one had heard from or seen him. I stayed at a friend's house that night but couldn't sleep.

I tried not to panic. Jay had been drinking at the cookout. We had the adrenaline rush of confronting the guy who pulled the gun on my dad, and from the police chase. He'd probably just crashed somewhere, exhausted, I reasoned. But a nagging feeling remained, preventing me from sleeping. As soon as daylight broke, I called everyone again. Their answers remained the same.

"Dad, go out back and see if he's knocked out or something. And check the highway, too." George Palmer Highway (now known as MLK Highway) divided the Palmer Park and Kentland neighborhoods. My dad called me back a few minutes later.

"Curtis, somebody's feet sticking up outta a hole in the alley. I'm calling the police."

"I'm on my way over."

By the time I got there, cruisers and crime scene tape blocked off the alley. My heart fell through my stomach. They'd removed his body before I arrived. Evidently, in the dark, he'd fallen into a recently dug hole, part of a construction project, which had been left uncovered. The construction, coincidentally, began the previous day. Neither Jay nor I knew about it. I pictured in my mind one of my best friends running through the dark. He tosses the pistol but can hear the cop behind him. He decides to try and cross the highway to lose the cop. He turns his head back, searching the night for his pursuer, and never sees the uncovered hole or the tape surrounding it. He falls, headfirst, striking pavement and pipes, his face submerged in groundwater.

They said he died of trauma to the head and drowning. I hope he felt no pain or fear. We also asked some questions: Why didn't the police officer pursuing him discover him there?

Could Jay have been pushed instead? Like so many deaths in the hood, those questions never got answered.

That was the worst day of my life. Jay looked up to me like I looked up to Twin. I acted as the older brother, the role model who tried to protect and guide. To lose him, especially in those circumstances, knocked me to my knees. For years, I avoided the alley.

In '94, Uncle Monk passed away from cancer. My father's best friend and the man at 1320 who gave me my first job, Monk wasn't my real uncle, but he played the part in my life. The man taught me honest work, showed me how to catch the bus by myself, and tried to teach me how to cook, Southern style. I could never sit still long enough to learn. When I asked him to put a basketball court behind my grandmother's building, he built one. That's the kind of man he was.

Randy, Ella C., Andre, Ken Freeman, Jay, Uncle Monk. For as much personal progress I made during the first half of the '90s, I also suffered losses and setbacks. My life felt constantly in flux. Like a tide, sometimes high, sometimes low, I navigated the ocean of my life as best I could. But by '95, I could see daybreak and, though I didn't know it exactly, saw the rise of DC Assault on the horizon.

From Planet Reebok to Team Assault

"So here's our promise to you," I told the crowd of players and some parents who'd gathered at the Columbia Park Rec to launch our AAU team. "If you commit to us, if you buy into what we're trying to do, then we'll commit to you. Our goal is to help you change your life. If you put in the work, if you focus on your grades and your game, we'll help get you into college. And with an education, you can do anything you want in life."

Troy, A. Brown, Damon Handon, Mike Sumner, and I had settled on this mission. We'd do whatever it took to help a player escape poverty or their environment. A kid's basketball skill couldn't save him on its own; these kids needed to develop responsibility and good character and stay focused on school. As a program, we agreed we would go to extremes to see our players be successful.

"If we need to hire you a tutor to get your grades up, we will. If you need to switch schools in order to receive the resources you need to succeed, we'll help make that happen…."

I did not speak about the real underlying problems for most of the kids in our community—stable homes and positive role models—but the five of us knew we would also need to provide both. We were all in our twenties. Troy and Damon worked as schoolteachers; Mike Sumner tried playing professional ball overseas; A. Brown worked towards getting into sports management with an agent. As for myself, well, I had a foot in two worlds. I'd played college ball, ran the streets, had owned a legit moving company. Each of us served as a role model of sorts, and those kids wanted someone a few years older to pay attention to them. Most came from single-parent homes; many lived in outright poverty. None knew that it took more than talent to play college basketball. They also needed to be academically eligible.

Over the years, we pissed off high school coaches by removing some of their best players and transferring them to other schools. Not all, but many, high school coaches will ride a talented player to a state championship without giving a damn about the kid's grades or family life, so long as the player remains eligible to play and shows up for games. The coach puts no further effort into him. Prominent college programs try to recruit the kid, which will literally provide the opportunity to change his life, just to find out he's not academically prepared to compete in a college classroom or does not have the qualifications needed to get accepted into college.

These types of coaches pad their win-loss records without helping the player. We decided to do the opposite.

We also realized how difficult family life could be for some. Growing up in the hood, we knew about empty refrigerators and crowded houses. Absent fathers were the norm. We could relate to our players while showing them a path out really did exist.

"I'm always going to love you. You've rode with me through a lot. But I've met someone else. I'm sorry, Darlene." I closed my eyes and rubbed my left temple, the phone cradled between shoulder and jaw.

"You son of a bitch. Our daughter is due next month!"

"You know I'll provide for you both. Neither of you will go without. . . ."

"How long you been screwing this new bitch?"

"Not long. It just happened. I'm sorry for hurting you."

"Come and get your shit," she said. I'd been living mostly with her and her mother.

"Okay. I'll get my stuff later this week." I was already pretty much living with my new girlfriend, Stephanie, who had a place in Largo, Maryland. I really did regret breaking up with Darlene, who, for twelve years, had put up with all my shit. I knew she loved me, but we'd also grown distant.

Curt Smith had introduced me to Stephanie Twyman. She was an outgoing woman who loved the basketball program and the kids we mentored. She opened her home to me and my players.

"Darlene, there's something else."

"What?"

"The thing about me having a daughter is true." After Darlene had confirmed her pregnancy, she was at the salon and told her hairdresser, Beanie. Beanie promptly replied, "Oh, how nice. Curtis will have two daughters," to which Darlene looked totally confused. Beanie told her about Tawanna and Tanay. When Darlene confronted me, I vehemently denied it and claimed Beanie was wrong or just starting shit. Now, I prepared my mea culpa.

"So, Beanie was right?"

"Yeah. I didn't know how to tell you."

"When?"

"When did this happen?"

"Tanay was born in '89."

"All this time...."

"Darlene, I'm sorr—hello?" She'd hung up on me.

I'd loved Darlene, and she'd loved me. Looking back, however, our relationship existed as a kind of prolonged high-school romance. It took me a while to mature. My strong connection to my neighborhood and childhood lingered, even in the dangerous adult world of drug dealing. Darlene served as yet another link to my past. Not that I rationalized this at the time. When I met Stephanie, we just automatically clicked. Immediately, I knew I wanted her in my life. I didn't want to (once again) go behind Darlene's back, and I doubt Stephanie would've let me had I tried. Our breakup was probably overdue and the timing terrible, but I vowed to be a good father to our daughter, Alexus.

The first player I welcomed into our home and treated like a son was Frank McQueen. Confident bordering on arrogant, with a cocky swagger, Frank's hard-knock home life forced him to act out. His attitude masked a lot of insecurities. He loved the game of basketball, usually on the court from sunup to sundown, and became one of our program's first standout players.

Frank lived in the high-rise projects on East Capitol Street. Troy and I jokingly referred to it as the "*Good Times* building," from the popular TV show. When we would go to pick him up for practice, we'd often find him at the intersection with a squeegee in hand, washing windshields for tips. To see this thirteen-year-old kid running from car to car for pocket change broke my heart. He could have easily gotten money from a drug dealer as a runner or peddling crack but chose to work hard and earn a dollar. He showed me a level of determination by not taking the usual way in the projects. I believed Frank a smart investment of my time and energy.

One day while at a convenience store after practice (I'd typically stop by with a carload of players and let them get whatever they wanted), I observed Frank steal a bunch of snacks. He stuffed shit down his shirt and pants. The scene reminded me of my candy-stealing days. I waited until we were alone in the car.

"Frank, I saw you stealing," I said.

The kid looked so embarrassed.

"Listen, whenever you're with me or Troy or any of the other coaches, you don't ever have to steal."

"I'm sorry, Coach Curtis."

"Why'd you take that stuff anyway?"

He looked out the window, and I knew he felt ashamed. In that instant, as his eyes focused on the poverty we passed, I realized why he'd done so, and I felt bad for asking.

"I just wanted some snacks to take home for my brothers and sisters and me if we got hungry later..." he finally explained.

"You don't have much food at home, huh?"

"Nah."

From that point on, I practically adopted Frank. He often stayed with me and Stephanie. I became his de facto father figure. His mother called me if he skipped school or got in trouble. I'd usually find him at the Watts playground playing basketball. It took a lot of hard work to get these kids to buy into what Troy, the others, and I tried to do. Keeping up grades and working your ass off at practice was a lot less appealing than making quick money selling drugs. But it would be worth it. To make them understand the larger picture, we needed to earn their trust and respect. Being a consistent, positive influence lessened that challenge.

In the summer of '95 I received my first official high school coaching offer from Coach McLeese at Dunbar High School. I met McLeese through my friend Butch Cherry, who served as an assistant coach at Dunbar. Coach McLeese wanted me to come onboard as an assistant beginning with the summer league season and continuing into the fall/winter. Dunbar competed in Sidwell Friends's summer league, and those games would be a great way to get to know the Dunbar team.

Coach McLeese also hoped to land Frank and another top player of ours, Kevin Johnson, whom we called KJ. This is a common practice at all levels of basketball: Hire a coach who knows and has earned the loyalty of top players as an assistant to lure their players. Top high school programs do it. AAU teams do it. College programs, especially, do it. An amateur coach who spent years developing a strong, healthy relationship with a top prospect can leverage that relationship to recruit the player. From the player's perspective, why not go to a Division I program with a coach you already know, like, and trust?

I am so grateful to Coach McLeese for the faith he showed in me and in giving me the opportunity to coach at Dunbar, even if it was Frank and KJ he really wanted. The Dunbar High School summer league team went undefeated and won the league championship. For Frank and KJ, the season was their first taste of success. It wouldn't be their last.

Though most of our AAU players were fifteen and sixteen, we decided to play in AAU's seventeen-and-under age group. A. Brown had recently joined Len Elmore's Precept Sports &

Entertainment management company and began representing pro players. He hooked some of his clients up with Troy, who ran off-season workouts. Walt Williams, Sam Cassell, Greg Minor, Joe Smith, and others could be found in the gym on any given day. I made sure to take Frank and our other players as often as possible, to show them we were legit in our promises.

Troy also created buzz as a fantastic workout guy and trainer. He and I had a great partnership: I provided the personality, he managed the game. His basketball IQ and growing reputation with soon-to-be-pro players drew the attention of college coaches looking to add a dynamic young assistant. We knew Troy would welcome such an opportunity, but first we had an AAU team to run.

A. Brown and Sam Cassell became close. As the season neared, A. Brown spoke with Reebok about sponsoring our team. Reebok had signed Cassell to a shoe contract, so A. Brown's connection to Cassell helped bring them in to sponsor us. They provided the team with shoes, bags, and apparel. We named ourselves Planet Reebok.

AAU basketball isn't a league, per se, but a loose association of teams across the country who play in sponsored tournaments. The big tournaments are hosted by the shoe companies: the Big Time Tournament by Adidas, the Peach Jam by Nike. As we began our first season, we entered regional tournaments up and down the East Coast. We won a few of them and the buzz back home began to build. Within a matter of months, local kids begged to join Planet Reebok. Troy and I realized we had the demand to expand the program beyond one team.

But our days of playing as a Reebok-sponsored team were numbered. Our kids played a lot of basketball, and shoes wear out quickly. After their initial donation, Reebok hesitated to provide more gear. While A. Brown scrambled to find a new sponsor, I used my own money to purchase gear for our players.

"It's a new shoe company," A. Brown explained.

"Aerial? What does that even mean?" I asked.

"Like up in the air, I guess. Anyway, they want Walt Williams to wear the shoe. Walt put me in touch with them, let them know he wants to help our team...."

"So, you're getting us Aerial shoes?"

"Aerial Assault."

We renamed ourselves Team Assault, after the shoe. If you've never heard of the Aerial Assault, it's because the company flopped. Since the shoe didn't take off, the money the company promised never came. This created problems when we got invited to the AAU national tournament in North Carolina.

The first issue was transportation. We didn't have credit cards to rent vans to transport all the players and coaches. We ended up putting the kids on Greyhound buses my father arranged for free. We gave each player money in case they got hungry. The bus would drive overnight, expected to arrive early the next morning in Winston-Salem. A few of the coaches piled into Stephanie's car and drove all night to make sure we arrived before the bus.

The second issue was the hotel. A major AAU sponsor, like Nike, would have paid for our hotel. But Aerial could not or would not. That meant we had to pay. To reserve the rooms, Troy used his personal, family credit card. A. Brown had promised to come up with the money. A. Brown made securing us a sponsorship his responsibility. As our "general manager," Troy expected A. Brown to solve the problem.

But A. Brown didn't come up with the money for several weeks. Troy's frustration created tension among us coaches throughout nationals, though we made sure the players never knew. They came to compete and have fun. By the end of the tournament, little known Team Assault finished fourth in the country. Suddenly, we landed on the map.

The first time I ever saw Kobe Bryant play, he scored forty-nine points against us, but Team Assault beat his Sam Rines team by thirty. I used to tell the kids, half-serious, "If we lose, you don't eat." It had a positive effect, as the kids loved going out for pizza, burgers, or Chinese food after a win. We were a scrappy bunch of inner-city bruisers. We played physical, gritty basketball, and such a style of play surprised some of the prima donna AAU teams we faced. This style arose from both our kids' upbringings and a lack of previous formal coaching. Players like Frank McQueen, Kevin Lyde, and Mark Karcher learned the game on inner-city courts against neighborhood opponents. Those games relied on a willingness to take a foul, draw a charge, or throw an elbow. None of them ever played in million-dollar gyms or branded fieldhouses or under coaches with pretentious pedigrees.

So, we surprised a lot of AAU teams and attracted the attention of prep school and college coaches, including Georgetown Coach John Thompson. Thompson had his eye on several players on Team Assault, but especially on Frank McQueen.

Frank had recently gone through a rough patch. He'd been arrested for gun possession. He claimed to have found the gun, but regardless, the police charged him and took him to jail. He called me and begged me to get him out. I knew he'd manage inside, so I decided to leave him there for a week to learn his lesson and think about the positive opportunities he had ahead of him. I think it worked, as he called me daily, begging and crying.

A few months after that, Frank and I met with Coach Thompson in his Georgetown office.

"I'm impressed with your game, son. But I don't tolerate troublemakers or bullshit in my program."

"Yes, sir."

"I think you could do well in our system and at this school. But Georgetown is an internationally respected institution. If I bring in kids who hurt our reputation, it'll be my ass on the line."

"I understand."

"You want to play college ball?"

"Definitely. That's my goal," Frank answered, looking at me for reassurance.

"I think you should go into the army. Do two years, get some discipline. You do that, and I'll have a place for you here. Scholarship money, a D-I program, a Georgetown education."

"The army?"

Needless to say, the idea didn't thrill Frank. Before we left, Thompson pulled me aside.

"Curtis, I'm impressed with what you're doing. You've got kids from all across the city as part of the same team. And I enjoy the aggressive style." Anyone who watched Thompson's Georgetown teams of the '80s and '90s would understand why he liked our style. "I hope you can keep this going."

My audacity still surprises me, but I was young, and we were desperate.

"Actually, Coach, we need to find a sponsor. Badly. We can't afford to pay for gear, uniforms, tournament fees, and travel out of our own pockets. We can't charge the families. They've got no money." I knew going forward our success relied on securing a major sponsor. A. Brown did his best but didn't have strong enough connections to bring in significant money. I used saved drug money to live and pay for our players. Troy and Damon earned teacher's salaries. We were strapped. Thompson had connections, though.

"Hold on, Curtis. Let me make a call." At the time, Nike sponsored Georgetown basketball. After a few minutes of waiting, I listened to Thompson's half of a phone conversation.

"George? It's John...yeah, everything's great, but I need a favor...I've got a new AAU team here in DC...finished fourth at Nationals...giving a great opportunity to these kids...need a sponsor...want ya to talk to my guy, name's Curtis Malone. Great! Thanks, George." Coach looked up at my raised eyebrow.

"George Raveling, top guy at Nike. He's an old friend. Says he's interested. He's gonna look into your program, wants to meet you when he comes to town."

"Thanks, Coach."

"No problem. Between us, I want to see you guys do well. Don't worry, Nike will come through. Now get Frank McQueen on track, alright?"

John Thompson was a great coach and truly cared about DC players. He'd also just taught me my first lesson in college recruitment. He wanted McQueen in his program. Calling George Raveling cost him nothing—Nike made a lot of money and gained plenty of exposure from Georgetown—but Thompson had done me a favor. The Nike connection would come through. He'd see to it. Now, I owed him. Whether it would be through Frank or another top Assault player, Thompson expected I'd repay him by promoting his program to would-be recruits. He eventually landed one of our players, Ed Sheffey.

As I prepared for the Dunbar High School season, we learned Coach McLeese had accepted the head coach position at Howard University. I really felt loyal to McLeese and thought about resigning, but my friend Butch Cherry, who coached the JV team, talked me into assisting him instead. We won the JV championship, while the varsity team lost in the DCIAA semifinals. I told Butch I wouldn't return the following season, as my attention turned back to Team Assault. I invited Butch to come over and coach with us, which he did.

Nike came through with gear and a little bit of money to help with travel expenses. George Raveling came to town for the Charlie Weber tournament. He took me and Troy to dinner to formally introduce himself. He told us he'd monitor how we did, and a long-term commitment would be contingent on our success.

Nike required us to attend a few of their marquee events, including the Boo Williams tournament in Hampton, Virginia, and the Peach Jam in Augusta, Georgia. We got excited about the Nike deal, even with its long-term uncertainty. The kids believed Nike to be the premier basketball brand in this time of Michael Jordan's supremacy. Troy loved Nike all the way. Just the name and swoosh on our jerseys gave us instant credibility. Within a few months, our scrappy group of street ballers suddenly belonged.

We competed in the Boo Williams tournament, fielding a team that included two of our youngest players, DerMarr Johnson and Keith Bogans. Being so young, neither got much playing time, and Bogans threatened to quit. One thing about kids from the hood: They're not afraid to speak their mind, no matter their age. Troy took no bullshit and certainly didn't put up with attitude from a fifteen-year-old. I convinced Bogans to stick with Team Assault, which he did, to our benefit in the years to come.

We didn't perform as well as we hoped at the Boo Williams tournament but played better at the Bob Gibbons invitational in Chapel Hill, North Carolina. Gibbons represented the big time in AAU tournaments, with top teams from all the major shoe companies showcasing their brands. In order to set expectations, we explained to the kids that this would probably be the toughest tournament of the year.

We played well enough to reach the semifinals but lost to Nike's top-sponsored team, Riverside Church. Making it to the semis really allowed us to gauge our talent against established programs. We turned heads and made a lot of people who had long been associated with AAU realize DC held tons of talent.

Team Assault's roster included Mark Karcher, our first McDonald's All-American, Kevin Lyde (McDonald's All-American), and Dalonte Hill, who was ranked top thirty nationally in his class. Bogans and DerMarr Johnson improved throughout the season and would provide depth for years.

After the Bob Gibbons invitational, we played in the Charm City Classic in Baltimore. Being so close to DC, the tournament felt like a home game. This time we made it to the championship against the Long Island Panthers coached by Gary Charles, who later became a good friend. Our scrappy group went up against Lamar Odom and Khalid El-Amin, two of the top players in the country. And this time we won. After the game, Gary came over to shake my hand.

"Really impressed, Curtis. Listen, you got to talk to my guy over at Adidas."

"Adidas? We're trying to secure our Nike deal."

"Listen, Sonny Vaccaro is the godfather of this shit. He signed Jordan when he worked for Nike. The guy's a legend. Adidas hired him to turn them into a basketball brand."

"I mean, we'll definitely talk to him."

"Oh, you don't talk to Sonny. He'll either adopt you or he won't. He's that kinda guy."

"I'll have our GM, A. Brown, call him."

"I've already put the bug in his ear for you."

Gary hinted at the gravitational force of Sonny Vaccaro but I just didn't understand at the time. I'd learn.

Sonny Vaccaro and DC Assault

"So, I talked to this guy, Vaccaro, at Adidas," A. Brown explained. "He's heard great things about us and is interested in sponsorship."

"What about Nike?" Troy asked.

"I explained that to him. He asked whether we had signed a contract or just verbally agreed. When I told him everything was verbal, he explained since we're not under contract, we could make a verbal agreement with him, too."

"So, what did he offer?" I asked.

"He wants us to come to Vegas and play in the Big Time tournament. He'll give us gear and cover all travel, meals, hotel. Everything."

Adidas sponsored the Big Time tournament, which featured nearly 400 teams from across the country. Its name was completely appropriate.

"We got the Peach Jam."

"I told him that, Troy. He says we can still attend that tournament. The Big Time is the week before."

"I don't want to renege on Nike," I said.

"This wouldn't be a conflict. Listen, I've asked around about this guy. Sonny Vaccaro is literally the godfather of youth basketball right now. He pretty much single-handedly developed Nike's grassroots program. He knows who the top high school kids are everywhere. He has almost unlimited resources, and he's connected to college coaches and pro agents. He's as powerful as they come. He left Nike, and Adidas has given him absolute authority to turn it into a top basketball brand."

"That sounds good, but I've been pushing this Nike thing," Troy added. "How they gonna feel if we get in bed with the guy who left to work for the competition? Curtis, we're supposed to meet again with George Raveling in a few weeks."

Troy was a Nike guy to the core. My loyalties were less defined.

"I don't see it as a conflict, Troy. If we were under contract, then, yeah, it'd be different. Maybe going to the Big Time will motivate Raveling to make a better deal?"

"There's another thing," A. Brown interrupted. "Adidas runs the ABCD Basketball Camp. Sonny suggested, pretty obviously, that sending some top Assault players there would help get us better sponsorship. It's a great opportunity for the kids, too."

"Jesus, we're committed to Nike's camp," Troy said.

"We can work around it," I replied. "We can send our young guys to ABCD. Karcher, Lyde, and Cosby can go to Nike."

Our younger players: DerMarr Johnson, Keith Bogans, and Dalonte Hill held tons of promise. I quickly calculated that if Sonny saw the potential future of our program, he'd want to sponsor us going forward.

"What did you tell him, A. Brown?" I asked.

"Well, obviously I said yes. It's too good an opportunity. The Big Time tournament will provide tons of experience, and it's free. How can we deny the kids, and our program, the chance?"

"And ABCD?" Troy asked.

A. Brown looked away. "Sonny probably got the impression we'd be sending some players."

Troy felt unhappy, but he was also a team player. He tried to keep his irritation from the players, but they picked up on it. Adidas mailed a check for $25K to cover expenses. They also sent gear; however, the jerseys were blank. No Assault logo, only Adidas's three stripes. Compared to the Nike equipment we had received, the gear was terrible, and the kids knew it. Still, it was free and came with an all-expenses-paid trip to Vegas. Who couldn't get excited?

The camp occurred before the Big Time tournament. We sent DerMarr, Bogans, and Hill. DerMarr Johnson left as an unknown and returned as the number one-ranked high school freshman in the country. Keith Bogans was ranked second. All our players performed well at both ABCD and the Nike camp. Our program's profile continued to rise.

I didn't say much to Sonny Vaccaro the first few times we met. In Vegas, he asked our staff to meet him at the gym where the tournament took place. I let A. Brown do the talking in his role as our GM.

"I hope you guys do well here," Sonny said after we'd introduced ourselves.

"We appreciate the opportunity to play," A. Brown answered.

"Let me explain how this thing works," Sonny continued. "I've got four hundred teams out here. Most of them are average. The players might make a D-II college roster. They aren't ever gonna win this thing. But they pay me to let them play, so they can tell the parents the team competes in major national tournaments. Those teams pay the bills.

"Then there's teams like you guys. Here's what I've heard: You all took a bunch of city kids, some whose families can't afford a pot to piss in, and you're beating major programs. I know Kobe Bryant. He's gonna be the friggin' face of the NBA, but some no-name team from DC beat him. Then I see your kids at camp. Johnson might be the best unrefined, pure talent I've seen in a long time. The others are fantastic, too. So, I'm rooting for you this week."

"Thanks, Mr. Vaccaro."

"Sonny. Here." He reached into a fanny pack and pulled out a wad of cash. "Use this to have a good time. If the kids need something, don't hesitate."

A. Brown counted the cash as we left. "Fucking four grand."

"This feels dirty. It's like we just met with Sonny Corleone," Troy said. His description felt right. I thought Sonny might be a mob guy at first, too. "He's trying to buy us like Team Assault's a prostitute."

I didn't agree with that. At this time, I may have been naive about how basketball truly worked, but I had begun to figure it out. Sonny didn't try to bribe us by handing A. Brown four grand. He didn't need to. He knew we needed him more than he needed us. But he also wanted to show us he could be generous. Throwing money around meant proving he had the resources to support the program. Would Sonny benefit if he could form a relationship with one of our top players? Of course. Especially if that player made it big in the NBA and remembered how nice Sonny Vaccaro treated him, or if his old AAU coach suggested he sign an endorsement deal with Adidas because Sonny Vaccaro sponsored their program. Sonny invested in Team Assault hoping we'd produce top talent who would ultimately wear an Adidas basketball sneaker. He was the spider weaving the web that entraps those in the basketball industry.

Troy's unease with the Adidas/Nike situation continued to fester, and after we met Sonny, he announced he wouldn't coach the team at the Big Time tournament. I didn't think this a fair thing to do to the kids, but Troy is a principled guy. The idea of wearing Adidas one week, then Nike the next, or kissing Sonny Vaccaro's ass, then sucking up to George Raveling, turned him off. We were an amateur basketball team made up of teenagers. Yet, as soon as money entered into it, our program and our players became commodities used to leverage any advantage.

To Troy, Team Assault provided a way for these kids to escape poverty and crime and gain a future. I believed, and still believe, the Sonny Vaccaros and George Ravelings of the basketball world exist as an unfortunate but necessary part of providing that opportunity. It's a system perfect for corruption and conflict of interest, as the recent situation with Louisville had exposed. But it's also a system that identifies, nurtures, and promotes talented kids. The shoe companies sit at the center of the web. I'd discover in the coming years how the influence peddling and conflicts of interest permeate the system.

Troy had another reason for being distracted that week. While in Vegas, he received a job offer to become an assistant coach at the University of Pittsburgh. He wanted to break into the college ranks with the hope of moving to the NBA in the future. He eagerly accepted the offer. I congratulated my friend and was happy for our program. Assistant college coaches do most of the recruiting. Having one of our own at Pitt provided the first branch of an Assault family tree that would grow into a network for our program.

I coached the team for the Big Time tournament with Mike Sumner and Damon Handon assisting. I think we impressed Adidas, as we made it to the final four before bowing out. No one expected this result. To be one of the top four out of four hundred pushed our program to national prominence.

But we didn't have time to celebrate. We flew back to DC for a few days, then headed to Augusta, Georgia, for Nike's Peach Jam. Given the tension between the staff, and my displeasure at Troy for boycotting the Big Time games, I decided to remain in DC. Many of the kids also wanted to skip. We'd just beat expectations in Vegas without Troy, and our team had grown close. Plus, I'd already formed strong bonds with the players, while Troy kept an almost professional distance from them. He provided food and rides, if needed, but otherwise played bad cop and expected the kids to respect him as their coach.

I took a slightly different approach. Since I conducted most of our recruiting, I allowed myself to get closer to the players, almost as a friend or older brother. As a schoolteacher, Troy knew how to command respect and keep personal affairs separate. I never learned how to completely do that. I had players living with me. My personal life and my life as a coach for Team Assault overlapped all the time.

This made the kids loyal to me and they trusted me. They also knew Troy had accepted the job at Pitt. However, I wouldn't have any rebellion. The Peach Jam remains Nike's premier tournament. It represented a great opportunity for our program and the exposure would create potential opportunities for our players. The kids who felt loyal to me—mainly Hill and DerMarr Johnson—may have wanted to remain behind, but I drove them to the airport, gave them money, and handed them off to Troy.

The team did very well, making the Peach Jam championship game, losing to Boo Williams. Only one tournament remained in the AAU season and the summer. We had to decide the program's future. Damon Handon and Mike Sumner were more than qualified to coach in Troy's place, but we still had to decide: Should we go with Sonny and Adidas, or George and Nike?

Before we'd left Vegas, Sonny invited us to his hotel room for dinner and made a pitch: gear and travel expenses paid for two years, beginning the following season. We'd compete in Adidas's major tournaments and send our top players to their ABCD Camp. Once committed to Adidas, we would not compete in Nike tournaments or attend Nike camps.

A. Brown took the lead in negotiations. I remained unaware just how widespread Sonny's influence was. A. Brown educated himself on the politics and strongly recommended we sign with Adidas. But we hadn't heard Nike's pitch yet, so we told Sonny we would get back to him.

After the Peach Jam, George Raveling asked to meet at the Twin Bridge Marriott in Rosslyn, Virginia. Troy remained as the only supporter of Nike, and A. Brown and I had already decided we'd sign with Adidas no matter what George offered. A. Brown strongly believed in Sonny's connections and influence and argued we'd be stupid not to align ourselves and get in bed with him. I blew the meeting off. A few weeks later I saw Raveling at a Georgetown game.

"You're the only person who has ever stood me up," he said. "You're going to make me bump my money up."

"It's nothing personal, George, but we're going with Adidas. Sonny Vaccaro's made a great offer."

Raveling acted graciously about the rejection, but I didn't realize Team Assault stood in the middle of a war between shoe brands. After Sonny left Nike, he moved quickly to capture as many top AAU teams—which we now were—as possible in the country. Sonny had been Nike's grassroots guy. Without him, they scrambled to regain ground. Both companies wanted to be the first to discover the next Michael Jordan.

Of course, I didn't know the animosity between Vaccaro and Nike. I wasn't too far removed from dealing cocaine on the corner. In Sonny, I saw someone respected and legit. I felt Sonny could help me on the straight and narrow path I so desperately wanted to walk. All around me, I saw guys doing well: Troy entering the college ranks; A. Brown moving up the corporate ladder at Len Elmore's management company. Then came Sonny. I thought if I could keep the program going, and Troy and A. Brown make it, maybe I could move up, too. If I remained loyal to Troy, A. Brown, and Sonny, surely they'd be loyal to me?

Over the winter of '95, A. Brown and I attended Adidas's yearly coaches meeting in Atlanta. Only the coaches from top programs received an invitation, which stroked our egos. We met the Adidas family and sat down to learn about the brand's plans for new gear and future basketball events.

I felt really impressed with how A. Brown represented us in the meetings. I understood why he moved up at Len Elmore. I sat in the background, observing and learning. I met Pam Vaccaro, Sonny's wife and right hand. I'm not sure he would have achieved the success he did without her. Meanwhile, A.

Brown spent time with Sonny and later broke the whole thing down for me.

"So, Sonny is at the center of it all," he began. "He has relationships with NBA general managers, college coaches, youth players and their families, and Arn Tellem." Arn Tellem represented a lot of the top talent in the NBA. "He forms the relationship with the player through sponsoring AAU teams. As the sponsor, he can invite the top players to ABCD and get to them and their families. If they emerge as a highly sought-after recruit, he can easily push the kid to a D-I coach. He promises to get him better and keep the bullshit away from him, like agents."

"An Adidas-sponsored program, right?" I asked.

"Of course. He wants the best talent wearing Adidas his entire playing life. So, Sonny influences where the kid goes to school. He speaks highly of the coach; the coach name-drops Sonny."

"What about Arn?"

"So, the player is ready to enter the draft...Sonny gives him a call. 'Hey, great player, if you want the best agent, sign with Arn Tellem. I've done a bunch of deals with him.'"

"Just like that?"

"Maybe not as blatant."

"So, if they sign with Arn, what's Sonny get?"

"Ah," A. Brown said with a twinkle in his eye. "Now, that's a good question."

And plenty of rumors circulated. Mind you, rumors run thick and plentiful, so who really knows the truth. But critics would point to Arn Tellem and Sonny's friendship and some of the many Adidas-groomed players who signed with Arn then received endorsement deals from Sonny: Kobe Bryant, Jermaine

O'Neal, Antoine Walker, Tracy McGrady, just to name a few. Rumors whispered of kickbacks to Sonny. Probably not illegal, but certainly, one must question how well the relationship protected the players' interests.

At first, I felt skeptical about all of this. My experience with Sonny to that point made me view him as a benevolent old man who loved basketball and deal-making. But as our relationship evolved, I learned how he operated. If he had a close relationship with a top player, he definitely leveraged it. If an agent or financial advisor wanted to speak with that player, they had to go through Sonny. And he'd make them pay, literally. He'd suggest they sponsor his All-American game or the ABCD Camp. If an agent wanted an introduction to a player or his family, then Sonny might explain how that player's AAU team could use another sponsor. If the kid had the potential for major pro money, these little requests by Sonny presented no problem, just the price of doing business.

I experienced this directly. At the same time we negotiated our first agreement with Adidas, Sonny and A. Brown introduced me to Bret Bearup. Bret worked for a financial management firm called Protrust Capital, and wished to make a connection with our program, mainly because we had several NBA prospects on our roster. For a guy like Bearup, meeting these players at a young age—and especially their families—provided a major advantage when they turned pro. Bearup spoke with Sonny. Sonny "convinced" Protrust to provide additional money to cover our team's travel expenses above and beyond what Adidas committed to. Protrust would eventually handle DerMarr Johnson's finances.

So, when I write of the spider's web, this is what I mean: The shoe companies hold all the influence. They connect with players through the AAU teams they sponsor and the exclusive camps they host. Once Nike, Adidas, or now, Under Armour, has a player wearing their gear, they use their connection to colleges to help the school land those top recruits. Once the player declares for the NBA draft, the shoe company leverages the goodwill they've established over all the years of supplying shoes and apparel to the player (and often his family) to push a specific agent. The player signs with the agent, who then "faithfully" represents the player's best interests to the same shoe guy who helped the agent land his new client. An endorsement deal gets signed with the shoe company who sponsored the player since age thirteen. The whole strategy paying off with every pair of Nike, Adidas, or Under Armour basketball shoes sold. Along the way, many people get "consulting fees," which some people would call kickbacks. The question remains, is it wrong?

Before A. Brown and I left Atlanta, the Adidas reps showed us our newly designed uniform.

"*DC* Assault?" I asked.

"We like our teams to represent where they're from," Jim Gatto explained.

"Alright. Well, we're DC Assault then," A. Brown said.

The time came for DC Assault's graduating seniors to select where they'd go to college, a new experience for most of them. College coaches expressed interest, and the kids got pulled in different directions. Some wanted to follow Troy to Pitt, while others wished to stay close to home at Maryland or Georgetown.

I supported Troy, and when a player sought my advice, I'd always ask them two questions: First, how many coaches on the school's staff did he know? And second, who is going to have your back if you get in trouble or are struggling in the classroom? Most of our players needed more guidance than coaching. Some needed a damn babysitter. A college program that would adopt the player and become family had to be the most important consideration. Troy would be there for them. I couldn't promise that John Thompson at Georgetown, Gary Williams at Maryland, or Todd Bozeman at California would be. Another consideration I pointed out was that most assistant coaches were more hands-on with the players than head coaches. Knowing an assistant coach and having a history with him benefit the player more than a high-profile head coach.

Frank McQueen's grades fell below NCAA eligibility, so I spoke with Coach Max Good at the Maine Central Institute. I knew he had a great track record helping academically challenged players. I figured sending Frank up to the middle of nowhere in Maine would keep him from getting into trouble. I sent Good a check for six grand to cover Frank's living expenses, put the kid on a plane, and kept my fingers crossed.

Three months later, Max called and told me they had expelled Frank. He just caused too many problems. I sent him to another prep school in Virginia, but he still couldn't improve his grades.

Ultimately, he went out to California to a junior college, but like me, he just stopped caring about academics once the basketball season ended. Frank would try his hand in the exhibition circuit and the various minor pro leagues, but he never caught a break. It's an all-too-common story: a kid with serious basketball potential, who may have blossomed if he'd played in a D-I program, but his game needed college to get that extra something required by the pros. Yet, because he made poor decisions and didn't focus on grades, he never got the chance.

He should have taken John Thompson's advice and gone into the army for a couple years.

But other DC Assault players did make it. Maryland aggressively recruited Mark Karcher, but he ultimately chose Temple. Attila Cosby went to Pitt, transferred to George Washington, but also had discipline issues.

A. Brown, Damon Handon, Mike Sumner, and I turned our attention to the coming season. Dalonte Hill, Keith Bogans, and DerMarr Johnson were all returning. Adidas fully backed us as our sponsor. The future felt full of possibilities.

The Game Won't Quit

On September 19, 1995, Darlene gave birth to my second daughter, Alexus. Though Darlene and I had separated, I vowed to provide for them both. The problem was, I'd run low on cash. I'd been living off money I stashed away during the height of my drug run with Pedro. But living expenses, combined with money I'd spent on tournaments and travel for Assault, drained my stash. Now, with a second child, I needed a way to earn a living.

Friends told me I was crazy for spending so much money on our program and my players. They didn't understand what DC Assault meant to me. Surrounding myself with guys like Troy, Damon, Mike Sumner, and A. Brown made me feel successful. For the first time, my friends succeeded without drugs. And the kids gave me a purpose. More than anything, helping those young men discover themselves and realize their potential helped me find my own path in life. Giving up on Assault just because I had money issues would never be an option.

Months had passed since I involved myself with drugs. Twin sat in prison doing time for the assault charge, and I truly believed I had ended the hustle.

"I'm making bread, Cuz," Cat Eyes boasted.

"You need to be careful. You know niggas put your name out there about Pedro. Mario's heard of it, I'm sure."

"Mario knows I had nothing to do with that shit. He's my man."

"They need all this money we bringing them down here. DC is a gold mine. But don't think he's loyal." Cat Eyes just shook his head.

"They got a car, all tricked out with hidden compartments and shit. I just drive back and forth to New York like a got-damn cash machine on wheels. I'll cut you in, Cuz."

The offer did tempt me. Pedro's supply had made me a lot of money. The fact his brother Mario worked with my cousin did show good faith. But I knew Mario cared more about the money flowing out of DC than any personal loyalty to Cat Eyes.

Ultimately, I said no. I couldn't jeopardize Assault's future. I still remembered being pulled out of the car as my players looked on when I coached for Columbia Park.

So, a few months passed, and I still bled cash. A friend of mine, G.R., called me up one day and asked to meet. I agreed and met him for a drink.

"I need a favor," he said after some small talk.

"What is up?"

"I've got a plug out of Cali. He's selling kilos for fifteen grand...."

"Alright. What's that got to do with me?"

"Just listen. I've got a way to bring the coke back, but I don't have the bread to make the trip worth my while. Put some money up so we can get a few kilos, and you'll come up at the end."

Again, I felt tempted. But I couldn't make a decision then and there. I told him I'd think about it.

In reality, I tried to avoid him. I knew if I had another conversation with him, I'd end up saying yes, and I really didn't want to. But I knew I'd have to do something soon. My thought process rationalized the decision: If I made enough money with this plug, I could help my players, provide for my own kids, and retire from the drug game for good. I called G.R.

"Alright...I'm in. I'll lend you fifteen and I'll buy two kilos for myself."

"My man. I'll make the call, get things set up."

A few weeks later, G.R. and I boarded a plane to California. A nice elderly Black couple who resembled something out of *The Cosby Show* accompanied G.R. and came on a later flight. PreSeptember 11th, airport security was much easier to navigate, and the elderly couple muled our sixty grand.

I didn't relax until we landed and safely arrived at the Marriott in Marina del Rey. Once G.R. finalized the deal and the plug's guys left, the older couple quickly stripped off their shirts.

G.R. covered the coke in mustard and coffee to disguise the smell in case we ran into any drug-sniffing dogs. Then he strapped the coke to their bodies and secured it with ACE bandages. I was impressed. G.R. knew his business.

We took a red-eye back to Baltimore, which would land at seven the next morning. As we sat on the plane awaiting takeoff, I almost pissed myself.

"Damn, G.R., who the hell is that?"

"Who?"

"The muthafucker wearing the FBI hat!"

"Be cool, Curtis. He don't know shit."

Somehow, we made it back just fine. I'd forgotten how the rush felt. As we left the terminal, I wanted to shout out in triumphant relief. Then I ran into John Thompson. The Georgetown coach stopped me with a genuine smile on his face.

"Curtis, how are you?" he asked.

"Just fine, Coach, you?" I said as I shook his hand.

"I'm fine. Where you coming from?"

I felt like I stood in some *Twilight Zone* episode where my two lives suddenly converged. I had to remind myself Coach Thompson didn't know where I'd been or why, so I lied through my teeth.

"Just coming back from visiting my uncle."

"Oh, that's great. Well, you must be tired. I'll let you go, but we should talk soon."

"Absolutely, Coach."

I power-walked out of the terminal, determined to get to Palmer Park and cook up my shit and move my kilos. Though I originally agreed to just one run, the money enticed me. I agreed to work with G.R. again.

These trips continued for a couple months. Then G.R. and I had our mules drive a camper with hidden compartments out to California and back. I easily doubled my money with every re-up, but I never fully trusted the connect. Eventually, the plug validated my mistrust.

"The shit's no good," I told G. R.

"What you mean?"

"You even sample it? It's cut. The quality is some shit. I can't cut this shit anymore…."

"You saying they played us?"

"I'm not saying, they did!"

I recouped my money on that last batch but told G.R. I was out. I wouldn't spend my money on product I couldn't sample. And I wasn't flying or driving to Cali every month, either. Byrd got me kilos for twenty grand, so my profit was less, but I only wanted to play the drug game when my money dipped. My old crew members all did their own thing, so I had no guilt about leaving them out. If I used Byrd to move some product in order to pay bills, I wouldn't need to touch my savings.

So, once again, I found myself with one foot in, one foot out of the drug business. I couldn't escape it. As DC Assault rose in prominence, other coaches would try to warn top players and their families to stay away from us by talking shit about me. I was a felon. I dealt drugs. I would be a negative influence. But in reality, I never mixed my drug life with my basketball life. I also practiced what I preached. Those players and their families witnessed my commitment to the kids, especially to two talented players, Dalonte Hill and DerMarr Johnson.

Dalonte and DJ

I'd known Dalonte Hill since I recruited him from Troy's team back when we'd coached at Columbia Park Rec. Dalonte grew up with his brother in a single-parent home but never caused trouble. His mother worked long hours, but the family still struggled financially. As Planet Reebok evolved into Team Assault, Dalonte emerged as one of our top players and we began spending a lot of time together. More often than not, Dalonte could be found at the apartment Stephanie and I rented.

As a high school freshman, Dalonte attended Bishop McNamara and won the city championship. After one season, the school fired his coach, and Dalonte decided he wanted to transfer. A small private school, Laurel Baptist, recently began accepting students, so he enrolled. The basketball coach, Coach Chris Chaney, had a fantastic reputation for looking out for his players. Laurel Baptist's basketball program only lasted about two years, but Chaney landed the coaching job at The Newport School. Over the one season Dalonte played for him, I really came to like and respect Chaney's approach. When Laurel Baptist ended their basketball program, Dalonte transferred to The Newport School to continue playing for him.

One day during Team Assault's first season, I received a phone call from my friend Curt Smith.

"Curtis, I'm over at Watts. You gotta come see this kid." Watts playground, in Northeast DC, was about fifteen minutes away from where I was hanging at.

"He's worth the trip?"

"Ever see a six-foot-seven fifteen-year-old dunking over grown men?" he asked with a smirk in his voice.

"I'm on my way."

When I arrived, Curt pointed him out to me.

"His name's DerMarr Johnson but he goes by DJ. Family's from this neighborhood, but he's living out in Maryland." DerMarr stood tall and lanky. I could tell he hadn't quite grown into his body, but his game already impressed me. When the pickup game ended, I called him over. He introduced himself and confirmed what Curt had told me about his family.

"You wanna play for the best team in the area?" I asked. I briefly explained what Troy and I were planning.

"Hell yeah, but you got to talk to my family," he said.

Never one to miss an opportunity, I immediately handed him my cell phone.

"Go ahead and call them."

He placed the call, and I heard him getting more excited. Eventually, he handed it back and told me his cousin Terry wanted to talk to me.

"Hello?"

"Curtis? This is Terry, Mann's brother from Riverdale." As soon as he said it, I knew DerMarr would be joining our team. Terry, his brother Mann, and I all went to Parkdale together. "We've been trying to track you down ever since we heard about your AAU team. We definitely want DJ on the team."

Terry and Mann talked me up to DerMarr and to his mother Sharon, who, like most mothers, felt a bit concerned at first. Eventually, she came to realize I really wanted to help her son. DerMarr didn't need convincing. From day one he began calling me to give him rides to the gym. He joined our program over the summer and worked out with Troy every day.

As fall approached, I needed to find out DerMarr's academic situation. He'd done his freshman year at Bladensburg High School and had failed the ninth grade. I didn't want him going back to Bladensburg and explained to his family that recruitment also depended on academics. We learned a valuable lesson with Frank McQueen and made it clear DJ had NBA potential, or the potential to forever be a playground legend. His grades would determine which.

Luckily, his neighborhood lied within Parkdale's school district. The basketball coach at my old high school, Brian "Ice" Waller, was a friend. Ice had been teammates with Len "Frosty" Bias, and I loved watching them play as I grew up. We spoke, and Ice knew what a come-up DJ would be for Parkdale. He also understood what Troy and I hoped to do with our program. If DerMarr transferred to Parkdale, it would be to turn around his academic performance.

Ice agreed and committed himself to helping DJ. I made it clear: If his grades slipped, I'd pull him out of Parkdale. I explained all this to his family, and they backed my plan. It didn't hurt that we'd sent him to Sonny's ABCD Camp, and he emerged as the number-one ranked freshman in the entire country.

I give a lot of credit to Troy for DJ's improvement. Troy worked him out hard. When you have natural athletic talent, it often comes down to polish. Troy polished DerMarr's game nonstop, and that made a huge difference for his future.

DJ and I became inseparable. Along with Dalonte, he felt like a son to me. Most days after practice, he'd want to come home with me. All the kids loved Stephanie and loved her girlfriends. My house became the place to chill and relax. One day, though, I drove DJ to his sister's home. When we pulled up, he noticed all his family's belongings piled on the sidewalk. They'd been evicted. I felt guilty. Had I known she had fallen behind on the rent, I would have helped his sister out. But DerMarr kept quiet about his family issues.

I told him to grab his stuff, especially anything important. He got lucky no crackheads or amigos took their shit. DJ was a shy, quiet kid who clearly felt embarrassed about the situation. On the way to my place, he asked me if he could live with me and go to school from there. I told him yes. Sharon seemed uncomfortable. I'm sure she felt like her son was drifting away from her, but Terry and Mann pushed the idea.

Once DJ moved in, he and Dalonte became very close. We always had a house full of kids, as all their friends hung out. One friend of DerMarr's, an Ethiopian named Yonnas, played an average game of basketball but had a great personality and was incredibly intelligent. The other kids loved Yonnas and wanted him around. Coming from an immigrant family, he had little money. I talked to Coach Chaney at The Newport School and got him to provide Yonnas with a scholarship. Chaney's loyalty to me helped make a difference in Yonnas's life. He'd go on to graduate from VCU.

Back then, we had a professional summer league in DC called the Urban Coalition. The Urbo, as we called it, was a big deal. The games took place at Dunbar High School and the bleachers would fill to capacity to watch college, semipro, and NBA players. A. Brown had a team sponsored by Len Elmore's Precept Sports & Entertainment. It featured some of his clients and future clients.

"What about having DerMarr play in the Urbo?" A. Brown asked.

"He's fifteen. I don't think there are any other high school players in the league," Troy said.

"He's also six-seven and the number one sophomore in the country," replied A. Brown.

"If he does well, it would really help give him some exposure," I chimed in.

"And if he doesn't?" Troy asked. But none of us thought he'd fail. The truth was, DerMarr Johnson probably could have gone straight from high school to the NBA. We didn't tell him that, as we wanted to keep him humble and hungry. He acted shy and polite, sometimes to a fault. But overconfidence can quickly lead to arrogance.

I asked DJ if he wanted to play, and of course he did. Fans packed the Dunbar gym for his first game. I sat with Terry and Mann behind the bench. Late in the first quarter, Roddy, the coach, called DJ's name. He jumped up and strode confidently to the scorer's table to sub into the game.

On his first play, he received the ball at half court. He took a few dribbles, then hit his defender with a crossover and drove the lane. It seemed like the whole defense waited for him. DJ literally launched himself at the basket and dunked over them all. The gym stopped, like a held breath, then the place exploded. People ran onto the court in shock and excitement over what they'd just seen. Guys high-fived one another for no reason other than just happiness for bearing witness to that dunk.

I don't think DJ even realized what he'd done. To him, it was just part of the game. The rest of us, especially Terry, Mann, and I, could only shake our heads in disbelief. I had just witnessed a fifteen-year-old kid dunk over an entire team of pros.

"Terry, I think DJ's legit," I yelled into Terry's ear as the crowd continued to roar.

"Yeah, Curtis, I think you're right."

Dalonte was two years ahead of DJ in school. For the entirety of DerMarr's freshman year at Parkdale, Dalonte nagged him about transferring to The Newport School to play for Coach Chaney. Several Assault players attended Newport, which quickly became a powerhouse. As Dalonte entered his senior year, and DerMarr his sophomore, we decided to send him to Newport. When Yonnas found out both were going, he asked if he could live with Stephanie and me during the week in order to carpool. We agreed.

When it comes to raising three teenage boys, it's best not to underestimate the role a woman plays. Stephanie and I had moved to a house in Greenbelt, Maryland, for more space and to make it easier for Dalonte, DerMarr, and Yonnas to commute to Newport. Then we broke up. Stephanie moved out, and, suddenly, I was left with three teenagers. Until then, I hadn't realized or appreciated how much she'd done for them. Whether it involved making sure they ate, had clean clothes, or did homework, or helping them through typical teenage angst, Stephanie had been a good mother figure.

Colleges recruited Dalonte. DerMarr's future was looking bright, barring fuckup or injury. Yonnas never got in trouble. My biggest challenge became keeping them humble. I emphasized school and doubled down when it came to girls. The last thing any of them needed was a baby. All three made it through, and DC Assault thrived, but it wasn't always easy.

Great athletes get pampered. It's just the way of the world. Shoe companies spoil. Agents kiss ass, and coaches sacrifice integrity in order to keep star players happy. I liked and respected Chris Chaney at Newport, but I also needed to keep DJ grounded in reality. When I found out DJ drove Chaney's car, and the coach provided him with a cell phone, I decided to pull him out. I called my friend Max Good at Maine Central Institute.

"I've got the top-ranked player in the country, and I want him to play for you," I told him.

"Jesus, not another Frank McQueen."

"No. He's never been in any trouble. But Adidas sends boxes of shoes to the house every week. *USA Today* wants interviews. Girls and adult women are throwing pussy at him, and his last coach let him drive his car and bought him a cell phone."

"So, I'm trying to save him?"

"He's schooling these kids and, I think, getting bored. At least up there he'll play against older guys. Plus, it's cold, snowy, and in the middle of nowhere."

"And what do I get?"

"The bragging rights of being able to say you coached the number one pick in the NBA draft."

"Hmmm. I think I like the whole savior thing better."

"Thanks Max. You're a good man."

"Don't thank me yet. Remember McQueen?!"

Neither DJ nor Dalonte was pleased about the transfer, but I held firm. Dalonte would be graduating and heading to UNC Charlotte. He'd have an average college career. I think he under-performed. He left UNC Charlotte his senior year and lived with me and enrolled at Bowie State, a Division II school. I convinced him to return to Charlotte so that he could graduate the following year.

After graduation, I suggested to UNC Charlotte's coach, Bobby Lutz, that his recruitment of Assault players would benefit from having a DC Assault alum on staff. He agreed and hired Dalonte as an assistant. I'd learned from Sonny and wanted our coaching network to grow. With Troy at Pitt and Dalonte at UNC Charlotte, we spread our influence and our Assault family tree. That would help get our players in school and, ultimately, out of troubled neighborhoods. Dalonte would also come back to coach with DC Assault, a decision which would have ramifications a few years later.

Meanwhile, DC Assault continued its success. In our first Big Time tournament as an official Adidas-sponsored team, we could only bring six players because Keith Bogans had to attend mandatory summer school at DeMatha High School. Our program supported the policy. Bogans would fly out for the weekend games, but at the start of the tournament, we played with a short bench.

One night, midway through the tournament, the coaches returned to the hotel after dinner and did room checks. One particular room smelled like weed. It pissed me off. Adidas paid for our accommodations, and I couldn't imagine the conversation I'd have with Sonny if he found out my players smoked weed in an Adidas-provided room. I confronted the players in the room and told them to pack their shit. I was sending them home—Al Miller, Derek Payne, and Omar Weaver, who were our gangsters on the court.

Back in my room, I fumed with Mike Sumner, A. Brown, and Damon Handon. "I'm gonna put them on a bus back to

DC. Two or three days crossing the country will give them time to think about how they let their teammates down."

"We'll be even more shorthanded if you send them home," Mike Sumner noted.

"How many guys were in the room?" Handon asked.

"Three, but they weren't smoking when I came in. I don't know whether they're all guilty or not, just the one whose room it is."

"We send anyone home, and they'll just spend the week in the city without any of us there. I mean, if they were able to find weed here, think how easy it'll be for them to get it in DC," added A. Brown.

"I told them to pack up already...."

The phone rang, and Damon Handon answered. He listened for a few seconds then turned to me.

"Curtis, it's Lyde. He wants to come up and talk."

Kevin Lyde was a team captain.

"Tell him to come up."

A few minutes later, Kevin arrived. He asked us not to send anyone home. "I'll take personal responsibility for them. We'll be on our best behavior the rest of the trip."

"I don't know, Kevin. This could have been a serious situation for us," I said.

"Coach, keep us all here, and we'll deliver a championship. I know we will. With Keith coming this weekend and the way we've been playing, I know we can win."

"All the more reason to teach you guys a lesson about messing up."

"Coach, please?"

"I respect that you came to talk with us, Kev. Us coaches will talk about it and make a decision. We'd better not hear one sound from that room all night."

We decided to keep the team together, but I didn't tell the players that. The next day, after winning an early morning game that I kept the three of them out of, we returned to the hotel. I pulled the players who had been in the room aside and pointed to the back of the hotel, where a parking lot was being constructed in temperatures of about 105 degrees.

"We decided not to punish everyone for a few guys making poor decisions," I began. "But you three do deserve some punishment." They all looked relieved at not being sent away.

"So, you're gonna run around the coaches until I tell you to stop." Their faces fell. I had the other coaches spread out around the perimeter of the vacant lot. The players not under discipline watched. After fifteen minutes, a couple wanted to quit, saying they'd rather go home. When Kevin Lyde heard that, he got in their faces. He felt disrespected, since he'd come to us asking for leniency. Kevin stood six-ten and about 230 pounds. The complainers quickly shut up.

"Man, Curtis, it's so damn hot, you're gonna kill one of them," Sumner said.

"Most of them from Southeast. Don't let them fool you, they'll keep running if it means they can keep playing. Besides, most of their houses are this hot in the summer," I half-joked.

The kids finished strong and so did DC Assault. Keith Bogans made it out in time for the semifinals and, without much trouble, we made the championship. Out of four hundred teams, it came down to two, and just as Kevin Lyde promised, we won the Big Time tournament.

Sonny beamed with happiness and pride. He also must have felt pleased that Adidas sponsored DerMarr. At this time, Lamar Odom and Tracy McGrady were considered the next "shoe guys," players who would receive big endorsement deals. McGrady, represented by Arn Tellem, got a huge contract from Sonny. The talk focused on DJ as the heir apparent. Sonny had his eye on the kid, and his success happened so quickly I struggled to manage it all. To me, Dalonte and DJ were my sons. But the line between serving as the protective, cautious parent became easily blurred as we got caught up in DerMarr's success. On one hand, I tried to keep his perspective on point; on the other, I contemplated how to leverage his talent for the benefit of us both.

My Vision

In 1997, the police arrested my cousin, Cat Eyes, and charged him in a drug conspiracy. I learned about his arrest on the way home from Oak Hill Academy, a preparatory school in Virginia.

I'd brought a young DC Assault player, James White, to tour the campus. Cell reception was nonexistent in the mountains, so I couldn't immediately check my voicemail. As I listened to the message on the ride home, I looked over at James sitting in the passenger seat. This basketball life held so much promise for me and provided so much more positivity for the kids I mentored, compared to street life. My cousin's arrest wasn't a surprise. We had heard earlier an investigation had been launched. He pled to a fifteen-year sentence. His conviction made me want to leave drugs behind even more.

For a few years, I'd watched with some envy as both A. Brown and Troy achieved professional success. As their careers took off, I decided I had to get serious about going legit (and staying legit). My vision included a job in sports management, continuing to help young men escape their troubled neighborhoods.

I just didn't know what, exactly, I'd do.

Other Assault players also received attention from colleges. Kevin Lyde received recruiting visits from Pitt, Auburn, UNLV, and Maryland. He became Assault's second McDonald's All-American and also played in the Adidas Roundball Classic. Maryland had a shot at Lyde. He was a local player who could have improved Maryland's program. They didn't recruit him as aggressively as some of the other schools, nor did they have any personal connections to Kevin or our program.

Instead, he chose Temple. Kevin remained close to Mark Karcher, who had chosen Temple over Maryland and Kentucky the year before. It disappointed me that Kevin didn't go with Troy. Troy acted abrasively as a coach. He took no bullshit. Though he established strong relationships with some players, others didn't like his style. They liked the guy who acted as a friend. Troy was no-nonsense, and kids thought he was too strict.

As our seniors started getting recruited, the strength of DC Assault's expertise and network emerged. A. Brown knew many NBA players and coaches and shared a lot of insight into the recruiting process. Wizards assistant coach Mike Brown trained DerMarr over the summer to improve his skills. Our growing web of preparatory-school coaches also watched out for our kids, helping them earn the grades to remain NCAA-eligible.

Ultimately, all of our graduating players landed at D-I schools that year. To name a few: Kevin Lyde at Temple; Attila Cosby at Pitt; and Ed Sheffey at Georgetown.

When we'd sent DJ to the ABCD Camp a few years before, the Assault staff simply tried to establish a relationship with Sonny Vaccaro. Though we knew we had talent, we didn't expect DerMarr to emerge from the camp as the top-ranked incoming sophomore in the country.

He continued to remain number one as he headed into his senior year. But critics love to attack the top guy, and DJ soon attracted their ire. They criticized him as lazy and of playing bored. They questioned his heart and his willingness to play hard. He'd also received awful grades his freshman year of high school, which made the haters wonder if he'd gain NCAA eligibility.

DerMarr worked hard to prove the critics wrong. But a lot of credit goes to Max Good, DJ's coach at Maine Central Institute. Max was crazy. Before DJ finalized his transfer to MCI, Max flew down to watch him play for us. Max got in DerMarr's face and cursed him out as if he already coached the kid. Max tested him hard. Here's a teenager being told by all his friends he's going to the NBA. He could have been an arrogant prima donna, like his critics enjoyed claiming. His reaction to Max could have been conceited disdain. But DJ wasn't that kind of person. He ended up loving Max Good and his no-bullshit style.

We sent another DC Assault player to Maine Central, Al Miller, who would go on to play at Central Florida. The school, and Max, really invested in their players. Remaining academically eligible and graduating remained the top priority for Max and his staff. The fact that the school existed so far from DC geographically and culturally also helped keep the kids grounded. Partnering with schools like MCI, Oak Hill Academy, and The Newport School allowed us to fulfill our promise to our players and their families: Buy into what we're trying to do, follow our rules, be a good teammate, and we'll help you escape the drugs and crime in your community and get an education.

My role with DJ centered around managing the agents, scouts, and college coaches coming at him. Whether he would go to college or straight to the pros was still unclear. Given what Sonny's connections said, DJ and the coaches felt one season of college would be worth it. Ending up an NBA draft lottery pick increased the payday compared to a mid-to-late first round spot. Sonny and A. Brown were my advisors through the process.

Numerous colleges tried to recruit him. No one bribed me, nor did I owe any favors. I wanted DJ to make his own decision. If a college coach contacted me, and I knew the school had no chance of landing him, I told the coach straight up so as not to waste his time. I remembered Freeman jerking around Coach Ford at Hampton. I wouldn't play such games.

DerMarr really wanted to go to North Carolina, but they passed. Many schools, UNC included, felt reluctant to recruit him because everyone knew he'd only play one season, then go pro. DJ's second choice was Maryland. Gary Williams had missed out on Kevin Lyde and Mark Karcher. Would he now land the top player in the country?

A. Brown and I asked Sonny to set up a meeting between us, DJ, and Williams. Sonny contacted Williams's lawyer, Rob Ades (who also represented Jim Boeheim, the head coach at Syracuse, and Bobby Cremins at Georgia Tech). Ades contacted us and wanted to meet. He ran interference for Williams. So, A. Brown and I agreed to meet at his office.

"You know, A. Brown, DJ might need some guidance. I don't want him to fuck up and mess his draft status up," I said as we drove to the meeting.

"What're you getting at, Curtis?"

"I'd like a job. You and Troy doing your thing. I want to move on with my life and if DJ goes to Maryland, if I worked there, I could watch out for him, too."

"What kind of job?"

"I don't give a damn. An office job or anything. Whatever. You think we can suggest something?" I only dabbled in drugs when my money ran low, hitting up Byrd a couple times a year. But I hated doing it and would've taken any job to avoid the drug game.

"I don't know. I mean, it's a common thing. Maryland gets the top recruit, DJ has someone he trusts to help him transition and you get a little paycheck. But…it's still kind of a touchy situation."

We arrived at Ades's office. Ushered in by his secretary, we found him behind a dark wood desk. His office displayed the legal practice standard: expensive furniture, big window, photos of him and well-known people. I let A. Brown do the talking.

"So, Rob, DJ likes Maryland," he began.

"I heard he likes UNC."

"UNC won't take a chance because they think he's gonna declare for the draft right out of high school, or, at best, play one season."

"Isn't he?"

"We," he pointed at me, "want what's best for the kid. We feel a college season under a great coach is important. But it needs to be the right school. The best environment."

"I think Gary and Maryland would be a great fit for DerMarr," Ades said.

"So do we."

"Well, that's fantastic. Gary will be thrilled."

"But there is something to consider." A. Brown paused. I could see him gathering his thoughts, and I knew my name was about to come up.

"DJ's done very well because of Coach Good up at MCI and 'cause Curtis here really took him under his wing. We feel that wherever DJ ends up, he'll be more likely to succeed if he continues to have his mentor around him."

"I see…."

"So, I'd like you to speak with Coach Williams about the possibility of hiring Curtis. He doesn't need anything special. But remaining with DJ while he's at Maryland would be the best. Coach gets a top recruit, DJ has Curtis looking out for him, and Curtis has a job."

"You want to join the coaching staff?" Ades asked me with skepticism.

"Not necessarily. With Maryland's alumni, I'm sure someone could hire me somewhere. I've been running DC Assault for a few years now and spending a lot of my own money on our players and the team. I need to find a new source of income."

"I see," he repeated. "Well, I'll need to discuss all this with Gary. I'll have to get back to you."

As we drove back to DC, I asked A. Brown how he thought it went. "Fifty-fifty, Curtis," he said.

A few weeks later, we scheduled a meeting at Maryland. We expected to meet with Gary Williams, or at least have an introduction, but when we arrived DJ, A. Brown and I met with Gary's assistants, Billy Hahn and Dave Dickerson. A. Brown began the meeting by explaining where we stood in our decision process.

"It's really as simple as this: If DJ chooses college, he wants to choose Maryland. We're leaning towards college but will make a final decision in a few weeks."

"Is Coach Williams coming?" I asked.

"Just us today," Dickerson answered.

DJ and I exchanged a look, and I knew he felt offended. The two assistants went through their sales pitch, which we listened to politely. Then A. Brown laid out our sales pitch.

"Landing DJ would be like opening the door for your program. He is a well-liked, highly respected teammate. DC Assault has younger guys coming up who will also be All-Americans and top recruits. DJ as a Terrapin instantly makes those other guys want to play here."

Billy Hahn broke into a grin and spread his hands. "DerMarr, you've heard what we have to offer. We understand we're your first choice, but we're a lot of guys' first choice. If you go somewhere else, we'll go and get someone better than you."

To this day, I have no idea Hahn's reasoning for saying something like that. Typically, schools fall over themselves trying to *flatter* a top player. Maryland almost acted like they didn't care. Maybe Hahn meant the comment to test DJ's reaction. But DerMarr was a humble player who did not need to be tested. Maybe the Maryland coaches felt sour over Kevin Lyde going to Temple and meant the slight for A. Brown and me. Whatever his reasons, the comment pissed DerMarr off. Combined with Gary's absence, Maryland already had two strikes.

As they continued their pitiful pitch, DJ whispered in my ear that he wanted to leave. Two weeks later Rob Ades called to say Gary Williams would not help me land a job. After filling DJ and Mike in, DerMarr decided Maryland, once again, lost out on a top local player.

Sonny recommended DerMarr go to college, and we officially announced we'd be making a decision on a school soon. Pitt, UConn, Cincinnati, and UNC Charlotte showed the most interest. I knew UConn assistant Dave Leitao and really loved their head coach Jim Calhoun's offense. I felt a bit guilty not backing Troy at Pitt, but UConn was my first choice. DerMarr liked UNC Charlotte because Dalonte was there, and DJ considered him his brother.

I also knew Mike Cronin, the assistant at Cincinnati. Bob Huggins, the head coach, had a personality similar to Max Good's: not a pushover. DerMarr felt sensitive over the critics claiming he lacked heart and couldn't handle a tough program. He wanted to prove he played hard and would succeed in the pros. Huggins's pitch played right into that.

I told DJ he'd have to make his own decision. We scheduled campus visits, and he wanted me to go with him. I refused. Not for any negative reasons; I just wanted him to feel free to make his own choice without my influence. Saying no was tough for me. DJ hated the college visit routine, and I feared he'd declare for whatever school got to him first just so he could avoid other recruiting trips.

Well, Cincinnati landed the first visit. Huggins met with him personally and told him straight up: *You'll only be here eight months. I'll toughen you up and improve your skills to get you ready for the pros. Choose the coach and program that will best prepare you to move on.*

Back then that pitch was novel. Coaches still lauded their school's record of academic achievement and the campus environment. Once the one-and-done rule went into effect, most coaches dropped the college life bullshit and hyped their programs for what they really were: one-year NBA minor league teams.

DerMarr announced he didn't want to make any other recruiting visits. He went with Coach Huggins and Cincinnati. I believed he made a rushed decision, but he wasn't swayed. He acted the same way over this major decision as he had while playing in the Urban Coalition when he dunked over pros. It was all just part of the game.

When DJ announced for Cincy, Leitao at UConn and Troy at Pitt were both pretty disappointed. Particularly my friend Troy, as neither Dalonte nor DerMarr had landed with him. But ultimately, though Cincinnati wasn't my top choice, I felt DJ had to make the final decision. I did make him call the other coaches to thank them for their interest prior to the announcement.

In addition to DC Assault, Sonny associated with a crew of top AAU coaches, including Wallace Prather from the Atlanta Celtics, Thad Foucher from the New Orleans Jazz, "Mac" Irvin from the Illinois Fire, the Pump brothers, Dana and David, of Pump-N-Run, Jimmy Salmon from the New Jersey Playaz, Gary Charles from the Long Island Panthers, and Chris Grier from the Michigan Hurricanes. Bret Bearup, in his work for Protrust Capital, also maintained relationships with us through Sonny and would recommend specific agents for our best players.

I'd met an up-and-coming agent, Dan Fegan, through Sonny and Bret Bearup. At the time, Fegan had two employees, Brian Dyke and Cindy Elgie, and worked out of his townhouse in Santa Monica, California. But he had eyes on DJ (everyone had eyes on DJ) and hoped to represent him if he went pro.

This happened before the NBA's one-and-done rule, which required all future NBA draft picks to be at least one year removed from high school and turn at least nineteen years old in the year they are drafted. The player could play overseas, go to the NBA's minor league, the G League, or could play one year in college, which is where the "one-and-done" saying came from.

Sonny monitored DerMarr's draft projection. If he went straight to the pros, he'd probably fall between the fifteenth and twentieth picks. A solid year of school in a top program would make him a top-ten pick.

As Fegan made his interest in DerMarr known, I moved to establish a solid relationship with him. I didn't know where it might lead. Sonny plotted DerMarr's future, but I knew expanding my network couldn't hurt.

As Fegan began networking and making a name for himself, Bret and Sonny both recommended him for DerMarr.

"Not Arn?" I asked Sonny. I knew Sonny gave endorsement deals to Arn's clients. I believed if DJ was going to see real shoe money, he'd need to be with the superior agent.

"Arn's talking retirement. Dan's up-and-coming. I like the guy. I think DJ should go with him."

"DJ's a shoe guy?" I asked, putting it out there and hoping for a commitment.

"He's the number-one prospect in the country, and he's wearing my shoe. Right, Curtis?"

True enough, but Sonny's answer was really no answer at all.

"I need a job, Sonny. I'm running through cash trying to support these players. Is Dan growing his operation?"

"Dan's just trying to land a premier client right now."

"But with the money he makes off that premier client, he could expand his business, right?"

"If that's what it takes. You know how this shit goes. If you want me to put the bug in his ear, just say so."

"Yeah. I need that."

I had known Fegan wanted to sign DJ for some time, but I also genuinely developed a good relationship with him. I liked Dan Fegan. After Sonny spoke to him, Fegan agreed to pay me $3,000 a month to work as a consultant. My job required me to identify prospects in high school and college and evaluate whether we should try to sign them in the future. I would act as Fegan's eyes on the East Coast. We finalized the agreement with a handshake. Nothing was ever put in black and white.

Once DJ finished his one season at Cincy and declared for the NBA draft, we officially announced that Fegan would represent him. Brian Dyke, who worked for Fegan, and who I also liked and worked well with, signed Kenyon Martin. Suddenly, Fegan + Associates represented two of the top prospects in the 2000 draft class. DerMarr and Kenyon led Cincy all year, then Martin broke his leg in the Conference USA tournament.

The draft quickly approached, and the NBA invited DJ to sit in the green room, typically reserved for projected lottery picks. In the beginning of June 2000, a Mercedes 430S arrived at my dad's house courtesy of DerMarr. DJ bought his mom a house in Bowie, Maryland, and hired Protrust Capital to manage his money. There was no shortage of lenders willing to give him credit. Fegan communicated with several teams, but we couldn't tell where DJ would end up. We knew he could be a top-three pick or drop as low as ninth.

Fegan also began negotiating with Sonny over an endorsement deal.

"Curtis, I'm just warning you, don't get your hopes up about a shoe deal," he told me.

"Sonny's been putting DJ in shoes for years and now he's backing out?"

"Says Adidas's budget isn't as big this year. Wants to see what city the kid ends up in."

"Why's that matter?"

"He can justify it better if he plays in a big media market, but...."

"What?"

"I'm not feeling it. I think it's all bullshit. You know he's in bed with Arn." Contrary to what we'd heard, Arn hadn't retired.

"So, we shouldn't expect a deal?"

"Don't hold your breath."

"If Sonny's only going to give endorsement deals to Arn's clients, why'd he help us connect?"

"That's a question you gotta ask him."

I met a D. businessman named Greg Holloway through a mutual friend, Mike Anderson. Mike wanted to break into the sports management business and thought we all might be interested in working together. But as I explained to both Greg and Mike, I felt loyal to Fegan, who'd given me a chance. I told them down the road, if things didn't work out with Dan, I'd be willing to reconsider. I think Greg respected my honesty and loyalty.

Greg was a foulmouthed, intelligent guy with a quick wit. We instantly took to one another. After our initial meeting, we kept in touch, and Greg became a donor for DC Assault. He donated money to cover miscellaneous travel expenses and mentored me as well.

I'd quickly seen how the game worked and decided I needed to start aggressively playing it. I began actively insisting anyone looking for a favor or my help must support DC Assault. Our mission centered around raising these kids out of poverty and crime by honoring their talent and focusing on their lives off the court—taking trips to prep schools to try and get them academic help, paying for meals (or groceries, so their brothers and sisters could eat), and helping to buy clothing and other necessities. These things all cost us money beyond what Adidas gave us. Yet, all were vital for us to fulfill the promise we made to our kids.

I'd witnessed Sonny engage in this kind of solicitation for his tournaments and camps: *Want to meet a player and his family, Mr. Agent? Then sponsor my camp*. I learned the lesson well and began doing the same thing. Agents, financial guys, college coaches...*support my efforts in helping to develop this player if you want access.*

Frankly, it was too easy for agents and financial planners to have me and the Assault staff raise a player, then come in at the end and benefit from their success. I believed, and still believe, that if an agent or financial planner wants to benefit from a top player at the end of his DC Assault career, he should support the program in its entirety.

In over twenty years of running DC Assault, the IRS only audited us once. Never were any monies misplaced or misused. We truly cared about the kids we helped and never took advantage of our situation.

"With the sixth pick in the 2000 NBA draft, the Atlanta Hawks select DerMarr Johnson of the University of Cincinnati."

After NBA commissioner David Stern announced the pick on June 21, 2000, DJ shook hands with some of us in the green room and hugged his family. We embraced and told each other that we loved one another. Then he confidently strode to the podium and held up a Hawks jersey. This was a dream come true for a kid who had a lot of shit go wrong in his life. I reflected back over the years: seeing him play at Watts; the day I brought him home only for us to find his family's belongings on the curb; the other coaches like Chaney at Newport and Max Good at MCI, who helped him arrive at this point in his life.

DJ signed a three-year, $6.8 million deal with a team option for a fourth year. Just days after the draft, we picked out an apartment in a gated complex in Atlanta. The Hawks held a press conference introducing DerMarr to the fans and media. Being the sixth pick in the draft, the spotlight shined on him brightly.

Sonny never came through with a serious endorsement deal. The money was so low both DJ and Fegan felt disrespected.

I also learned that Fegan + Associates would merge with Assante Sports Management, run by Leigh Steinberg, one of the top football agents at the time. Typically, when a larger agency buys another, it's based on the smaller firm's client roster. Until DerMarr and Kenyon Martin, Fegan didn't have a large roster. Those two put his name on the map, and he became an easy acquisition for Steinberg, who wished to expand into pro basketball.

Fegan made the deal without consulting Brian Dyke, Cindy Elgie, or me. Brian and Cindy were pissed. Brian quit, and Fegan gave him a severance of a couple hundred grand out of the large amount of money Steinberg had paid for the client roster. Under the terms of the agreement, Steinberg paid Fegan a lump sum for the sale, and he would stay on with Steinberg at a nice salary.

Brian approached me and asked if I'd like to leave and go into business with him. Fegan had given me a $45,000 bonus after the merger, and I felt a strong loyalty to him because he gave me my chance to fulfill my vision for my future. I believe in loyalty, and, though I liked Brian and felt badly about his situation, I couldn't leave Fegan, and our arrangement continued.

Brian invited me to his wedding many months later, which took place in Houston. While in town, I called Moochie Norris, who played with the Rockets at the time and was a friend. While we hung out, I asked who represented him. He told me he planned on signing with a new agent the following week. I explained my association with Fegan and asked if Moochie would be willing to at least speak with Dan before signing. He agreed. A couple weeks later, my phone rang.

"Curtis, it's Moochie."

"Hey, Mooch. What's up, man?"

"Curtis, give it to me straight. Is this guy Fegan legit?"

"Completely, Moochie. I'd never recommend him to you if he wasn't, and Steinberg wouldn't have brought him in otherwise."

"You think he'll get me the best deal?"

"I trust him, bro. You know I don't endorse a guy unless I know."

"Alright. Just wanted your opinion."

"You going with him?"

"I think so. We met and he impressed me. Not one hundred yet, but definitely leaning his way."

"I don't think you'll go wrong if you sign with him."

"I'll let you know. Thanks, Curtis."

Moochie did sign with Fegan. I felt so happy, as he became the second player I'd brought to Fegan. I felt like I contributed. I saw my vision coming true.

Part 4

The Trouble with Guys like Gary Williams

2001–PRESENT

Monica, Nolan, and Sydney

In the summer of 2001, DC Assault held our first DerMarr Johnson Basketball Camp. I had worked all year on the camp, which I planned to use to recruit top talent. We invited the area's best eighth-grade players to attend for free, including Kevin Durant, Nolan Smith, and Michael Beasley. Troy, Kenyon Martin, and Notre Dame coach Mike Brey all spoke to the campers, reinforcing Assault's mission and message.

Durant played for Ms. Tillman's PG Jaguars. I knew Durant's father, Wayne Pratt, who lived for a time in Palmer Park on Muncy Road when we were young. I really wanted his son on our team, but Wayne had little influence. Kevin's mother, Wanda, made decisions regarding where he played. She always treated me well: allowed me to buy her lunch and make my pitch, but ultimately said no. Durant turned into a superstar and a fine young man. I have nothing but respect for him and Wanda, but damn, he would have looked good in an Assault jersey.

I had no connections to Nolan Smith or his family. Nolan's father, Derek Smith, played in the NBA for nine seasons and also coached with the Washington Bullets. Tragically, Derek suffered a heart attack during a cruise in 1996 and passed away.

Nolan's mother, Monica, and sister, Sydney, dropped him off and picked him up each day at camp. Though Derek had worked for the Bullets, the family home was in Louisville, Kentucky. Monica debated whether to go back to Louisville or stay in Maryland after Derek's death.

I hoped to recruit Nolan, who stood around six feet tall with a size fourteen shoe. Monica had learned of me and DCA through Kris Vance, who coached Nolan's dad's AAU team in Louisville, the Derek Smith All-Stars. That program also received sponsorship from Adidas, and Kris knew me.

Monica had heard good things about me from Doug Overton, one of Derek's former players with the Bullets, whose opinion Monica really respected. Given the positive recommendations, the ball was in my hands to land Nolan. I asked Monica to have lunch with me.

The first thing I noticed about Monica was her attitude. Monica grew up in Kentucky. She acted poised, confident, and intelligent but also laid-back, in the Southern way where nothing appears urgent. She conveyed a quiet intensity. Certainly not naive, Monica had done her homework on me and my program. She wanted to make the best choice for her son and her family. She knew, because of her years with Derek, how the basketball business worked. Nolan had skills. Making the right choice now would go a long way towards securing his future.

Monica was a few years older than me and came across as more mature. I'll admit, she had me on my heels during our lunch.

"I've heard good things about you, Curtis," she said as she dug into her salad.

"That's good to hear. I appreciate the support. We really try to offer our players a chance to succeed."

"Johnny Dawkins put a good word in, too." Johnny worked as an assistant coach at Duke.

"He and I have talked about some of my kids over the years."

"Is it true you had some of your players live with you?"

"Yeah. Four, actually." I told her about DerMarr, Dalonte, Yonnas, and Frank. We shared single-parent horror stories, and Monica began to relax. As she drank coffee after her meal, she turned serious again.

"I've also heard some bad things, too," she said, staring straight at me. I'd had to deal with this kind of thing before, and I had my answers ready.

"What, exactly, did you hear?"

"You did jail time, and you're still involved in the street life."

All the bad-mouthing really pissed me off. My conviction hung over me, a storm cloud. Whenever another coach feared losing a player to DCA, he'd tell the player's parent I dealt drugs.

"That happened a long time ago. Nine years. I'm a completely different person now. These kids give me a purpose drugs never could. But other coaches bad-mouth me because they don't want their best players coming to my program."

"So, you swear you're not involved in drugs?"

I swore and didn't lie, exactly. I hadn't moved any product for a couple of years. With my consulting gig for Fegan and Adidas, as well as a monthly allowance from DJ, I made good money. But obviously, I led her to believe I left the game in '92. So, our relationship began, built upon a false foundation.

Monica seemed to accept my explanation. She told me they were thinking his options over. We promised to keep in touch.

The more I scouted Nolan, the more impressed I became with both him and his older sister, Sydney. Monica ran a tight ship, and her efforts clearly paid off. Both kids acted respectful, polite, and proper. Monica didn't allow cursing. She banned rap music in her house and car. Nolan's and Sydney's intelligence showed. A bit innocent, even. I would probably be a corrupting influence, but I also realized I wanted to protect them. You have to have some street smarts even if you are book smart.

I connected with the kids quicker than I did with Monica. They'd lost their father and had disliked Monica's previous boyfriend. I knew how to relate to and treat teenagers. Sydney was a great kid. I really bonded with her. Tall, athletic, and smart, she came across extremely mature and self-possessed, like how most teenage girls try to act, but for her it was genuine. She knew who she was and what she wanted and had the confidence to avoid negative influences. But she and Nolan still needed my street savvy because the streets would eat kids like them up, given the chance.

Nolan, too, impressed me with his maturity and kindness. I think the death of their father forced the kids, and Monica, to close ranks with one another. They protected and loved each other.

Monica valued family, and her dedication as a mother really showed through her kids. So, I think I loved Nolan and Sydney before I fell in love with Monica. I've always wanted to guide and mentor young people, but I realized I wanted to protect these two fantastic kids. Because of them, I really looked at Monica carefully. At first, she was just a potential player's mother. Just someone I needed to win over to get Nolan on my roster. But after getting to know her children, I discovered an intelligent, classy, and sophisticated woman, whom I believed to be a step above my own station in life. Monica was less street, more cultured. I would have to be a better person to have her in my life; I'd need to grow.

These things swam in my head as our first lunch led to another, then another. I'm not really sure what Monica saw in me. Maybe she recognized a certain amount of strength; an eagerness to succeed. She immediately embraced DCA's mission and my personal role in achieving it. She knew I acted righteously when it came to my players, and perhaps she saw a man who would protect her children.

She told me she was in a relationship, but also made it clear she was unhappy. I felt hesitant. I'd dated the mother of one of my former players after Stephanie and I split. The relationship went poorly, and I vowed never to date another mom. But Monica intrigued me.

A few months into our courtship, I ate at Jasper's Restaurant in Largo, Maryland, just across the street from Monica's townhouse. Dalonte and our friend Roland Powell were with me. Roland grew up on Muncy Road with me and was like a little brother. Suddenly, my phone rang with her number on the caller ID.

"Hey Monica, how—"

"Listen, muthafucker. Stop calling my woman. I'll fucking have you killed, you son of a bitch. You don't know who you're fucking with."

"That's a big threat. Who the fuck is this?" I asked, already guessing it was Monica's boyfriend.

He didn't answer, just hung up. A minute later my phone rang again.

"Curtis, it's Monica. I'm so sorry about that. Listen, Thomas is leaving. I told him to get out of my house."

"Are you okay?"

"Yeah. He's an asshole, just ignore him. I'm sorry. I got to go, though."

After we hung up, I quickly paid our bill and told Dalonte and Roland we needed to leave. They didn't have a clue as to what was going on. Less than five minutes later, we sat in my car outside Monica's house, waiting for Thomas to leave.

"Curtis, what are we doing?" Dalonte asked.

"This sucker just threatened me. I gotta teach him a lesson. You two post up behind the tree, just in case."

I got out and sat on the steps to wait for him. A few minutes later, Thomas came out the front door. Monica looked at me from behind Thomas. I stood up and faced him.

"Gonna have me killed, huh?" I asked.

He looked like he'd swallowed something cold and slimy. He must have realized who I was but couldn't have understood how I'd gotten to Monica's house so quickly.

Then I punched him, my right fist connecting with his jaw so fast and so hard, he dropped like dead weight, unconscious across the doorstep.

Monica had the door open to put him out, but now he was halfway in, halfway out the front door. Monica tried to close the door, but the chump, out cold, blocked it.

"Oh, my God." She had never seen this type of violence before.

"Sorry," I said. But I had a smile on my face. The truth is, I really wanted to hurt him much more than I already had. Where I'm from, you don't just threaten murder and expect nothing to happen.

After that, Monica and I began dating for real. I learned from Sydney that neither she nor Nolan had liked Thomas, but they approved of me. Over time, I began spending nights and weekends at their house, and things got serious pretty quickly.

I'd thought my confrontation with Monica's ex would be the end of him, but unfortunately it wasn't. Thomas pressed assault charges against me. He described me as six-foot-three, over 200 pounds. I turned myself in, but when the cop compared the description he provided to me, they dropped the charges. I love tough guys who run to the authorities when their threats don't work.

Michael Beasley

Michael Beasley, a tall, left-handed, uncoordinated, big-footed kid with a ton of potential, also attended our DerMarr Johnson camp over the summer of 2001. He and Nolan quickly became friends. I also liked him. He played AAU for Ms. Tillman's PG Jaguars, but I immediately began recruiting him for DCA.

"Hey, Beasley, who's your father?" I asked him on the second day of camp.

"Mike Beasley, like me."

"Where is he?"

"He in jail."

I wondered at the coincidence. I happened to know a Mike Beasley. Back when I was at Alvin Community College, in Texas, I'd hosted a young player with the same name. I'd kept in touch with him over the years, and knew Big Mike was now serving time.

"Your dad a tall, light-skinned lefty with big feet like you?"

"That's him."

Well, it's a small world.

Michael lived with his mother, Fatima, in Landover, one of five kids from four different fathers. I contacted her and began to make my pitch for DCA. Meanwhile, Michael and Nolan became very close. In most ways, they were opposites: Nolan came from a family-oriented home with a strict mother; Michael was out of control. He had little supervision and consistently got in trouble. Nolan earned good grades; Michael failed almost all his eighth-grade classes and his school, National Christian Academy, threatened to expel him. They'd already taken his scholarship away.

As I got to know Michael and began talking to Fatima, I learned Michael had been charged with vandalism and some other bullshit and faced an upcoming court date. A juvenile jail sentence was a definite possibility.

DCA's mission focused on providing players an opportunity to succeed on and off the court. In our short history, we had already gone above and beyond other programs to help a kid outside of the game of basketball. But Michael would be our biggest challenge. Never had I recruited a player with this much baggage at such a young age. Frank McQueen was difficult; Michael would exceed him.

But his potential made the challenge worth it. I met with his mother, explained our mission and our record of success. I explained how our sponsorship with Adidas would expose Michael to the best competition and biggest opportunities across the country. Then I told her I would take him to his court date, I would explain to the court that I was his mentor, and I would take responsibility for him and his actions.

She didn't trust me at first. Here I was, some stranger who suddenly appeared in her life, making promises hard to believe. But she also felt desperate to do something to point him in a better direction. She didn't commit him to DCA just then, but she let me take him to court. The judge sentenced him to four months house arrest and a fine for the stuff he'd damaged. Before we left court, I paid the fine, for which Fatima seemed grateful.

Nolan hung out at Michael's house almost every day of his home confinement. Once it ended, Michael came to Monica's house. I'd moved in with her and she'd bought into DCA's mission. Michael became another son for us both.

During the winter and spring of 2002, we worked hard to help him pass his classes. First, Sydney tried to tutor him. Then Monica and I hired a private tutor that the coach recommended. Our efforts failed. He ended up getting kicked out of National Christian Academy. Luckily, there were only a couple months left in the school year. I used my connections to enroll Michael into a school in North Carolina for that short time.

The time for choosing had come. The AAU season would begin soon.

"Fatima, Michael is the perfect example of the kind of kid who needs a change of environment. I can help him—not only with basketball. We'll find him a new school, get him some structure. He could play in the NBA someday, but only if we help him now."

Silence greeted this statement. Fatima had pride and loved her son. When you have someone outside your family telling you he can help your child, it must feel a little insulting. Maybe she felt like she'd failed. That wasn't the case, nor my intention. So many single mothers in the hood do the best they can, without much money or support from the father. Sometimes it isn't enough. She may have felt insulted, but she also loved her son.

After a moment's hesitation, she looked at me and replied, "Okay. You do everything."

We spoke a while longer, and she opened up about Michael's behavioral problems. She seemed exhausted and unsure how she could help him. I think she saw in me a potential father figure, the male mentor he lacked. She needed a break, and I offered her an out.

At least, that's what I thought.

The 2002 DC Assault sixteen-and-under roster became one of our most talented and one of the best in the country. Head Coach David Cox led the team with assistant coaches Melvin Middleton and Dalonte Hill. Nolan and Michael joined Chris Wright, Adrian Bowie, and NaVorro Bowman, while Austin Freeman came later. They did well in their first season together despite their youth. The following year they'd win the 2003 sixteen-and-under AAU National Championship.

My relationship with Michael Beasley really developed off the court. Once Fatima entrusted him to my care, he basically moved in with us and became our other son. We couldn't have gotten him to leave if we'd wanted him to. Our first big decision surrounded school. I'd visited IMG Academy in Bradenton, Florida, several times in the past, and I knew their coaching staff. The school strongly focused on athletics, counting many professionals and Olympians across multiple sports as alumni. Michael's basketball talent earned him a scholarship. I felt pretty excited about this opportunity. He would live in Florida most of the year. Hopefully, the new environment would help improve his behavior. If he performed well in the classroom and on the court, IMG provided a fantastic pedigree to attract Division I colleges.

Michael and Nolan had attended Sonny's ABCD Camp and Michael emerged nationally ranked. IMG wanted him at their school as badly as Monica and I wanted him there. I bought him a one-way plane ticket, and we hoped for the best.

Meanwhile, Nolan was about to attend St. John's High School in Washington, DC, for ninth grade. He would join Sydney there, both on scholarship. Monica and I had grown extremely close, extremely fast. We decided to buy a house together. While we got our credit in line and awaited pre-approval for a mortgage, we rented a three-bedroom apartment just ten minutes from St. John's.

I made good money as a consultant, Monica worked in the legal department for Washington Sports & Entertainment, the company which owned the Wizards and Capitals, and our family lived comfortably. Monica had bought into helping DCA's kids, and I bought into family life with a commitment I'd never shown to anything else. Crack, Premier Movers, CM Entertainment, and Palmer Park seemed very distant.

I remained close to my own family, and Monica fit right in. She accepted the Malones and my family loved her. We'd meet up on Sundays at my mom's house for family meals. Sharon married Aaron Gaddy, who served in the army. They had two kids together. Brenda married Craig Robles. She already had a son, Kenny, from a previous relationship. Beverly had two kids of her own, Shavon and Ebony, but could never shake her drug addiction. My mom took care of her kids and raised them after my grandma, Ella C., passed away. Bev cycled in and out of jail and on and off drugs. Bev is my best friend, though, a bond strengthened by our both being the black sheep of our family.

My dad and mom got along perfectly fine after separating. They never divorced. My father never had another serious girlfriend. "Your mom is the only woman I ever loved," he told me. As I got older, my father and I became closer. I suppose that's normal. As a younger man, I moved too fast and thought myself too cool to appreciate him.

Throughout the winter of 2002 and spring of 2003, Monica and I came into conflict with both Nolan's and Michael's high school coaches. The problems began with Michael.

IMG gave him an entrance exam and his test results came back so low they wanted him to repeat eighth grade. He'd be a fifteen-year-old eighth grader, and if he developed into a professional player, it would delay his career by a year. We thought it was alright. He needed all the help he could get. But we also wanted Fatima's input. Even though she'd given me carte blanche to make decisions, we never wanted her to feel abandoned or ignored.

"His test scores were really bad," I explained. "They want him to repeat eighth grade."

"He's probably angry about that," she replied.

"Fatima, we know he's a slow learner. Monica thinks he might have a learning disability, but I'm not sure. Could just be laziness."

She didn't reply right away, and I sensed some resentment from her whenever I mentioned Monica.

"What do you think?" she finally asked.

"He's going to need to go to college. It's his way out. But to get recruited, he has to get good enough grades. Keeping him back would probably help, long-term."

"Do what you think is best, Curtis."

Once we situated Michael at the right academic level, we enjoyed a few months of peace. Then the calls started coming in, reporting his bad behavior.

Michael wasn't the only athlete at IMG on scholarship. But the majority of students came from privileged backgrounds. Michael, reportedly, acted like a bully in the dorms. The incidents were never too serious, but they began piling up. Parents spent a lot of money for their kids to attend IMG, and they weren't about to let some bully treat their child however he wanted.

But IMG also didn't want to lose a great player. Their solution was to remove him from the dorms and have him live off campus.

"He can live with me," said Dan Barto, an IMG assistant coach. "I've got a two-bedroom apartment."

"Well, that's great of you," I replied. "It sounds like a perfect solution."

"I don't mind, Curtis. But I think it's only fair you help with the rent. And if he's off campus, I'll need to feed him, too."

I thought about it for a second or two, silently cursing Michael for putting me in this position. "How much you think is fair, Dan?"

"I figure, for room and board, eight hundred a month."

"Let me talk to Monica and get back to you. We want what's best for Mike."

"Don't take too long; we need to do something to address this now, because they want him off campus ASAP."

I sat down with Monica and explained the conversation.

"I think we should consider homeschooling him," she said.

That option hadn't occurred to me.

"How do we do that?"

"I'll do it. Maybe get a tutor for specific things I can't teach him. I've been thinking about it for a while. Just need to get more information."

"You think we should pull him out of IMG so soon?"

"Maybe next year. Give me time to get everything settled."

"And it gives him a full season down there..." I trailed off.

"So, we pay the eight hundred?"

We agreed to do so while Monica explored the homeschooling option.

As the school year ended and AAU season approached, Nolan's coach at St. John's told his players they were required to play for the school's summer league team. This created a conflict between DCA and the high school summer league schedule, which I tried to explain.

"The Adidas Super 64 tournament in Vegas cannot be skipped," I patiently told Paul DeStefano, Nolan's coach.

"The colleges look at a player's high school career. I got coaches on my phone all the time. Nolan's made a commitment to St. John's and he should be here to play."

"I disagree with you. The AAU season is important."

"Nolan needs to make St. John's his first priority. AAU should come second."

"I'm one of Adidas's top programs in the country. I'm one of their consultants when it comes to talent in our area. I happen to live with and date the mother of Nolan Smith, one of the best players in the country. You expect me to have to explain to Adidas that Nolan is skipping their premier tournament to play high school summer league?"

"Well, maybe he can attend the Vegas tournament every other year?"

I wanted to bang my head against the wall.

Me, Monica, and Coach DeStefano couldn't come to an agreement over Nolan. We already had decided Michael would leave IMG. We then told DeStefano Nolan would transfer.

Monica took care of the requirements for homeschooling Michael. We had to hire two certified teachers to tutor him, which Lou Wilson helped me with. Lou led Riverdale Baptist High School basketball and built a powerhouse program. I'd known Lou for close to twenty years. He coached me in the PG County All-Star Game back in 1986. Monica and I happened to have two of the best players in the area. When she confirmed a homeschooled student could participate in athletics at the school of his choice—sending Nolan to Riverdale, while teaching Mike at home and having him play for them—it seemed like a perfect solution. Plus, Riverdale was only five minutes from our house. Nolan and Michael loved playing for Lou. They finished the year ranked in the top twenty-five in *USA Today* and top five in the *Washington Post*.

The Biz

Just prior to the opening of training camp for the 2002 NBA season, DerMarr crashed his car. I received a call early in the morning from his mother.

"Curtis, it's Sharon Johnson." She sounded panicked.

"What's wrong?"

"DJ's been in an accident. He's in the hospital."

"My God. What happened?"

"I don't know everything. They're worried about his neck."

"We'll get a flight right away," I answered. I immediately called Fegan, who arranged our flights. He'd fly in from LA later in the day. Fegan didn't know much more than me. DJ had left a club early in the morning with a couple friends. He'd crashed the car and had been rushed to the hospital.

When Sharon and I arrived, we learned DJ had broken his neck in four places. The doctor recommended surgery, effectively ending DJ's playing career. We waited until Fegan arrived to get his input. He had his assistants find the best neck and spine specialist in Atlanta, and we had DJ transferred for a second opinion.

The specialist examined DJ and declared surgery unnecessary. Instead, he would wear a halo, immobilizing his head and neck, then go through some intensive rehab. He'd miss the entire season but keep his career. I admit I felt concerned over DJ's future career, but more than that, I felt helpless. DJ grew up in my home; he was a son to me. Seeing him, big and strong, laying in a hospital bed, his head in the halo, made me realize even he could be vulnerable and weak. So young, he seemed immortal, especially on the court.

The accident occurred because DJ fell asleep at the wheel. He'd been drinking at the club but was not drunk. He'd never been a big drinker. The car hit a tree. His two friends escaped from the car with minor injuries. Unfortunately, DJ was stuck in the driver's seat, unconscious. He drove a Mercedes 600 Series, a tank, but the impact was so vicious the car crumpled.

Then it caught fire.

Fearing an explosion, DJ's friends frantically dragged him from the car. With a broken neck, they could have done more damage, but they didn't know the extent of his injuries. They feared for his life.

So regardless of how his rehab turned out, DJ was blessed. If he could come back and play, then even better. Fegan acted great, at first, but as time passed, he checked in with DJ less and less, which bothered me. Loyalty is my creed and I thought Fegan's lack of attention spoke volumes about his character. He'd moved up in the agent world. Arn Tellem never retired, but Fegan landed marquee clients on his own. He only signed top first-round draft picks now. DJ had been one of his first big clients. I was disappointed in how he treated him throughout the year of rehab.

I also felt let down by the Atlanta Hawks, who declined to pick up DJ's option year for the 2003-2004 season, which would have been his fourth with the team. The doctors cleared him to play, but the Hawks let him become a free agent due to the injury. They thought him fragile. Their hesitation caused other teams to pass on signing DJ. He would eventually come back and play but bounce around from team to team. In truth, his game did suffer because of the injury, but it also declined because he never got a fair shot at stability with a long-term contract.

Though my opinion of Dan Fegan began to change throughout the early '00s, our business relationship still held. I had recommended Fegan to Stephen Jackson when I happened to see him at a hotel during the Boston Summer League in '01. I introduced Stephen to Fegan while we had dinner with DJ and Kevin Lyde. A few days later, Stephen called me to get my opinion of Dan and also asked to borrow a couple thousand dollars. This was just one of the numerous occasions when he asked to borrow thousands of dollars. He promised to pay me back. He never did, but I still got a commission from Fegan once Stephen hired him.

Fegan treated us guys in his circle well enough. I brought Juan Dixon to him, and Dan flew us out to LA, threw a big barbecue at his house, took us out for an expensive dinner at a five-star restaurant, and got us into a Playboy Mansion party. But as he continued to succeed, I began to feel less important to him.

In 2002, DCA's Adidas contract expired. I began negotiating a new deal. But this time, we had to work with Jim Gatto and Daren Kalish. Sonny Vaccaro was out.

The trouble had begun several months before when LeBron James declared for the NBA straight out of high school. Adidas had hired Sonny in the early '90s to build a grassroots network, which would identify the next Michael Jordan and launch Adidas as a major basketball brand. He'd already nabbed Kobe Bryant. LeBron represented the culmination of his vision. Sonny had found LeBron early on. He invested heavily in the phenom. LeBron James wore Adidas sneakers his whole playing career.

Until he entered the NBA.

Sonny began negotiating a shoe deal with LeBron as soon as he declared. I'm sure Sonny thought the negotiation would go like most others he'd engaged in; James was an Adidas kid, after all. But Nike, realizing they'd missed Kobe and knowing their brand depended on a new superstar, came in aggressively. Sonny threw everything he had into an endorsement deal.

Nike countered.

Ultimately, Sonny needed somewhere between $10–20 million more to beat Nike's offer and probably land LeBron. Adidas said no. He threw his hands up in the air. In the mid-'80s, Sonny Vaccaro told Phil Knight to mortgage everything on a player named Michael Jordan. Knight did so, and Nike never looked back. Sonny never got the credit he deserved for his insight. Now, he recognized LeBron as the second coming, he had developed him as an Adidas talent for years, and his bosses were too nearsighted to realize the opportunity they threw away.

So, Sonny left.

He took a job with Reebok (the redheaded stepchild of athletic footwear), where he stewed over the disrespect he'd been dealt. His two underlings, Gatto and Kalish, worked feverishly to keep Adidas's grassroots program intact.

Now, I liked both Jim and Daren. They were decent guys, but neither conveyed the same dominating presence as Sonny. But they offered DCA one hell of a contract: a five-year sponsorship deal, including tournament fees, hotel, travel, a budget for miscellaneous expenses, and gear for all our teams.

Additionally, Gatto and Kalish decentralized control by forming a board of directors for their grassroots programs. DCA would have a representative on the board. They also organized their platinum AAU teams into a group called the Super Six. DCA would be included in that elite group. As our rep for the Super Six and president of DCA, I sat on their grassroots board. I earned a consultant's fee with the primary responsibility of vetting all players in the mid-Atlantic and Southern regions of the country. Anyone who wished to attend ABCD Camp or Adidas tournaments, gain sponsorship, or otherwise deal with Adidas had to go through me.

In short, Gatto and Kalish allowed me to become the Sonny Vaccaro of my own little fiefdom. I had absolute control over all player and team development from Maryland to North Carolina. Through the Super Six, I also had a voice on which teams attended Adidas tournaments or received sponsorship money.

"I can't match this. Not even close," Sonny told me over the phone. My loyalty remained with him, and I had asked him to review Kalish's offer. I knew Reebok didn't have the resources or network of AAU teams, but I wanted him to try. He wished me well, emphasizing how good this deal could be for me personally, and we hung up. We renewed the Adidas deal shortly thereafter.

In 2002, Mike Sumner introduced me to a small-time agent named Joel Bell, who worked out of an office in Gaithersburg, Maryland. Joel had asked for the introduction. So, the three of us had lunch while Mike and I attended ABCD Camp in New Jersey. The contrast between Joel and Fegan couldn't have been starker. Fegan closed deals at the St. Regis. Joel did them in the lobby of the Comfort Inn. He came across as a used-car salesman, but, in fact, did a good job representing players.

"I've been following Assault for a while now," Joel began as we sat around the table awaiting the waitress. "You've done an amazing job."

"Thanks. We put a lot of work into the program," I responded.

"Mike told me you're working for an agent?"

"Yeah."

"I'm doing well, but would like to get to Dan Fegan status someday," Joel said. I raised my eyebrow at this. "Curtis, I know he's your guy. Right now, I'm representing some lower-tier guys, mostly overseas players."

"Dan worked his way up, too," I replied, thinking of Fegan back when he operated out of his house with just two employees.

"I wanted to meet you, Curtis, 'cause we know a lot of the same people, come from the same area, and might be able to help one another."

"I'm a pretty loyal guy." I wasn't sure what Bell wanted, exactly, but I wasn't ready to leave Fegan, even if I felt disappointed in how he had treated DJ after the accident.

"Oh, I know. It's something everyone says about you: 'Curtis Malone is loyal,' But I'm not trying to step on Dan's toes. I want to develop a relationship with you and DC Assault, prove my value to you."

"So, what do you have in mind?"

"Let's be real. Anyone can represent a DerMarr Johnson or some other top-ten draft pick. But DCA is full of depth. You're sending about ten guys a year to D-I schools. Not all of them will go to the NBA."

"Most of them won't," I agreed. "We try to get as many as possible into college as a way of bettering their lives."

"But they grow up dreaming of the NBA."

"Of course. We all do." Mike and Bell had played basketball for American University. We knew every kid in the hood who had any talent dreamed of making it big.

"So, all I'm saying is, allow me to be a friend of DCA. I can help the kids Fegan doesn't want. I can get them contracts overseas—Europe, China. While Fegan cherry-picks his first rounders, I'll work for the guys he overlooks."

Bell knew how to appeal to me. His pitch was no different from the salesman on a car lot asking, *What will it take to get you into this beauty today?* But his offer also made sense. For every DJ, five or six players' careers would end with college. Joel had a good overseas practice, and with that, he represented a way DCA could further help them improve their lives and possibly their professional careers.

I made no commitments at lunch, only promising to keep in touch. As time passed, Joel Bell continually showed his interest in helping our program He'd tip me off to talented players, donate money to help cover our traveling expenses, and promote DCA in the area. In return, I recommended a few of our alums whom Dan didn't want, such as Darren Kelly from the University of Texas and Rob Little from Stanford.

Over that same period of time, Fegan and I began having disagreements over my pay. We'd never signed any contracts or legal agreement; provisions in the NBA Players Association charter forbid AAU coaches from employment with agents. I never would have pressed a legal claim in court anyway. Where I came from, you didn't handle your problems by running to court. Frankly, I felt so thankful Fegan had given me the opportunity to break into the agent side of the business. Again, loyalty. But I also felt that Fegan had moved on from me. His success changed him. I saw it in the way he'd treated DJ, in how often he passed on DCA players who weren't going to become NBA superstars. When he began balking on paying me what I believed he owed me, based on our verbal agreement, I felt fucked over.

Meanwhile, Joel Bell continued to prove he meant what he'd told me at our initial lunch. He heard the rumors about Fegan and me disagreeing, and always made it clear I could come work for him.

As we entered 2005, I began asking my pro contacts about Bell. Most warned me against him. They criticized his character and spoke badly of him. I'd always believed Joel to be a genuine person. I decided the one person I could trust to give it to me straight was Sonny. So, I arranged for the three of us to have lunch in New York. Prior to meeting, I filled Sonny in on how close Bell had been playing me. I meant for the lunch to be a tryout or an audition, of sorts, for Joel. If he could win over the great Sonny Vaccaro, I'd strongly consider leaving Fegan.

"I don't like him," Sonny declared the day after our lunch. "Seems like a sleazeball to me. Don't make a decision you'll regret."

"He made a strong offer."

"I haven't spoken to anyone who thinks well of him," Sonny answered.

I asked a few NBA scouts and a couple front-office execs I knew. They all said the same: Joel Bell was no good.

I felt torn. I wanted to make my own decision. Lots of other AAU and high school coaches spoke poorly of me out of spite, not knowing or caring how deeply I believed in helping the kids in our program. I knew what it felt like to be judged.

I considered things from a business perspective. Bell offered me a monthly stipend similar to Fegan's. He also offered a higher percentage of profit off contracts and endorsement deals. Further, he promised to represent all DCA players talented enough to play pro ball, whether a projected first rounder, a player expected to go undrafted, or someone developing a career overseas.

Still, the relationship between Fegan and I remained in place. We acted professionally about our disagreement. On June 1, 2006, he let me use his condo in Miami, where Monica and I got married in a small, private ceremony. We exchanged vows on the beach and used the condo to celebrate our marriage.

By that fall, Fegan and I reached an agreement: He would continue to pay my commission on the guys I'd delivered to him, including Moochie Norris, Stephen Jackson, and Juan Dixon, among others. I received $7K a month just off the Norris and Jackson deals. I would weigh my options for the future. He and I remained cordial. It was a business decision, nothing personal. I realized he'd come up in the agent game. I was the last of his original staff remaining. He no longer needed me.

I talked to and met with a few different companies, but I felt comfortable with Joel Bell. When he heard I'd split with Fegan, he increased his original offer, so I'd make up what I'd lost with Dan. Joel agreed to match the monthly pay Fegan was giving me plus more. He was willing to do whatever he needed to become the next Arn Tellem or Dan Fegan of the world. That included indulging "pay-to-play" when he deemed necessary.

I envisioned my future. If Bell became successful like Fegan had, I'd have a true partner to help me transition from AAU to sports management—my long-held dream. And as I accepted Bell's offer and officially became his consultant, I believed I had the perfect player to launch our relationship. His name was Michael Beasley.

Converging Paths

In late 2005, Monica and I bought a $525,000 home in Upper Marlboro, Maryland. We moved in with the kids. Sydney was in her senior year at St. John's, Nolan was a sophomore at Riverdale, and Michael continued catching up in his classes under Monica's watchful eye. The house was even big enough that my daughter, Alexus, had her own room when she came to visit.

Homeschooling proved to be the best choice. Mike had made up his ninth-grade courses, and the state considered him a sophomore. He and Nolan had a great season at Riverdale. I began to see serious basketball potential in Mike and Nolan. Both steadily rose in the national player rankings. I hired an agility coach and they hit the gym, weight training to bulk up. Both worked hard. With Monica as his surrogate mother, Mike's attitude improved. She didn't put up with any bullshit. Sydney and Nolan also provided role models. Monica and I believed we were seeing the potential person he could become.

Then Lou Wilson called me.

As a homeschooled student who participated in athletics at Riverdale, Michael could be on their campus for a few hours each day. The school year had nearly ended, when Mike was caught hooking up with a female student in a bathroom. We couldn't believe he'd gone almost an entire year without problems, and then got in trouble with just weeks left in the term.

Michael passed his tenth-grade tests and advanced into eleventh. But Riverdale banned him from campus. Luckily, the season had finished. Now we needed to find another school for him. Nolan, who'd grown extremely close to Mike, decided he'd transfer to whatever new school Mike attended.

I decided to send both to Oak Hill Academy in Mouth of Wilson, Virginia. I'd sent players to Coach Steve Smith before and knew his style. Combined with Oak Hill's remoteness, it would be good for Mike. We never worried about Nolan; he'd adjust and do well anywhere. Monica and I sent a few thousand dollars for each of them to attend; athletic scholarships paid the rest of the tuition. Monica made sure Michael's homeschool transcripts got sent out, and we filled Fatima in on where Michael transferred to and why. She had gone to the disciplinary meeting at Riverdale, along with the parents of the girl caught in the bathroom with Mike, so she understood the need for us to find a new school.

Once Michael and Nolan left, and with Sydney now attending the University of Louisville, Monica and I had the house to ourselves. With no longer needing to handle Mike's schooling or drive him around to games and practices, we didn't know what to do with ourselves. I focused on remodeling the basement, and Monica wanted to get new furniture. Unfortunately, at this time, money ran a little low. I'd left Fegan but hadn't lined up anyone with Bell just yet; DJ's monthly stipend had dried up, and I lived off my modest Adidas consulting fee.

A friend of mine, whom I called Shorty, owned a recording studio just down the street. Shorty knew of my background and needed a favor.

"Curtis, I need to count some cash, but I got clients in the studio all day. Any chance I can use your place?"

Monica was out at work, and I had the house to myself.

"You just need to count it?"

"Yeah. Won't take long."

"Alright. Come on by."

Shorty brought his cash-counting machines to my house, and we huddled in the basement. He fed about $700,000 through the machines and passed me five grand as thanks for letting him use my place.

Seeing all that cash gave me the itch. Shorty told me his supplier had an eighteen-wheeler come right to his studio. I'd seen the truck at the studio countless times.

"How much a kilo going for nowadays?" I asked him.

"Depends. If I fronted you, I'd need about twenty-one grand a piece."

"Hmmm. I might be interested. I'll let you know."

I called around and found out I could get twenty-three grand a kilo around DC. I decided to dip a toe back into the drug game. Shorty fronted me five kilos, I made two grand on each, and suddenly Monica and I could start furnishing the house and finish the basement to our high-end taste.

Both Nolan and Michael had successful junior years at Oak Hill. The team finished the season ranked first in the *USA Today* High School Basketball Power Rankings. Both boys earned good grades. Schools began recruiting Nolan, though most believed he would play for the University of Louisville, his parents' alma mater and where his sister Sydney attended.

Jerryd Bayless, a top player out of Arizona, had committed to Duke but then backed out. Suddenly, Duke needed a guard out of Nolan's class. A family friend, Johnny Dawkins, who knew Monica, asked her if Nolan was truly committed to Louisville. When she told him nothing had been decided, Duke entered the conversation.

Coach K and his staff aggressively recruited Nolan once his junior year ended. Monica and Nolan took a trip to Durham to attend a game. When they returned, Nolan was sold on Duke. I'd seen this before with DJ; a campus visit or even just going to a game can easily sway a recruit. So, I took Nolan to see John Thompson at Georgetown. Nolan liked Thompson's personality. He also did research on Georgetown, Louisville, and Duke's basketball programs.

Nolan thought about going to school with Michael, but ultimately, he saw Duke's extended basketball family and could envision a life after basketball. He knew, regardless of how well his playing career went, that he'd want to coach or stay involved in the game in some capacity once the ball stopped bouncing. Duke could best help him achieve that goal.

I'd never been the biggest Duke fan but held a ton of respect for Coach Krzyzewski. When he came to the house for the official home visit to meet our family, I felt about as proud as a peacock. Coach K in my house! Though I knew Duke alums Johnny Dawkins and Brian Davis, and knew of Grant Hill, who had played with my friends Curt Smith and Henry Hall, Duke's basketball program wasn't my top choice for Nolan. However, I knew the school would prepare him for life, which was more important.

He was (still is) a very self-aware kid who knew what he wanted, had done his research, and made his own decision.

Nolan's recruitment ended up being easy. Michael's would be another story. Monica and I knew we'd need to be really involved and selective in where he went. He needed the right place with the right coaches if he was to succeed. Michael verbally committed early to attend UNC Charlotte because Dalonte worked as an assistant there. Dalonte coached Mike's DCA team and had become a mentor/big brother to him. He wanted to go where Dalonte worked. This suited me fine, as I knew he'd need a babysitter wherever he attended.

This validated itself near the end of his junior year at Oak Hill when he decided to autograph the bumper of the principal's car. Oak Hill told us Nolan could come back for his senior year. Michael could not.

"Shocked" barely covers how Monica and I felt, though I suppose we shouldn't have been. Once again, Mike had waited until the last few weeks of the school year to act like an asshole and get himself expelled.

Shortly after the end of the school year, Coach Bob Huggins left Cincinnati to become the head coach at Kansas State. He called and told me he wanted to hire Dalonte as his assistant. Michael had emerged as a top recruit, and Huggins knew Mike would go wherever Dalonte coached. Coach wanted to make an impact at Kansas State by immediately landing Beasley. I told Huggins it would be Dalonte's decision, but that I knew Huggins ran a great program based on DJ's experience there. I encouraged Huggins to call Coach Bobby Lutz at UNC Charlotte and discuss Dalonte personally with him.

Obviously, Coach Lutz was pissed. He felt betrayed by Dalonte but was also mad when Mike changed his commitment to Kansas State. I could understand Dalonte's reason for leaving. He had a young family and Huggins offered nearly $100,000 more in salary. But I've never understood why coaches get angry when a recruit changes his mind. More often, a coach changes jobs and leaves his recruits out to dry, yet he expects the player to never reconsider.

Dalonte prepared to pack up and move to Manhattan, Kansas. Before he left, I tasked him with helping me find a new school for Mike. Coach Smith promised not to bash Mike if other coaches asked, instead saying Mike was considered a fifth-year player and Oak Hill didn't want to take on the academic risk of forfeiting games with a fifth-year player. Dalonte began his search.

I've never forgotten where I came from. Perhaps, in some small way, things would've turned out differently if I had. But even when I started rubbing elbows with Vaccaro, attending the NBA draft, or hosting Coach K at my home, I still considered myself a street guy. I never changed my company of friends. My everyday life included the friends and old heads I'd grown up with. Whenever I wasn't busy with DCA, I'd go pick them up. I didn't care whether they were crackheads or dope fiends. I'd drive them to the liquor store or take them out to eat. I would also help pay for funerals and sponsor after-party celebrations of homegoing services and Palmer Park Reunions.

If an old friend was using, I'd encourage him to get clean. If one was sober, I'd use my contacts to get him a job. I gave away old clothing, so my friends looked sharp, and gave them money whenever they needed it. I wanted my friends to feel my success and hopefully feel motivated by it to try and succeed on their own. We all looked up to Sugar Ray Leonard as our hero in Palmer Park. The hood thought that Ray turned his back on us. I always said if I made it, I would never turn my back on the hood that made me.

I knew I couldn't save everyone. I took the same approach with my players. I gave as much of myself to as many as I could. I might buy a Thanksgiving dinner for a poor family, give away thousands of dollars' worth of clothing or shoes, dedicate all my free time to mentoring a young athlete, or just be a loyal friend to one of my mentors.

But I also knew remaining true to my roots could come back to haunt me. Thinking of myself as a drug dealer, a product of Palmer Park, kept me tied to the kind of criminal thinking and street codes that, at any time, could lead to trouble. If Monica represented a higher social class—a step up and beyond my own background—then my attachments to my past created a tension in my life. So many times, I could have outgrown Palmer Park. So many times, I could have turned my back and moved on. I never did. Whether dropping out of college or failing to fully commit myself to go legit through the opportunities DCA presented, I continuously turned back to drugs.

I don't regret that. There are absolutely specific decisions I've made which I'd re-do, if I could. But remaining true to my upbringing isn't one of those regrets. I do wish I'd found a better balance. Could I have achieved success while keeping my old friends and mentors and moved beyond my drug dealer self-image? Perhaps. But that's not what happened.

You learn things growing up in the hood. Rules, creeds. If you're in a good situation and a homie comes home from prison, you're expected to help him jump-start his life. Guys like Irvin, Tydie, Twin, and Byrd would have killed or died for me. The same expectation applied to me. Tydie caught a case, netting him a life sentence plus fifty years. But when he won some appeals and came home after twenty-five years behind bars, I remembered how he'd put clothes on my back. I tried to help him with money, tried to get him up on his feet. But some guys, they're too institutionalized as criminals. Making slow money by working an honest job isn't good enough. Tydie couldn't be patient. He wanted quick money and ended up robbing a store in Virginia. He was sixty years old and got a fifty-two-year sentence. Some of us just don't learn.

I always considered Irvin my godfather. I felt so thankful that he'd been in my life as a kid and young man. He never told me no and always encouraged and saw the best in me. So, I would always be there for him, no matter what he needed. After he suffered a heart attack in the early '00s, I would drive him to his doctor's appointments and buy his medications. Sometimes we'd spend hours at a natural health store buying all kinds of miracle remedies he wanted to try. He would suffer a second, fatal heart attack on September 30, 2011. That hit me hard. I'd lost many friends before, but Irvin was family. Slowly, year by year, I lost my ties to Palmer Park. But their imprint upon me would always remain.

Michael and Nolan's final AAU season began. DCA had so many players in the age group, we made two seventeen-and-under teams with nine players on each. One of my proudest achievements. Every single player, on both teams, signed a letter of intent to play Division I basketball. Some of the eighteen players would leave troubled neighborhoods to go to college. We lived our mission.

Of course, with so much talent, egos got in the way. At sixteen and seventeen, kids start smelling themselves, especially when they're being aggressively recruited. Everyone's telling you you're special; teen girls (and some grown women) throw themselves at you. It's easy to get full of yourself. The job of us coaches became less tactician or strategist and more mentor and babysitter. We existed to provide a reality check.

We attended Adidas's ABCD Camp in Atlanta, then stayed in Georgia to participate in a tournament. Our game was scheduled for noon the following day, so we imposed a midnight curfew on the teams. Typically, I did room checks, and, when I did, the kids tended to behave. I made an example out of anyone who broke the rules. I always acted like the nicest guy among our staff. But teen boys will take kindness for weakness if you let them, so we strictly enforced curfews.

I sat in the hotel lobby with Damon Handon, Mike Sumner, Butch Cherry, Pierre Allen, and Curtis Richardson at ten past twelve. We were about to head upstairs to do room checks when Michael, Nolan, Austin Freeman, and Jamar Samuels strolled in.

"So, they said 'fuck curfew,'" I mumbled to the others. "Hey, Nolan, you guys come over here!"

I was pissed. Had Michael arrived late, I wouldn't have been surprised, but this was really out of character for Nolan and Austin. The group walked over to us, Nolan looking apprehensive, Michael defiant.

"What time is it?" I asked.

"Twelve ten," Nolan replied.

"When's curfew?"

"Twelve, but—"

I cut him off with a look and held up my hand. "Get upstairs. You four gonna owe me tomorrow."

Sure, they were only ten minutes late, but if small things start to slip through, then big things come next.

We won our game the following day. As the players began piling into the rented vans, I pulled Michael, Nolan, Austin, and Jamar out of line.

"You four will follow us to the highway," I said.

"What do you mean?" Michael asked.

"Jog or run behind the van. We'll pick you up once we get to the highway."

It was about a hundred degrees and probably two miles to the freeway. I drove slowly, constantly keeping an eye on them. They jogged, walked, cramped up, and hated me for the punishment.

Sometimes players resent the nice coach they force to discipline them, but I felt it worth the risk. Curfew was midnight. Not 12:01 or 12:10. The fact that those four were our best players also sent a message: No one breaks the rules.

Except for me, perhaps. While in Atlanta that weekend, I ran into Mario, Pedro's brother. I hadn't seen him since Pedro's death. He had a nephew playing in the tournament. Talk about coincidence. We exchanged phone numbers and got together the next night to catch up.

We made small talk and reminisced about old times in DC and Maryland.

"You know, Curtis, I'm living well in Miami now. It's like paradise."

"Living that well, huh?"

"Curtis, the kilos and work are even better now than in the nineties...."

"Mario, I want you to know, my cuz had nothing to do with Pedro's murder. I swear it. He was with me all day. We both found out together."

"I believe you. We heard he had nothing to do with it, and later on we found out who done it," he replied.

"How is he?"

"Locked up. Got fifteen. Are you still doing your thing? Pedro always respected how you conducted our business."

I hesitated for only a second.

"No. I'm done with that game." Helping Shorty count cash was one thing, flipping some kilos to buy furniture was one thing, but getting back in the game with Mario would be a whole different level. "What I'm doing now, it's rewarding. And I like being legit."

I went on to explain my role with DCA and Adidas. I told him I could help his nephew attend ABCD the following year if the kid wanted to. Mario offered to host me in Miami if I ever found myself in "his city," and we both promised to keep in touch. I walked away feeling like I'd just spent some time catching up with an old acquaintance whom I'd probably never see again. Boy, was I wrong.

Dalonte found a school in Finchburg, Massachusetts that specialized in qualifying a kid for NCAA eligibility. Notre Dame Prep would help Michael get his grades up and score decently on the SAT. The NBA had instituted the "one-and-done" rule, so Michael couldn't skip college. He only had one option: Gain eligibility to play college ball on his way to the pros.

And he'd end up in the NBA. Over the past two years he'd blossomed as a player. Entering his senior year, he ranked as the number-one high school senior. We all knew he'd have a pro career so long as he could get that one year of college out of the way. Michael knew it. Adidas knew it. And Michael's mother, Fatima, knew it. Oh, how success can lead to selfishness.

Fatima

By June of 2007, Michael graduated from Notre Dame Prep. Coach Bill Barton deserves a lot of credit for Mike's achievement. Not only did Barton and NDP keep Mike's grades high enough to remain NCAA-eligible, but he scored well enough on the SAT to pass through the NCAA clearinghouse. His path to Kansas State opened up.

Nolan graduated from Oak Hill Academy and prepared to head to Duke. Monica and I rented an apartment in Durham so we could attend as many of his games as possible. I would also be flying back and forth to Manhattan, Kansas, Mike's soon-to-be new home.

But Mike's accomplishments really caused Monica and me to exhale with relief. We'd held our collective breath as he had struggled through National Christian, IMG in Florida, Riverdale Baptist, Oak Hill Academy, and Notre Dame Prep. Monica singlehandedly set him straight by homeschooling him. Had you asked any of his teachers over the years, no one would've thought he'd amount to anything, regardless of his basketball skills. But Mike had come through and graduated, now eligible to play D-I ball. His future stretched out before him, if he wanted to grab it.

He had also emerged as a basketball talent. He earned McDonald's All-American honors and an invitation to play in the Adidas Roundball Classic. Nolan also made All-American and would join Mike at the Roundball.

As Mike's on-court talent emerged, and it became clear he would play in the NBA, Monica and I began to hear from more of Mike's family. For almost five years we had fed, clothed, and housed Mike. We never received so much as a can of beans from any of his real family during that time, and we certainly didn't receive any financial help raising him. But as he moved closer to a pro career, and pro money, all sorts of voices piped up, all giving him advice; all of them trying to exert some level of control over his future. No one inserted him- or herself more than Mike's mother, Fatima.

To understand why we felt Fatima interfered—after all, she is his mother—I need to provide some context. For all the years Mike lived with us, Fatima had remained an arm's length away from her son. Whenever we had a big decision to make regarding Mike, like whether to send him to a new school, we included her in the conversation, made our recommendation, and explained why we thought it the best choice. She always agreed. Whenever Fatima wished to attend one of Mike's games, whether a DCA game or high-school, we made sure she got there and even paid for a hotel, if needed. During this time, we all understood I made basketball decisions, Monica made academic decisions, and Fatima had a say.

Mike lived with us exclusively during this time. On school breaks I'd fly him back to Maryland. He would hardly ever stay with his mother—maybe for one day, if that, but very seldom overnight. He would go visit with his family, but everyone understood our house was his home. Nolan was his brother, Sydney his sister, and he called Monica "Li'l Ma." At no point did Monica nor I want to, or try to, supplant Fatima. We never spoke unkindly or disrespected her to Mike, but we also believed he was part of our family. Everything went well until Fatima and Mike's other relatives began whispering into her and his ears.

The problem began with Nike. I don't exaggerate when I describe the animosity between the shoe companies as a war. Mike had emerged as the top player in the country. He wore an Adidas shoe. Nike wanted in. The strategy the brands typically use is to find the weakest person in the player's family and try to exploit that person, gain their trust, sell them on the brand, then convert them into an advocate for the brand. That's what Nike began to do with Fatima.

The Nike rep called her directly. He would complain that I isolated Mike and wouldn't give Nike a chance to make a deal. He suggested I was on the take with Adidas and only looking out for myself. He reminded her of Nike's vast resources and of the NBA greats who had worn a Nike shoe: *Wouldn't it be amazing to go to Footlocker and see a Michael Beasley sneaker on the wall?* he'd ask. Then he began sending Mike boxes of Air Jordans. And not just a couple pairs. Every week more would arrive. There I was, a consultant for Adidas, with a house full of Jordans. It was disrespectful. I finally had to call him.

"You need to stop sending these shoes to Mike," I began.

"You need to let us try and make a deal with the kid."

"I'm not trying to stop you. When the time comes, and he declares, whichever brand makes the best offer will get the deal."

"I'm trying to show him some love, now."

"And telling his mother a lot of bullshit. Listen, Nike hasn't been around, helping him out for all these years. When Mike was a goofy kid who couldn't walk and chew gum, you were nowhere to be found. Don't try and jump on the bandwagon now."

"Curtis—"

"No, listen. If you send one more pair of shoes to him, the next time I see you, I'll smack the shit out of you."

I also called the rep's boss and told him to stop sending shoes and wasting his company's money.

Mike couldn't understand why I was so pissed. I had to explain everything to him.

"Mike, Adidas sponsors our program. They pay me as a consultant. The food I put on the table, the clothes I buy you, all that is thanks to Adidas."

"But Nike is just showing me they like my game."

"When you got kicked out of IMG, Adidas still put you in shoes. When you got expelled from Oak Hill, Adidas didn't drop you. You don't whore yourself to every shoe company out there. Show some loyalty to the guys who have supported you since you were fourteen."

"But my ma says you're only looking out for yourself."

"When you get to the show, Joel will get you the best deal with whatever company offers it."

Both Fatima and Mike already knew—and accepted—that Joel Bell would represent him. It was one of the few things at the time Fatima didn't challenge us on. I'd introduced her to Bell, and she liked him.

Monica and I had a few rules we enforced with the kids: They had a strict curfew; we didn't allow girls over after a certain time at night, nor could girls go to either Nolan's or Mike's bedrooms; both had to keep their hair neat, with no braids or cornrows; we forbade tattoos; we didn't allow saggy pants. Monica pushed these harder than I, but we both understood appearance reflected character. If you looked, dressed, and acted respectfully, others would respect you.

Monica and I attended a game in New Jersey. As we sat together in the stands, Monica leaned over and pointed out a dark mark on Mike's arm.

"What's that?" she asked.

I looked closer during a time-out and realized it was a tattoo.

"Did you tell him he could get a tattoo?" I asked.

"No, of course not."

After the game, I asked Mike about it. "My mom told me I could get it," he answered defiantly.

I was really pissed. All these years, Mike had accepted our rules, and now he played Fatima against us. We were strict, but Mike needed that level of attention and structure. I told both Mike and Fatima that if she continued to undermine us and go against our rules, then Mike could move back in with her and live by her rules. She would have loved that. By that point, she'd realized Mike was her cash machine. But Mike had grown too close to Nolan and Sydney to leave. He liked the lifestyle we provided him. Moving back in with his mother didn't appeal to him at all.

"We've treated her like our sister, and I just have a feeling she's going to turn on us," Monica said.

"She's seeing dollar signs, but in the end, she knows we're looking out for Mike's best interests."

"My intuition tells me she's going to cause problems." I should have trusted Monica's intuition.

Mike and Nolan had been selected to play in the McDonald's All-American Game and the Adidas Roundball Classic. Once again, Nike began interfering by inviting Mike to play in their Jordan game. He could only play in two games, and the McDonald's All-American Game was a must. Fatima wanted Mike to play in the Jordan game.

"You know, I work for Adidas," I told her. "Adidas sponsors Assault, the team Mike played on all these years. How's it going to look for the kid I've practically raised to choose the Nike game over the Roundball Classic? Especially since Adidas has been putting custom-made, size-twenty shoes on his feet."

"But if he doesn't play, they might not offer an endorsement deal," Fatima complained.

"If Mike is good enough to get a shoe deal, they'll make an offer. That's business. Of course, we'll give them a shot. I want what's best for Mike."

"I don't see what it'll hurt," Mike chimed in.

"What? You don't think Nolan would like to play in the Jordan game? But he knows I work for Adidas. He realizes how bad that would look for us. And who do you think feeds you and your mother and keeps the lights on?"

I thought I'd squashed all the Nike crap, but Fatima still took their calls. She loved the attention they gave her. The change in Fatima happened so quickly, we had a hard time grasping it. I don't think she even appreciated what Monica and I had done for Mike. The time and effort I'd put in—hell, I gave him more attention than my own daughters—meant nothing to her. She only saw the end result—a future NBA contract—and wanted her cut.

"I need you to believe in me, Fatima," I said. "We have a game plan: college, the draft, endorsements...you gotta trust me and Joel."

I wanted to give her the benefit of the doubt. We paid for her plane ticket and we all flew up to Finchburg, Massachusetts for Mike's graduation. She threw shade at Monica and gave me attitude the whole trip. Monica, Sydney, and I wanted to celebrate this really amazing accomplishment of Mike's. Instead, we got mistrust and attitude.

"I think she wants to move us out of Mike's life," I told Monica.

"It's just a matter of time," Monica predicted.

At the McDonald's All-American Game, I introduced Fatima to my friend Greg Holloway, a DCA booster. I recommended Greg serve as Mike's business advisor. Greg was a certified public accountant and a tough businessman. Although Mike would most likely hire a firm like Protrust Capital or Merrill Lynch, Greg would oversee their work and could advise Mike on specific investments. Greg offered to do this for free. He already had money and didn't need to make any more off Mike. He wanted to see him succeed and not squander his money like so many other athletes. Fatima agreed to sit down and talk to Greg once we returned to Maryland.

In the late spring of 2007, I received a call from Bob Huggins. He'd been offered, and accepted, the head coach position at West Virginia. The news would break in the coming hours, but he wanted to speak to me first. I felt pissed he would bail on Kansas State and Mike just before the season, but I also knew this kind of thing happened all the time.

"Is Dalonte going to West Virginia with you?" I asked.

"No. I want you to be patient, Curtis. I'm going to recommend Frank Martin to the university's president to be the next head coach. Dalonte will be promoted to associate head coach."

It would have been hard for Dalonte to leave Kansas State anyway. In short order, he'd recruited Mike and other DCA standouts such as Jamar Samuels, Ron Anderson, and Dominique Sutton, as well as Jacob Pullen out of Illinois. Plus, the following year, he secured commitments from Rodney McGruder and Wally Judge (two of DCA's up-and-coming stars). Judge would be named a McDonald's All-American his senior year of high school. Dalonte didn't want to pull out of his commitment to those kids and to Kansas State.

Frank Martin had more experience than Dalonte, but I believe Dalonte had more appeal to potential players. In hindsight, I should have tried to push Huggins to make Dalonte the head coach. Martin ended up being a good coach, but I really thought Dalonte would help Mike more.

As it turned out, the university president hired Frank as head coach and named Dalonte associate head coach. At twenty-eight, Dalonte secured a $420,000 salary. He became the highest-paid assistant in college basketball at the time and it totally changed his life.

I spoke with Frank Martin and Dalonte about hiring one of DCA's coaches, Bruce Shingler, as an assistant coach. I considered Kansas State one of DCA's colleges now—part of our growing network. Bruce proved a great mentor to some of our younger players, but I also knew another DCA alum at Kansas State watching over Mike couldn't hurt.

For almost ten years, Kansas State had been the Big 12's doormat. Dalonte and his pipeline to top Assault players began to change that. In large part because of their connection to DCA through Dalonte, Kansas State ended up back on the map.

This contrasted starkly to Gary Williams, who, while at Maryland, refused to bring in young assistants with ties to local players. Dalonte had built a relationship with Mike since the kid was thirteen years old. Mike trusted Dalonte. That relationship helped Dalonte land the Kansas State job (and, I have to emphasize, Dalonte is a great coach). His connection to our program, our players' familiarity with him, led to a strong recruiting class. Martin and Dalonte hired Bruce, which solidified McGruder and Judge's commitment to KSU thanks to the relationship they both had with Bruce.

Meanwhile, these kids received solid educations through DCA's network of prep and private schools and, eventually, a chance to play college ball and go pro. They made it out of their neighborhoods and—once in the NBA or playing professionally—could provide for their families by making a decent living.

Now why couldn't a coach like Gary Williams provide that chance? My players would've loved to stay local, playing games in front of family and friends at Maryland, rather than moving to Kansas or Durham or halfway across the country. Williams could have built up Maryland as a perennial contender while helping local players. Only his corrupted sense of integrity prevented him from doing so.

The whole situation created an interesting paradox. As the years passed and my criminal life caught up to me, Williams and others would be quick to criticize or make it clear they never approved of me. Some men who would've stood shoulder to shoulder with me suddenly turned their backs when my arrest hit the news. Yes, I sold drugs. I did it to continue my lifestyle but also to help my players. Despite what my detractors say, and yes, some are rolling their eyes right now, I always wanted to help kids succeed. But who is worse—the drug dealer who mentors and guides countless kids to college, or the college coach who could easily help raise the kid out of poverty (who literally holds the kid's future in his hands) but instead says no out of some sense of prideful morality?

With Mike set to leave for Kansas, Fatima declared she, too, wanted to relocate. Initially, Mike told us coaches he didn't want her out there with him. But he never had the balls to say it to her face, so we kept quiet, too.

Dalonte helped her find a job as a receptionist in a medical office, and she looked for a house to rent. I told her to call Greg Holloway to help get her established.

"Curtis, you're going to have a problem on your hands," Greg told me.

"What do you mean?"

"I met with Fatima and her sister. Those two are already counting that boy's money and figuring out how to spend it."

"She's been seeing green ever since Nike put the bug in her ear."

Fatima called Greg and told him she wanted to move to Kansas. He offered to front her the money to make the move. He paid for a moving company, the deposit plus first-year's rent on a house, and he bought Mike a used Tahoe (Monica and I had told Mike no on the truck. We thought him too immature to drive, and freshmen weren't even allowed vehicles on campus—Fatima overruled us). The cost for Greg totaled about $37,000. He told Fatima the money was a no-interest loan, and when Mike signed his pro deal they only had to reimburse him.

This was both generous of Greg and foolish of both him and me. I involved Greg to help watch out for Mike because I knew a lot of people would come for his money. After Greg had met with Fatima and her sister, we both should have known she had plans for Mike's money. Plans that didn't include paying Greg back.

Fatima and Mike settled in Manhattan, Kansas. The media projected Mike as a top-five pick in the 2008 draft. Fatima became a pain in the ass for everyone at KSU. She made demands as if she were the star athlete who needed to be pampered. She even started a blog on the local newspaper's website, dishing out her opinions on the university, the team, and many other topics.

During this time, Joel and I had agreed to give Fatima and Mike a monthly stipend. She received $3K and he got $2,500 per month, in cash. I did all of the transactions either by flying to Kansas or making other arrangements. This way nothing could come back on Joel. We certainly didn't need any more bumps in the road like the ones Fatima was already causing.

Monica and I spent what little free time I had attending Nolan's games. I also flew out to visit and watch Mike play a lot, but I wanted to avoid Fatima. I could only shake my head. When Mike, as an awkward eighth grader, constantly got in trouble, Fatima practically handed him off to strangers. I'd only known him a few months when I stood up in court and promised a judge I'd be responsible for his behavior.

Yet, as soon as Mike became an asset, Fatima reasserted her claim of mothership she'd abandoned all those years before. Days when Monica argued and struggled with Mike over a school lesson, Fatima wasn't around. Days when I had to deal with pissed-off school officials because Mike had messed up, again, Fatima wasn't around. Now, she resented us being around. The woman had no shame.

The Beginning of the End

My relationship with Joel Bell had progressed well: I brought NBA guys like Bobby Jones, Solomon Jones, and Bernard Robinson over to Bell Management, plus numerous overseas players. Joel and I talked about making me a partner once Mike was drafted. I'd always been upfront with both Fatima and Mike about my business relationship with Joel. I stood to benefit from Joel's representation of Mike, but I also believed Joel would do a great job for him. Joel had put in the effort to develop a relationship with both Mike and his mother. Plus, he knew the challenges Mike created for himself. Joel would defend and fight for him.

But Bell Management wasn't the only agency game involved in our lives. In early 2006, Monica took a job with Perennial Sports and Entertainment, which represented Major League Baseball umpires, NBA referees, and had a football division overseen by Tony Paige. The job change came out of the blue. Monica had previously worked in the legal department for Washington Sports & Entertainment.

Lamell McMorris, a young brother, ran Perennial. Monica's job, event planning, seemed to consist of doing very little and getting paid for it. Lamell developed a close relationship with us, attending Nolan's games and sponsoring DCA. At first, I suspected he and Monica might have had some funny shit going on. Over time, Lamell's motivations became clearer.

My wife and I had also launched the Curtis and Monica Malone Foundation, which held golf tournaments and other events to raise money for local charities supporting diabetes research and nonprofit organizations like the Fishing School in Washington, DC. Monica had served as vice president of Behind the Bench, NBA Wives Association and had gained experience in fundraising. The foundation allowed us another way for us to give back.

As 2007 came to an end and 2008 began, only our deteriorating relationship with Fatima caused us any stress. Well, that and my growing drug business.

I had continued to allow Shorty to use my basement to count his drug money. I'd also contacted a friend—I'll call him D—to see who had paper and was looking for kilos with a quick turnaround. I did this just to find out how the street felt, in case I needed to make some quick cash.

After we bought the house in Upper Marlboro, we began spending money like it meant nothing. The basement renovation cost almost $100K with the interior designer, and we spent tens of thousands more on furniture. Then, we rented an apartment in Durham to be close to Nolan. With my consultant fees from Adidas and Joel's commission, plus Monica's salary, we made good money on paper, but I made even more off the books.

Shorty introduced me to his suppliers from LA, Psych and Cat Eyes, as well as his man KD, at a dinner one night. Over

T-bones and Veuve Clicquot rosé champagne, we traded stories of our drug lives. I gossiped about the inner workings of the college and pro basketball game.

"You know," I said, "if this basketball shit doesn't work out, I may need you guys' help."

Fatima's reemergence and control over Mike had made me nervous. I made no secret that Mike's NBA career would be the catalyst to launch my next move in the sports management business. I'd worked towards that goal for seven years. But as our relationship began to change, I panicked and tried to find a plan B.

Plus, I was greedy and really loved easy money.

"You know we'll help you out. Whatever you need, I can get," replied Psych.

"What about PCP?" I asked. "Back in the day, I made some good money moving gallons."

"Sure. I can get you a gallon for ten grand in LA."

I did some quick math. A buddy of mine purchased PCP for twenty grand. If I arranged the deal and charged fifteen, I could make a quick $20–25K if he bought four to five gallons for literally thirty minutes of work. Too tempting.

"I'll let you know. Need to make a few calls."

I ended up making the PCP deal with Psych. The extra money ran through my hands like water. Monica never asked too many questions about where the money came from. She first thought it came from counting Shorty's cash. But Monica knew my history, knew who I spent time with, knew I always remained loyal to my roots. She must have known something less than legal went on. Perhaps my street life disappointed her, but she certainly enjoyed spending the money. It became so lucrative, she just turned a blind eye.

A few months later, my friend D contacted me, requesting five kilos of cocaine. Psych was on his way out with a delivery, so I grabbed five kilos from Shorty once Psych dropped it off. D had his money ready, and I quickly sold the coke. Again, easy money.

We got together for dinner, as we typically did whenever Psych made a run east, and Psych asked me if I'd gotten some of the work. I told him I grabbed five kilos.

"What did Shorty charge you?" he asked.

"Twenty-one, five," I said. I'd flipped them for $25K each.

Psych looked at Pretty (Shorty wasn't there) and said, "That's too high for him." Looking at me, "We give it to him for seventeen, three."

I didn't complain because it had literally taken me thirty minutes to make almost twenty grand. But from then on, I got the kilos directly from Psych and Bald Head and increased my profit margin. I gave little thought to the lives I was impacting with my quick money.

My stepson's career at Duke was rocky. Nolan didn't get much playing time and his performance suffered from the lack of consistency. Had it been Mike, he would have done something foolish and acted out. But Nolan was the complete opposite. We never had to baby him because he acted mature and responsible. Sometimes, that causes a parent to pay less attention to a kid, and that, in turn, can cause resentment or jealousy. But Nolan has always been, and still is, an independent person. So is his sister. Monica raised them well.

She attended all Nolan's games, and I attended most to support and encourage him. I advised him to fight, to work hard, to be the first in the gym and the last to leave, and to study film. His work ethic was fantastic, but the team lacked the strength of most Duke teams and lost early in the 2008 NCAA tournament. Nolan planned to stay in school and earn a degree—another difference between him and Mike.

Monica would chide me for focusing too much attention on Mike and not enough on Nolan. But Nolan didn't need me on his case every day. If I gave him some advice on an aspect of his game I thought needed improvement, he just went out and put in the work. Nolan had a lot of other men in his life who supported him and had his back, whereas Mike had no one to help him except for the people who had their hand out. Hell, Nolan would come home two hours before his curfew if there was nothing to do. Mike would've found trouble.

So, I hope Nolan doesn't feel as if I neglected him. I am so proud of him. I think I may have learned more about being a good person from Nolan and Sydney than anything they learned from me. But I hope I provided the love and stability they needed during that time in their lives. I couldn't (and didn't try) to replace their father, but I hope I did a good job filling in.

Mike ranked as one of the top college players in the country and earned a nomination for the John R. Wooden Award. The awards dinner and ceremony were held in LA. Monica, Sydney, Nolan, and I flew out to attend and support him. Fatima flew in from Kansas.

After the dinner finished, but before the ceremony, a female player brought her family over to our table to introduce them to Mike's family. He introduced Fatima as his mother and then referred to Monica as Li'l Ma. He'd given her that nickname because of Monica's height and how he towered over her.

After the awards ceremony, Mike climbed into our car for the ride back to the hotel, while Fatima had gotten her own ride. Mike had tears in his eyes.

"What's wrong?" I asked, thinking he felt overcome with disappointment for losing out on the award to Tyler Hansbrough.

"My mother's tripping," he answered.

"Why?"

"As we were leaving, she grabbed me and cursed me out."

"What's her deal?" I asked.

Mike glanced at Monica, then looked out the window. "She told me never to call someone else 'Ma' in front of her. That she's the only mother I got."

Monica looked at me. But there really was nothing to say. I reminded him that Monica had been Li'l Ma since the eighth grade and nothing would change that. Fatima's attitude that night just piled more bullshit onto the ever-growing pile she was creating for her son and for us.

Mike had an issue with marijuana. While at Notre Dame Prep, he began smoking weed. We knew about it, and Bruce Shingler tried his best to keep Mike clean. The NCAA tournament was about to being, and Joel and I worked hard for Mike's NBA draft declaration. We didn't need any distractions or problems.

At the NCAA tournament, we got a tip that the NCAA would drug test after the game. I called Mike's hotel room and asked him when he last smoked. He told me a day or two ago. THC, the compound in marijuana, can stay in the blood stream for a month, depending on how much and how often the person smokes. When I heard he'd gotten high within the past forty-eight hours, I cursed him out like I'd never done before. Here we were at the NCAA tournament and the draft just months away. What a PR disaster it would be if he failed a drug test and got suspended. The timing of Mike's fuckups remained consistently awful.

I called 411 information to find a health store in Omaha, Nebraska, the site of the game. I then ran around that afternoon buying all types of cleansers and herbal teas. I had him drinking all this shit all afternoon to try and clean his urine out. During the game that night, the managers replaced his Gatorade with a fruit punch-flavored cleanser. Every time-out he'd guzzle it down.

Kansas State would go on to lose the game. The NCAA only drug tests the winning team, so we'll never know if Mike would have passed. We did our best to make sure he would. He must have pissed a hundred times that day.

Leading up to the NBA draft, DeAndre Jordan, out of Texas A&M, also signed with Joel. He and I now had two top prospects on our roster. We began having meetings with reps from Nike, Adidas, and different financial management firms to plan out each player's options.

We always included Fatima in the meetings, especially those with the financial advisors. I wanted her to be involved, though I didn't trust her. Steve Reed, who owned Capital Advisors, impressed us, and we all liked him. He seemed like a stand-up person, and after Joel did some research on Steve's background and history, we felt good about hiring him. But before we recommended Mike sign on, Steve wanted to meet with me.

He flew me out to San Francisco to lay the groundwork for how his company could manage Mike's money.

"You've been a mentor to Mike for a while now. What would you like out of this?" he asked.

"Really, I just want you to make sure Mike supports DCA. Assault gave him all the opportunities to develop his game and get noticed."

"So, a donation?"

"Yes, him giving back. We are a 501(c)3 nonprofit. I think some money every year would be fair. He should give back and help the younger kids coming up," I explained.

"Curtis, what's it gonna take to get Beasley, DeAndre, and maybe some other players to sign on with my company?" asked Steve, matter-of-factly.

"How about a hundred grand a year to DCA? And by the way, this rug you have here in your office is beautiful."

"One hundred grand to DCA is doable. And I'll throw in my rug."

It was a large amount of money. By that time, we knew Mike would be either the first or second overall pick and knew what his rookie contract would be. Mike would be a lucrative signing for Steve, not mentioning the other players who I could get to sign with him.

"That would all be really generous," I replied. I understood how the game was played. I knew $100K a year from Steve was so easily attainable, be it from his pockets or his clients making donations through his company.

"Curtis, I really appreciate your support here. You're my man. If Mike brings me onboard, I want to make sure you get what you need. I'll also share the profits I make off Mike, DeAndre, and anyone else you bring me once they have serious money put away. That's my commitment and promise to you."

"Well, I really appreciate that, Steve. I want the money to be strictly for DCA and not one dime for me."

After I left San Francisco, Steve flew Fatima out and wined and dined her. He put her up at the Four Seasons and pampered her with massages, fancy dinners, and nice Louis Vuitton bags. He also entertained all her hair-salon business ideas Greg Holloway had warned me about.

With Joel, me, and Fatima all endorsing Steve Reed, Mike hired him to manage his money. He immediately told Steve he wanted a Range Rover. Keep in mind, Mike had yet to sign a pro contract. He hadn't even been drafted. But, like DerMarr, a top prospect will receive lines of credit and loans well before he signs a deal.

Mike told Steve to deliver the truck to my house. Somehow Fatima got wind of this and told Steve to send it to her house. When Steve called me and asked for my advice, I told him to speak with Mike. Mike still lived with Monica and me, and he wanted the Range Rover sent there. Steve complied but got an earful from Fatima. If it were up to us, Monica and I wouldn't even let Mike drive. We thought him too immature, so we did not care where they parked the truck. Fatima's reaction just further divided us and caused unnecessary problems between Monica, me, and Mike.

Steve Reed played a shrewd game. He knew he had to impress me because I still held influence over Mike and had a business relationship with Joel Bell. He also knew he needed a harder sell to win me over compared to Fatima. He realized early how much control she would have and knew allying himself with her would put him in a powerful position should she emerge as Mike's top influencer. He played us all against one another while kissing everyone's ass. As he propped up Fatima's fragile ego with grand promises and flattery, he promised me he'd "support DCA for life." Steve did a great job playing both sides and was very quick to throw shade on someone else when they weren't around.

Boy, was I naive.

Joel began negotiating with the shoe companies. Nike continued to try and sow discord by badmouthing Joel to Fatima. I eventually called William Wesley, known as World Wide Wes (WWW), and Lynn Merritt at Nike and told them if they wanted consideration to begin working with Joel.

Adidas had verbally agreed to an endorsement deal, but we hadn't discussed numbers. Both companies told us the weakening economy would mean less money than previous years. With the housing market crashing, the whole mess created havoc throughout the economy. Kevin Durant received the last big contract, $60 million over seven years, and we knew Mike's money wouldn't come close.

Nike offered $750,000 a year for three years with performance bonus potential of up to $3 million. They claimed they offered Mike, O.J. Mayo, and Derrick Rose all the same money. Adidas initially offered $1.25 million a year for five years, and with performance bonuses, the deal potentially could be worth up to $10 million. Clearly Adidas's offer blew Nike's away. Joel and I discussed how we'd approach the negotiation. Joel wanted my opinion on the number of years involved.

"Honestly, Joel, we want the longest deal we can get."

"Mike might want more money on the front end and the flexibility a shorter deal will give him."

"And with Mike's issues, he may fuck himself and never get another shoe deal. No, we lock Adidas in long-term, so even if Mike's attitude, or his mother, screws things up, he's financially secure."

Joel set a meeting up with Adidas in New York. He and Mike invited Fatima along. She really had no business being there. What could she contribute? She knew nothing about negotiating an endorsement deal. But her ego made her stubborn and Steve Reed probably put her up to it. Had she not been brought in, she would have caused trouble, so Joel appeased her. Players hire agents to do the hard work for them. Typically, their mommy doesn't hold their hand.

When Joel, Fatima, and Mike arrived for the meeting, Steve Reed surprised them at the hotel. Fatima had invited him. This was not only unusual but insulting to Joel. Steve worked as Mike's financial advisor. In that role, he took the money Joel negotiated for Mike, and invested it so Mike could live comfortably after his playing days ended. His role did not include helping negotiate a deal. He wasn't even a licensed agent.

I heard from Adidas contacts afterwards that the entourage puzzled them and made them unsure who represented Mike's interests. In truth, he was getting screwed all around by the competing interests of his mother and Steve Reed. Mike lacked maturity to understand all the implications of the power struggle raging around him, and his mother had badmouthed me enough to cause my advice to have zero impact. In hindsight, I feel bad for him; he was caught in a tug-of-war. But at the time, I also felt frustrated he had allowed Fatima to reassert herself in the first place.

Joel felt comfortable with Adidas's five-year offer. Derrick Rose, who had worn Nike sneakers his entire life, had signed with Adidas. He had felt insulted by Nike's $750K per year offer. Adidas offered him a few hundred grand more, and he went with them. This meant Mike's $1.25 million per year was a flattering offer, one that showed Adidas's loyalty to a kid who had worn their brand since thirteen. The five-year deal would also give him some stability after his rookie contract ended, or if he got hurt.

But Mike hesitated to sign the deal. Joel got pissed that Steve attended the meeting, believing Steve's lack of support prevented Mike from signing. Also, Kevin Durant's mother, Wanda, whom I took to dinner in 2001 as part of my DCA pitch, told Fatima Mike could've gotten a better offer if he had a better agent. She recommended Durant's agent replace Joel. But neither Wanda nor Fatima understood the economics of the NBA in 2008. The shoe companies knew a recession loomed, and luxury goods, like overpriced basketball sneakers, wouldn't sell as fast. The money just wasn't there. The deals the following year were even lower.

The NBA held their draft lottery and, afterwards, we knew Mike would either land in Chicago with the first pick, or Miami at number two. I threw a pre-draft lottery party at my house with catered barbecue. Of course, I invited Fatima and her clan, as well as Mike's management team: Joel, Steve, and Bruce Shingler, who had recently been hired as Mike's personal assistant (or professional babysitter). Joel and Bruce attended, but Steve couldn't make it. DeAndre and his mom, Kim, came too.

Mike had asked me if Bruce could come with him, wherever he landed. Bruce had become a mentor to Mike during their time together at Kansas State. I knew having him around would do Mike good. So, I called Frank Martin and asked whether Bruce could take a one-year hiatus to help Mike get settled. Frank agreed, promising to hire him back, a considerable favor to me. Most assistants, once they leave, don't get hired back. But I asked Frank because I knew he wouldn't tell me no.

At my party, I watched as Bruce sucked up to Fatima. I'd helped get him a job on Frank's staff and had arranged for him to leave work for Mike, yet he clearly saw the shifting power dynamics and aligned himself with the Fatima faction.

Joel and I had done well for Mike. Not only had Adidas offered a generous shoe deal, but Joel had secured sponsorship deals with ESPN and a water company. Growing up, I had learned that loyalty was one of the most important and valuable characteristics a man can possess. I looked at all the smiling faces eating overpriced barbecue in my basement, all waiting to live off Mike's dime. I wondered: What had happened to such an ideal? I also knew anyone from the Beasley family would cut my head off the first chance they got.

As the draft neared, teams began doing their background checks on the top prospects. I spoke to all of Mike's former high school coaches, and they all agreed to give positive reports to the organizations that might call. The organizations also interviewed Monica and me as part of the process. Monica feared Fatima would tarnish her pristine reputation she had around the league. As a former spouse of a pro player, and with her work history at Washington Sports Group and Behind the Bench, she still had strong ties to the league.

Ed Maull, the Miami Heat's personal advisor/assistant to Pat Riley, knew Monica's new boss, Lamell McMorris, and set up an interview with Monica at the Perennial offices. Ed then called me to discuss Mike. Miami held the second pick, so a successful background check could set him up as a top selection.

Ed fell in love with me, Monica, Nolan, and Sydney. Of course, sitting down and talking to Monica and her perfectly polite, mature children did not accurately reflect Mike's personality. Though we raised him and tried to instill certain values and positive characteristics, Mike was not Monica's blood. To compare Mike and Nolan would be comparing apples and oranges.

But Ed told us that he would convince Riley, the Heat's president and GM, to draft Mike if Chicago didn't take him with the first pick. Mike's future seemed bright. I still wonder, to this very day, how something so good could go wrong so quickly. Fatima reasserted herself so aggressively, Mike had a hard time saying no to her. She began spending his money before he had any. Suddenly, designer clothes and suits arrived at the apartment he'd rented, all of it on credit. Fatima then announced she wanted to throw a post-draft party for Mike at Dave & Buster's in NYC and wanted to invite 200 people. It would cost Mike $30K. Joel needed his approval to plan the party.

"No," Mike said. These young players all wanted to attend the official draft parties thrown by hot promoters and other sponsors in NYC. He didn't want to spend draft night with his mom at Dave & Buster's. Nor did he want to spend $30K to do so.

Joel told Fatima Mike said no, so she cut her plan down to a hundred people for $15K.

"I don't even know a hundred people in my family," Mike complained to Joel, "and I definitely don't want to go to no party."

But Fatima pressed her advantage, and the kid backed down.

"At least it's not at Chuck E. Cheese," I joked with Bruce.

"Curtis, I don't know what you did to this woman, but Fatima hates you all."

I told Monica about Bruce's comment, and she just shook her head in disbelief.

"Remember a few years ago, when she was in trouble?" Fatima had had some legal trouble and potentially faced jail time for outstanding traffic tickets and moving violations.

"Yeah, no shit," I replied.

"She asked me, crying, if I would watch over her two youngest. She said she'd even give us guardianship if she went away."

"Money changes people."

Fatima became so vile, vindictive, and petty, every week brought something new. I once drove Mike's Range Rover on an errand because my car was blocked in the garage. I passed Fatima's brother, and not five minutes later, Fatima called me, requesting the truck. She claimed she needed it.

The NBA asked Mike whom he wanted to sit with him at the draft table. Fatima made an issue about Monica's presence. Monica threw her hands up and said she would sit in the stands, but Mike begged her to sit with him. It was his choice, not his mother's, but at times it became tough to tell who was being drafted, Mike or Fatima.

On draft night, Joel gave all the tickets he'd purchased for Mike's family and friends to Fatima. Monica and I had passes because we'd be sitting at the table in the green room, but Nolan and Sydney would be up in the stands.

Just an hour before the draft started, Monica got a call from Sydney asking where they should pick up their tickets. Fatima never bothered to give them their tickets and stranded them outside Madison Square Garden. Nolan would have been devastated if he missed his brother getting drafted to the NBA.

Luckily, Lamell came through for us again. He called up one of David Stern's guys from the league office already at the arena and got Nolan and Sydney passes. They got in just in time to cheer Mike on.

"With the second pick in the 2008 draft, the Miami Heat selects Michael Beasley, Kansas State University."

The DC Assault cheering section went wild. The water company that signed Mike sponsored buses for our kids, so they could travel to New York and attend the draft. It allowed us another opportunity to reinforce our promise to our players. Seeing one of their own up on stage with a Heat jersey held up in front of him made these young kids realize they, too, could succeed.

The next morning Mike, me, Joel, Fatima, and her sister Mona flew to Florida for the introductory press conference to the Miami media and Heat fans. Mike had invited Monica, too, but she politely said, "Hell no."

Joel and Ed Maull had briefed Pat Riley on me and my relationship to Mike. When we got to the arena, Pat greeted me like an old friend, and we talked for quite a while. I could see Fatima getting more and more upset over the lack of attention and knew she'd get payback, somehow.

Riley had not wanted to draft Mike. He and Dwyane Wade really liked O.J. Mayo. But Joel and Ed sold Riley on the kid; however, he still had some doubts. The day after the draft in Miami, Riley warned Mike about breaking team rules, saying he didn't put up with bullshit. Mike was now Miami Heat property and couldn't party on South Beach every night. A typical speech you'd give a nineteen-year old about to sign a contract for $12+ million, completely guaranteed. He ended his lecture with this warning: "Don't fuck with me or I'll ship you to the worst team in the league."

The press conference went well enough, and I breathed a sigh of relief. Mike had made it through. He'd been drafted, Joel would oversee his endorsement deals, Steve Reed had promised to look out for DC Assault, and I could finally get away from Fatima.

Then Mike fired Joel.

The Downfalls of Success

I believe Steve Reed acted behind the scenes to have Joel fired. Joel wasn't feeling Steve and vice versa. Everyone got caught off guard. Mike wouldn't have understood the process of firing Joel on his own. I believe Fatima and Steve arranged everything. Chrysa Chin, who oversaw rookies for the NBA, and Steve eventually pushed Mike to Jeff Schwartz, his soon-to-be new agent, and Jeff in turn recommended Steve to his clients. Jeff also had many more clients than Joel.

At the same time, several internet sites reported Mike had severed ties with me as well. We certainly did not agree on Joel. The agent had done a good job representing a very challenging client, while walking a tightrope trying to please an overbearing mother. But neither did we have a falling out. Mike was as much a part of our family as anyone, at least Monica and I felt so, and we wouldn't turn our backs on him.

My income dropped as an immediate aftereffect of Joel's firing. It also very much clouded the picture of my future in sports management. Without Mike's endorsement and future NBA contracts, my commission would be severely reduced. Plus, Joel and I had discussed becoming partners using Mike as the foundation of building up our clientele. Without him, the partnership went on hold. Greg Holloway also got cut as Mike's business consultant, as Fatima and Steve Reed consolidated their control over Mike. They would never pay back the $37K Greg had lent.

Still acting as Mike's financial advisor, Steve finalized the endorsement deal with Adidas. Adidas offered the same amount of money, but Steve shortened the deal to three years. The only benefit: He could earn a bonus more easily. But this shorter deal also meant no long-term security. Both Mike's rookie contract and endorsement deal would end around the same time. If the kid flopped, he'd have serious money problems.

Part of the Adidas deal stipulated that Adidas would give DCA additional money, $75K a year. The money would be paid to Mike, who would then donate it to Assault as a charitable tax credit. Steve handled his money. The first year we got $40K, the second year $30K and nothing in year three. When I asked Steve what happened to DCA's money, he told me Fatima wanted to help sponsor her brother's AAU team.

So much for looking out for Assault.

While in Miami to celebrate my fortieth birthday, I had lunch with Mario. I filled him in on what happened with Mike. He couldn't believe everything had changed so quickly.

"Yeah. Well, this shit's going downhill so fast, I don't know what to expect day-to-day."

"Fuck the kid. He's gonna turn his back on you. Wipe your hands of him."

"It's not him. Not really. It's the damn people around him. You know his mom rents a house in Pat Riley's neighborhood for over ten grand a month? Why does she need a house like that? The woman's never had a house her whole damn life. But she spends his money like it's her own."

"Hey, if he's too dumb—"

"That's what pisses me off. She takes advantage. He isn't the brightest kid. Get this, he flipped out because someone told him Adidas paid me to bring him to them."

"I thought that's how this whole thing works?"

"There was no bribe. I'm a consultant for them. They pay me to identify top players and bring them into the Adidas family. Hell, if it wasn't for Adidas, Mike wouldn't have eaten. Adidas raised him as much as Monica and I."

"So whatcha gonna do?"

"Might need you. Money is slowing down, for real. I had a plug out in Cali, but my boy got busted the end of last year, and he's pulled out for now."

"You sure you want back in? I've tried talking to you about this before and you always say no."

"I gotta do something. My whole plan to go one hundred percent legit just been blown up. Next time you come up, stop in and see me."

Shorty had been busted in 2006 and Psych, out on the West Coast, fell back to see where the chips would fall. He'd be back, but until then, my drug business slowed down. Mario could help me get some quick cash.

We had a few more drinks: Bacardi and Diet Cokes for me. My drinking had really picked up. I could always function and would never drink the night before a morning meeting, but sometimes functioning required a drink, too.

As Joel and I scrambled to figure out what to do next, Monica continued to thrive at Perennial. Lamell paid her okay, and most days she didn't even have to go into the office. He let Sydney keep his INFINITI G37 Coupe and use it whenever she wanted. He attended Nolan's games at Duke, sitting with us like family, and brought me to the World Series and the NBA finals. I became more suspicious. Why all these special favors? I again thought Monica might be having an affair with him. But I trusted my wife and couldn't quite believe she'd cheat. Still, he had to have a motive. What was his agenda?

Meanwhile, Nolan struggled at Duke. He broke into the starting lineup early in his sophomore season, but Coach K benched him after one particularly bad loss. I could tell he'd gotten into his own head, thinking too much. The best players play with confidence, not self-doubt. Out on the floor, you make split-second decisions. Once you start overthinking, you make mistakes.

The situation made Nolan unhappy. He worked hard and felt that he should have been a starter. When other teams heard the rumors, my phone rang constantly. A number of teams, including Kansas, wanted him. But I didn't like the idea of him transferring. Finally, I sat him down to talk face-to-face.

"Are you willing to fight through this, or you want to pick up your toys and run away? 'Cause that's what some people will say. They'll write blogs and give interviews and say, 'Nolan Smith couldn't handle the pressure at Duke, so he ran.'"

"I don't know. I don't think I fit into Coach's plans here."

"Nolan, I never knew your dad, but I know a lot of people who did. I don't think he'd want you to quit. Transferring is running. Coach K is challenging you. You gotta meet the challenge. What do you think?"

I'm not sure I completely sold him, but he agreed to stay. At the end of the 2008 season, he'd watched a bunch of his teammates go "one-and-done." Plus, with Mike's entrance into the league, I could understand his self-doubt. But Nolan always planned to stay and get his degree, so his lack of confidence was shortsighted. If he busted his ass for four years, he'd improve. Coach K wasn't going to give him anything; he needed to take it for himself.

Joel and I got a call from Pat Riley sometime in August 2008. He wanted to meet about Mike's attitude and behavior. Neither Joel nor I had much control over the situation. Joel didn't even represent him anymore, but we agreed to sit down. Pat wanted the team around Mike who had gotten him to the NBA.

Pat and Joel had a good relationship. That's why Joel felt meeting Pat was the right thing to do. Plus, Joel also held out some hope that Pat could mend the fences between everyone, and then Mike would rethink hiring a new agent and stick with Joel. Unfortunately, that did not happen.

Mike's endorsement and NBA contracts with bonuses came out to about $6 million a year for three years. By the time he finished his second season, he owned nine cars. His mother rented that expensive house for $10K+ a month, and now she wanted to buy a $3.3 million house in Prince George County. Mike blew through money like nothing. Eighteen million dollars doesn't last long when you spend it before you have it.

Mike's firing of Joel surprised Riley; so did Mike putting distance between himself and me. At the meeting, we sat around a conference table with Fatima, Steve Reed, Ed Maull, Chrysa Chin, and Pat. Mike didn't show up. Riley patted a thick file folder of papers.

"These are all Mike's fines since the draft," he began. "What I want to know is, how are we going to help save this kid before he self-destructs?"

When Riley called Joel to arrange the final details for the meeting, he asked the same question: How can we save the kid? Joel told him that I was the only person Mike respected and that the other adults in his life catered to him so they could live off his success. So, Riley looked at me after he asked his question.

Well, talk about an awkward situation. Mike's main problem sat across the table from me. But I couldn't (or wouldn't) start an argument in front of Pat Riley. I looked at Fatima and started to speak, but Pat cut me off.

"What exactly is the problem between you two?" he asked, looking at Fatima and me. A good question; one I'd asked myself. All I did was raise her kid, give him the opportunities he needed to reach his dream…she'd hit the lottery and hated the guy who gave her the lottery ticket.

"Me and Curtis don't need to discuss our issues here. We can do that privately," Fatima huffed.

"Well, I suggest you do. You both are the most important people in his life, and he's getting closer to crashing every day."

The meeting devolved into Mike's main issues. Chrysa told us what resources the league could provide to help Mike, while Steve Reed assured everyone he closely controlled Mike's finances. By the look on his face, I could tell Riley thought Steve a slimeball.

Within a month after the meeting in Miami, another issue came up with Mike. On September 4, 2008, while Mike participated in the mandatory NBA rookie orientation symposium, the league expelled him and two other players from the program for smoking weed in their hotel room. Mike was also later fined $50,000. Riley had warned Mike that everything he now did reflected on himself and the entire Miami Heat organization. Pat was upset, saddened, and embarrassed by Mike's latest debacle. And training camp hadn't even started yet.

That meeting in Miami was also the last time I ever spoke to Fatima. I no longer travelled to Miami, only attended a few Heat games, and didn't go out of my way to speak with Mike. Everyone, from Pat Riley to Bruce Shingler to Mike's own father, told me Fatima hated me. I still don't know why.

About four to five months after the meeting with Riley, Steve Reed called and told me Mike wanted to give both Monica and me a monthly stipend of five grand. The stipend would begin in January of 2009 and would be sent the first of every month. At this point, I really wanted some space between Mike and me, but my precarious financial situation meant I couldn't say no. Plus, I believed Monica deserved some love for all the energy she had invested in the kid. I didn't quite understand Mike's motives for giving us money after all that had happened. Perhaps it was guilt.

The financial arrangement lasted only nine months, until September of '09, and the money almost always arrived late. On September 20th, I called Steve and asked what's up. He gave me the runaround until the 25th, when I was informed Mike would not be sending any more money. I called Monica and asked her if Mike had given her any warning. He hadn't. Losing the money did not upset me that much, though it did help, and we gladly appreciated it. I felt angry Mike hadn't warned us to at least give some time to prepare.We had no communication with Mike about giving us money or cutting us off. Steve became Mike's spokesman, so we really didn't quite get the whole thing. Mike never told us anything. Steve delivered all the good and bad news. He also told Fatima everything, such as Monica and I were looking for a handout. The truth is, we never asked Mike for a dime.

A few weeks later, the Miami Heat sent Mike to the John Lucas Rehab Center in Houston. His drug use had become a problem, and the Heat had had enough of his bullshit. Dalonte and I flew down to visit and support him. Fatima never visited at all.

The following summer, the Heat's "Big Three" of Dwyane Wade, LeBron James, and Chris Bosh formed. The Heat needed to dump some salary in order to make the numbers work for their new contracts and for everyone else's—except for Mike.

Riley traded him to the Minnesota Timberwolves, one of the worst teams in the league at the time, keeping his promise that if Mike fucked with him, he'd be shipped out of Miami. Because Mike had basically failed in Miami, it didn't surprise me when I later found out that Ed Maull, Riley's right-hand man in Miami and the one who convinced him to draft Mike, had been demoted to a scout.

During Nolan's off season, we hired Gary Lampkins, a highly respected trainer who I'd known for years. Troy, who now held the assistant general manager position at the Oklahoma City Thunder, also recommended Gary. Additionally, we brought in Alonzo Ruffin, a specialist in resistance training. We wanted to get Nolan to the next level. He'd been up and down his sophomore year. Knowing he was in the game for all four years meant we could plan out his development. Both Gary and Alonzo had great effect, and we saw immediate results.

Since Joel Bell no longer represented Mike, we scrambled to sign other players. If Nolan decided to go pro, Joel would represent him, but that was a decision two years away. DCA had other great players in top college programs, so we moved to secure new clients from the ranks of DCA alums.

One of those players, Jeff Green, played college ball for Georgetown. Joel and I thought Jeff would sign with us until the Georgetown coaching staff told us that other agents would be considered. They called us into a meeting at the university.

"I don't feel good about this," Joel said.

"Why?"

"Big John is running the meeting." Big John was John Thompson's father. Though not the coach, players and parents listened when he spoke.

"You two got issues?"

"No. But David Falk is Big John's guy. Look back on every great player to come out of Georgetown and who's their agent?"

"Falk?"

"Exactly. Big John will listen to our pitch, smile, might even laugh at a joke. Then once the meeting's over, he'll tell Jeff to go with Falk."

That is exactly what happened. John Thompson III, the coach of Georgetown at the time, knew he had screwed Joel and me over by allowing his father to influence Jeff's decision. It caused bad blood between us. I retaliated by not referring top DCA players to Georgetown. If one of our better players expressed interest, I would steer him away toward another school. Maybe that seems petty, but by allowing his father to influence Green's decision, Thompson III looked out for his own interests while fucking us over.

Coming on the heels of losing out on Mike, combined with the fact that DeAndre Jordan had also fired him after the draft, Joel began to lose faith in me. I helped him sign DCA alum

Dante Cunningham, but he hadn't landed a huge contract yet. Nolan had the potential to go pro if he got his act together and played consistently. Joel felt really let down by Mike, especially after spending lots of money on the kid and his family. I think he resented me because he believed my issues with Fatima ultimately led to Mike firing him. Joel was my guy, and Fatima purged anyone connected to me. Not fair, but I can understand why he may have felt jaded.

Conversely, I also think Joel was the reason why Mike and Fatima left. He never met Fatima's opinion of a power agent, and his reputation was criticized by others around the league. The two of them were so disappointed that I stood by Joel and supported him. But I just didn't believe you use a guy for his money, then renege on everything you told him you'd do. I could have taken Mike to any agent. I had so many of them reach out to me trying to sign Mike. Some even promised me a lucrative job. But to me, loyalty means more. Joel had done a lot; he deserved it.

My income shrank to the stipend from Joel and my consulting fee from Adidas. Adidas's money arrived in January and June. Monica's salary was just okay, not nearly enough to cover our lifestyle.

We could have cut back, but that was never my way.

Throughout my life, whenever I came to that proverbial fork in the road, I'd look left, then right, and if one direction offered a hill to climb while the other offered an easier path, I chose easy. Adjusting my lifestyle to the reality of my financial situation would have been difficult. It would have meant getting rid of the apartment in Durham (or, even harder to contemplate, the house in Upper Marlboro), driving cheaper cars, cutting back on eating out, and, worst of all, explaining to Monica how tight money had become. I expected to live at a certain level. Anything short of that expectation? Unacceptable. My other option—to work harder, to find another, legal source of income—did not even enter my mind. I was ready to go back to what I knew: the streets.

Moving into the drug game again didn't require any special changes on my part. Monica and I led very independent lives. Most days we didn't even know one another's schedules. Plus, with Nolan in school and Sydney out on her own, the bond we'd formed through the kids started to wane. We loved one another, but hiding my drug life from Monica was extremely easy.

Whenever she asked where money came from, I'd tell her, "None of your business." This pissed her off, rightfully so. But I grew up learning never to let a woman know your business so she couldn't screw you over. It's not a lesson I would ever teach Nolan, but Nolan's not a criminal. For her part, Monica eventually stopped asking. She must have known, but she also enjoyed the lavish lifestyle we lived.

In hindsight, my decision to reenter the drug business helped begin the downward spiral which would end my marriage. But by the end of 2009, we still lived it up.

My first call was to Mario. Psych still held back because of transportation issues but had promised to come east again soon. In the meantime, Mario could provide between fifteen to twenty-five kilos of powder cocaine per trip. They drove a pickup truck, tricked out with a hidden compartment, from Miami right to my front door.

I got in touch with my friend D, who I'd done the PCP deal with, and off-loaded the twenty kilos within a week. Mario loved how quick we moved the product. He began making runs at least once or twice a month.

I only made $1,000 per kilo. But I couldn't complain. As the middleman, I literally just accepted the delivery, called D, and passed the cocaine off. Most trips, I made $15-25K. Some months that equaled nearly $50,000. *In a single month.*

Here's the thing...taking the easy path allows anyone to criticize me. Hell, I criticize myself now. But I would never even consider asking a family member or friend for money. Why beg a man to take care of me, and owe him something, when I had the ability to look after myself and my family? My pride would never allow me to beg Joel or a kid like Mike for money.

I rationalized the decision like this: Eventually, Nolan would go pro, sign a decent contract, and take care of Monica. I only needed to do the drug thing for a short time, like I had several times before.

Lamell McMorris at Perennial also invited me to join him when he would get his basketball division up and running. The transition from referee agent to players' agent would take some time, but he promised to bring me in when he launched and pay me $10-11K a month. At least that's what he told me. I now started to understand his plan.

So, I believed the drug hustle would be short-term.

I lied to myself so well.

Psych and Bald Head came back east with a new setup: Their guys would drive a tractor-trailer from LA to Maryland. They would park at a truck stop and their guy, called Sticky Fingers, would meet them and transfer the kilos to the Cadillac Deville I'd bought for him to use when he came to town. We called him

Sticky Fingers because he only had nine fingers and every time he delivered the money, it came up $5-10 thousand short.

Sticky usually stayed at this low-end hotel filled with junkies and fiends. I hated the place and called to complain to Psych about it often. One day, I got the call that Sticky Fingers would be at the house in ten minutes. He had already picked up the Cadillac the night before. I was there and waited around for him, finally getting another call from Bald Head in LA.

"You're not gonna believe this," Bald Head said.

"What? He got locked up?"

"The dumb muthafucker stopped at his hotel to take a piss and got car jacked."

"Someone stole my Caddy?"

"Got pistol-whipped. They robbed his ass and stole the car."

I went into panic mode. Do I try to find out who robbed him and have to deal with it myself, or do I call the police? The car was registered in my name, to my house. I decided to report it stolen.

"I called the police," I explained to Bald Head.

"There were fifty fucking birds in the trunk," he said.

"I'm mad as a muthafucker," Fifty kilos, fifty grand for me, or close to $100K if I could get $2K off each bird, depending on my price for the shipment.

The next day I got a call from the police: The car was found and impounded in Forestville, Maryland. I went and picked it up. Of course, the cocaine had disappeared. I put feelers out on the street to see who might be trying to move quantity, but I couldn't track down the coke.

We traded in the Caddy. The connect must have really had love for Sticky Fingers because anyone else would've been dead after losing fifty kilos. Instead, they just fell back for a few months.

Eventually, Psych and Bald Head began making runs themselves, meeting the trailer and then meeting me. The frequency of the deliveries picked up. For a stretch, it became really convenient because the tractor-trailer would literally drive down my neighborhood and use a church parking lot to turn around. I'd pick up the work not even a mile from my house.

With Mario's kilos plus my LA connect, I averaged almost $100K a month, but neither was consistent. I might have one really good month and then two months with no action.

So, what did we do with all the money?

Most of it I saved for rainy days, which always occur in the drug business. But the rest, we enjoyed spending.

I brought Monica with me to LA. While I met with Psych and Bald Head in the city, Monica shopped. She had claimed a room in our house for herself and wanted to decorate it. She found a $12,000 sofa and a nice rug for another fifteen grand. The more money you make, the more money you spend. If we travelled to a big city, we shopped and sent the bags home by mail. We always bought too much to carry on the plane.

We also had faux marble painted around our fireplace, installed dark walnut hardwood floors, and painted the ceilings a light sky-blue. I bought an eight-thousand-dollar TV. Whenever we travelled, we stayed in five-star hotels. During Nolan's basketball season, we practically lived in Durham, eating out every night and keeping pace with the snobby families of the other Duke players.

It became normal for me to give Monica four or five grand as pocket money. Early on, she never saw any drugs. If she questioned the money, or walked in on me as I counted it, which happened a couple times, I fell back on my "none of your business" line. She never knew exactly what I did then, but she knew I wasn't robbing banks.

Later on, around 2009, Monica did walk in a few times while I had drugs laid out in front of me. She would say "excuse me" and go the other way, or just back out the door.

Sometimes, success can blind a person. Often, the signs of a coming downfall surround you, but dollar signs blot out the warnings.

At 2:20 in the morning on April 9, 2009, police pulled me over about four miles from my house. I'd been speeding and flew through a speed trap. After pulling over, the cops asked me to take a sobriety test, which I refused. They claimed they smelled alcohol and weed in the truck, giving them probable cause to search my Toyota Tundra.

My drug game was slowly coming to an end. I was just too greedy to see it.

The Fourth Quarter

"Mr. Malone, you're under arrest for driving under the influence and possession of marijuana," Officer Jason Jones said as he handcuffed me. "You were also clocked going seventy-nine miles per hour in a fifty-miles-per-hour zone."

Several officers had searched my truck and found some trace amounts of weed. I didn't smoke, but I often let a few guys borrow my vehicles. I could've killed whoever smoked that shit in my truck. There ended up being around ten cars at the scene. The bright, flashing blue-and-red lights practically blinded me.

The officers also found and confiscated a white bag of cash in the back seat and later said it had $26K in it, but my man who dropped off the bag to me claimed there was much more than that. He had owed me well over $50K.

And because I'd refused the sobriety test, they claimed I was drunk. As they searched the truck, I stood in the back behind it and called a member of my crew whom I called Big P. I used one of the four cell phones I had in my pocket.

"Man, the police got me pulled over. They found the cash in my car. I need you to get to my house now."

"Whatcha need?"

"I got work," meaning thirty kilos, "in the garage supposed to go out tomorrow. They might get a search warrant or something. Go get them out of there."

"Aight, you got it."

After I hung up with him, I ditched all four cell phones under the police cruisers while they were still searching my truck. My mind raced with possibilities: This could be a simple traffic stop, or it might be part of a bigger investigation. I only operated a small crew. Most people only thought of me as the president of DCA and a consultant for Joel. Unfortunately, as the cocaine had increased, I had to expand my circle. Though still small, my crew had grown bigger than I really wanted. Could someone have ratted me out?

"Mr. Malone, where'd you get all that cash?" Jones asked as he pushed me into the back of his cruiser.

"I'm on my way home from Atlantic City. I won it."

"Won it? You must be one lucky guy."

Like I said, when I'd picked up the money, my man told me it was $50,000. He owed me for kilos I'd fronted him. I was released on my own personal recognizance the next day, and the county court commissioner claimed there was $25,790 in the bag, just like the officers had said. I'm not sure whether my man screwed me, or the police stole some of the money, but of course I trusted my man.

I ended up pleading guilty to driving while impaired. The marijuana possession charge was thrown out because the amount of weed found in the truck equaled about five bucks on the street. My license was suspended for six months, and I paid a $500 fine.

But I didn't get my money back. My lawyer at the time, Harry Tun, missed the petition deadline to get the cash back.

We then found out the police tested the money for drug residue. It came back positive for cocaine, and they turned it over to the Drug Enforcement Administration (DEA).

The Feds began civil forfeiture proceedings on the cash. As part of the investigation, the police had contacted every damn casino in Atlantic City. None knew of a Curtis Malone who'd won money on April 8th or 9th. So, then I claimed the money a loan to cover DCA expenses. That would lead to the one IRS audit DCA ever suffered. The audit came back clean, of course, but the Feds knew the money, covered in coke residue, was connected to drugs.

I found out later that after he pulled me over, Officer Jones contacted Prince George County Narcotics Detective Thomas Eveler and asked him if he knew anything about me. Eveler had never pursued an investigation into me, but back in 2007 a confidential informant had told Eveler I sold large quantities of cocaine. Either way, Eveler's information, combined with the Feds' drug test on the money, put me squarely on the police's radar.

I didn't know that then, however, and losing my license for six months and a $500 fine did not slow my drug business down at all. Some negative press followed, but DC Assault's program was so strong at this point, nothing could derail us. I continued my double life, moving Psych and Mario's kilos and turning my attention to a new legit opportunity: Lamell's basketball division at Perennial.

Ever since I'd helped raise DerMarr and guide him into the NBA, I had dreamed of entering sports management and leading a legit life. Fegan gave me my first opportunity; Joel Bell had promised a partnership. Neither worked out, and I had returned to street life. Now, Lamell McMorris asked me to help him put a staff together to find future pro players.

"Think about a few brothers who we could bring in as agents," Lamell said. "We need to get to these kids early before the Fegans and Falks sign them."

"What about Joel Bell?"

"I want to give some brothers a chance. Already enough white agents running the show...."

I disagreed with that. I thought a diverse group could attract a broader range of potential clients.

"What's my role going to be?"

"You're going to be my main man. Oversee all these other guys. Like my point man. I'll pay you six figures to basically recruit. More or less, you'd be a consultant."

That sounded perfect to me. I wasn't a lawyer and couldn't be an actual agent, but identifying talented players and connecting them to our agents seemed ideal. So, I put out feelers to some friends in the business. I spoke with Wallace Prather Jr., Kim Grillier and Mitchell Butler and invited them to a meeting with Lamell. Wallace's father ran the Atlanta Celtics, a top AAU program, so I knew he saw great potential players every day. Kim, an agent, and Mitchell both had strong connections to youth programs. I also had good relationships with these guys, and they trusted me.

Lamell flew us all to Atlanta, and we met at the Ritz-Carlton. We sat down with him, and, of course, my three recruits acted like know-it-alls. Kim told us in order for him to join Perennial, he needed to bring his partner, agent Bill Strickland, on board. Bill in turn would need to bring his secretary with him, too.

I had wanted Kim, not Strickland, who was nearing seventy years old. Bill had been a pioneer in the agent business, but I felt his time had passed. Bringing Bill's secretary along as well cost too much. Hell, we could have made Monica a secretary since she already worked at Perennial.

Lamell offered Wallace a contract, and I again brought Joel Bell's name up.

"You know, Lamell, you really should think about Joel. He and Nolan have a great bond, and hiring Joel means you automatically get Nolan on your client roster." Even if Joel and I had experienced some stress in our relationship, I liked the guy. I felt bad over how Beasley had treated him and wanted to remain loyal to him. But Lamell wouldn't listen.

He ended up hiring Kim, along with Bill Strickland—and his secretary as well. Guess who never received a contract? I'd brought these guys in, landed Lamell an instant team, and received nothing. The six-figure job never materialized. What pissed me off even more than Lamell's treachery was that neither Wallace nor Kim spoke up for me.

When Nolan became a starter at Duke during his junior year, his NBA chances increased. The team won the '09–'10 national championship. Nolan dominated throughout the NCAA tournament. He considered leaving school early, but we nipped that in the bud.

The following year, Duke lost to Arizona in the tournament, but Nolan earned All-ACC first team, ACC Player of the Year, and ACC Defensive Player of the Year honors. He also made it as a finalist for the John R. Wooden Award for player of the year. He'd been the senior captain, and all those years of hard work paid off.

It became very clear Nolan wanted Joel to represent him. Still, to be fair to all, he met with several different agents. Mike Siegel came in and Wallace Prather, Jr., represented Perennial. He also met with Jeff Schwartz, one of the biggest NBA agents out there, who represented Blake Griffin and Mike. But Joel had put the work in all those years, and Nolan felt comfortable with him. I asked Joel to discount his agent fee: 2 percent instead of the typical 4 percent, and 10 percent on marketing and endorsement deals instead of the typical 20–25 percent. Joel agreed, and Nolan signed with him. I declined to receive any of my standard commissions off any of Nolan's/Joel's future deals.

After he signed with Joel, Larry's long-term agenda became clear. He fired Monica. He also took back his G37 that he had basically given to Sydney. I'd always felt like there was an ulterior motive behind his kindness towards us. He used me to build up a basketball division, and used Monica in hopes of landing her son as a client. I'd warned Larry that Joel already had developed a strong relationship with Nolan and recommended he bring Bell into Perennial. But Larry didn't listen; he wanted (and probably felt he deserved) Nolan as his client.

In the 2011 NBA draft, the Portland Trail Blazers selected Nolan Smith with the 21st overall pick. Nolan became the third NBA first-round draft pick to live under the same roof as me. He's the one I felt the proudest for. Unlike Mike and DJ, whose talents made them immediate prospects, Nolan had to work his ass off to develop. He put that work in without complaint. He played selflessly and led by example. Unlike Mike, Nolan's attitude became one of his positive characteristics. Monica was right. I hadn't paid Nolan as much attention growing up as I did Mike because I didn't have to. Nolan grew into a fine young man, a role model for others, and I knew whether his playing career lasted years or decades, he'd be successful.

Meanwhile, DC Assault continued to thrive. While in Vegas with the team at the Adidas Super 64 tournament, I got a call from Bald Head asking me to fly out to LA. He knew I was already in Vegas, but one of my teams tipped off the championship game at three p.m.

"When's it over?" I told him, and he said he'd have a private charter waiting for me at the airport.

"Got someone here who wants to see you. We need to meet. It's urgent."

"Who?"

"Just win your game and get your ass here. A plane will be waiting at six p.m. Go to the desk, and they'll escort you straight to it."

The team did win, but I didn't have time to celebrate. I gave a short speech congratulating the kids, then handed Damon Handon a few thousand dollars to take the players and their families out.

"Where you going?" he asked.

"Gotta take care of something for a few hours, but I'll be back later tonight." I figured by the time the kids got back to the hotel after their celebration, I'd be back.

I took a cab to the airport and went to the desk. They pointed out which plane waited for me and then walked me across the tarmac to this tiny-ass six-seater. The one flight attendant immediately handed me a Bacardi and Diet Coke and told me if I needed anything at all, just call her and she'd be right there. Forty-five minutes later we landed in LA.

A black SUV sat idling, ready to bring me wherever Bald Head wanted me. I didn't care where I ended up. Right then I was in my moment: DCA still dominated, my drug empire ran smoothly, the Bacardi flowed, and I got flown on private planes and chauffeured in style.

After a while, we pulled up to this gated community in Chatsworth, California. The driver called someone who opened the gate. We pulled into the driveway of this fucking huge house. At the front door, my Mexican supplier, a member of the Sinaloa Cartel, and his beautiful wife greeted me. Bald Head arrived a few minutes later, and we sat down for dinner.

"This is our good friend from DC, Curtis," my supplier introduced me to his wife. They served a delicious Mexican meal with chicken breasts, steaks, Mexican rice, and veggies. My phone rang. It was one of my players.

"Coach Curtis, where you at? We're all looking for you."

"Just taking care of some business, but I'll be with you all later tonight." I hung up and shut my phone off.

"Curtis, I asked you here because I want you to know how much we appreciate your friendship," the supplier said.

"And I appreciate yours," I said. We toasted to friendship.

"We regret what happened, losing the fifty birds." He meant when Sticky got robbed. "Sticky won't be coming back."

"Is he dead, or we just won't use him anymore?"

"We'll take care of Sticky…we now have a better way to transport. Could you handle more work?"

I saw dollar signs floating in front of my eyes. "Of course. I can move however much you give me."

"Good." He nodded his head. "I wanted to introduce you to my family. To show you how much we trust you. Bald

Head will give you the details of our new arrangement, but you should expect a delivery in a few days."

We drank to our relationship and enjoyed dinner. At one point, my supplier pulled me to the side and gestured to several beautiful women in attendance.

"Please, choose one. She will go back to Vegas with you, or spend the night with you here, as my guest."

The women were some of the finest I'd ever laid eyes on. I had to keep my cool and politely declined. I had my wife and family waiting for me. But damn, that was a hard choice. I probably could've had two if I wanted.

"Thank you, but give me my plain-Jane wife, whom I wouldn't trade for the world," I told him.

"I respect that, my friend," he said.

I drank a few more Bacardis, then Bald Head drove me to the plane. On the flight back to Vegas, I downed another four or five Bacardi and Diet Cokes. The alcohol had hit me, but I hoped the kids would just assume I'd been celebrating their victory. I smiled ear-to-ear that night—maybe because of another DCA Adidas championship, but more likely due to the high caused by the thought of the money coming my way.

After the proposed deal with Lamell fell through, a friend of our family named Earl Badu contacted me about starting a sports management business. Earl suggested we bring in an agent, while he would oversee finances for the players.

I had met Earl a few years before through Mark Karcher, a DCA alum. Earl had walked on at Maryland, played with Juan Dixon, and went into day trading and portfolio management.

Over the years, he became a close family friend. He attended Nolan's games at Duke and shared a lot of dinners with me, Monica, and the kids. He had also donated about four grand to DCA.

I told Earl to get the money together we'd need to start a business, then we would talk more. I wasn't going to hop in bed and get screwed again. "Show me you have the finances in order so we could build up the business, and let's put it in black and white," I told him.

A few weeks went by, and I heard nothing from Earl. An old friend of mine, Lamont Gore, called and asked to meet me. He wanted to talk about Earl. The call was pretty random. I hadn't had any real conversations with him since his cousin, Chris Wilcox, began playing in the NBA years before. I was at Ruby Tuesday's when Lamont called; I agreed to meet and told him to join me, and we could talk.

"What's up with Earl?" Lamont asked after some small talk.

"I don't know. Why you ask?"

Lamont continued, "I made some investments with him, and he owes me money. But every time I try talking to him, I get the run around."

"That's funny, 'cause I got another friend that told me Earl owes him about forty grand. Says Earl keeps playing games."

"You think he's doing some underhanded shit?" Lamont asked.

"I invested thirty thousand with him, but when my homeboy told me Earl was playing games with him, I pulled out. He gave me my money back. What's he telling you?"

"That once you and him launch your company and sign Beasley, he'll have my money. He said he's loaned it out to you."

That shocked me.

"Now that's a damn lie. Earl's donated a few grand to DC Assault over the years, but I've never borrowed money off him, and we aren't in business together."

Lamont held up his hands, "Hey, I'm just telling you what he's saying. Some shit is going on with him, for real."

Later that day I called Earl. What Lamont told me sounded sketchy, and if Earl was fucking my friends around and using me as his excuse, I wanted to know why.

"Hey, Earl, it's Curtis," I said when he answered the phone.

"Oh, Curtis, hey, how you doing?" Earl sounded as if he didn't want to talk.

"Earl, what the hell do you have going on? I'm hearing all sorts of shit about you owing guys money."

"Listen, we need to talk, but now's not a good time for me. Can I call you tomorrow?"

"Earl, are you telling guys I owe you money?"

"Nah, it's not like that. But let me call you tomorrow. We'll meet up, and I'll explain, okay?"

We ended the call, but I didn't hear from him the following day. He eventually called me two days later, a Wednesday, and we agreed to meet later in the week. He didn't sound like his usual, confident self. He really wanted to meet that night, but Wednesdays were my date night with Monica, and I couldn't skip out on her. The next day, Lamont called me.

"Curtis, you're not gonna believe this shit," he said.

"What's up? This about Earl? I'm supposed to meet him later this week."

"Earl's dead."

"What?"

"Killed himself this morning. Jumped off the got-damn overpass!"

"What the hell was going on with him?"

Come to find out, Earl ran a Ponzi scheme, taking people's money, never really investing it, and paying fake returns from the money of other "investors." When he couldn't deliver a return for his clients, he used me or DCA as excuses, saying he had invested money in me. Maybe he thought none of those people knew me and never talked to me. But that was stupid because I knew half the city. Of course it would eventually get back to me.

I felt guilty at first. Perhaps if I'd met him Wednesday night, he would have confided in me. I would have tried to talk him out of killing himself, and at the very least, told him to turn himself in. Going to jail is better than suicide. Earl wasn't a bad person. He'd been a great mentor to Nolan, who took his death hard. But ultimately, greed got to him, too.

Earl represented my last chance to finally work in sports management, even if his proposal wasn't serious. I'd burned my bridge with Fegan; my relationship with Joel was strained with little commission coming in; Lamell never kept his promise.

I gave the dream up.

Ever since I'd met Sonny Vaccaro and guided DJ to the pros, I'd wanted to be legit in the business of basketball. Nothing worked out. I decided drugs would be my business, one I'd always been good at. I continued to serve as DCA's president, continued to help talented kids escape their lives, but thought of myself first and foremost as a hustler.

I suffered from depression as a result. All my life, I'd tried to become a success, and every time, I experienced failure. It weighed me down, this duplicity. To the outside world I was a power player in AAU basketball. The godfather of DC basketball. Connected and influential. But inside, I knew the only thing I really did well: move drugs.

As a result, my drinking spiraled out of control. Growing up I hadn't been much of a drinker. I took my first drink after my high school graduation. But I'd spent my twenties partying every night, and I'd developed a taste for alcohol. I craved Bacardi and Diet Coke like a man in the desert craves water.

I was a functional alcoholic. I never blacked out, and bills were always paid on time, though at times I did lose control. I never missed important meetings or events because of drinking, but I usually needed a drink to get me through them. I began to act out because of the alcohol.

One night I joined one of my former Columbia Park players at the bar at a restaurant owned by LaVar Arrington, the former Washington Redskin. We ate wings over drinks.

Unbeknownst to me, my former player had a run-in with the female bartender before I arrived. As we sat there, he made a comment that offended her, and she called the bouncers over. Two big guys approached us and told my friend he needed to leave. He then got into an argument with them. As a regular at the restaurant, I knew one of the bouncers and LaVar. I urged my friend to leave, but he wanted to get the last word in, raising his voice and acting belligerent.

Evidently the bartender had called the police, because a Prince George County sheriff came running into the restaurant. He saw us all grouped up and arguing as he came in.

"You and you," he said, pointing to me and my friend. "Get the hell out of here."

"Me?" I asked, incredulous. "I'm not leaving. I've got nothing to do with this."

The cop grabbed at me, trying to push us both towards the door.

"Hey, get the fuck off me, man. Don't touch me!"

I'd had several drinks but wasn't drunk. The cop pissed me off by putting his hands on me. Before I realized what happened, he had me in a choke hold. The bar descended into chaos.

I got out of the choke hold and swung at the cop. My punch connected, just enough to put him down on one knee. The bouncer I knew grabbed my arm before I swung again.

"Come on, Curtis, I got you." He ushered me to the door, but by now more police had shown up. The restaurant emptied out into the parking lot, providing plenty of witnesses, which prevented the cops from fucking me up more than they already had.

They did get some punches in. An officer who I hit landed a punch with his cuffs wrapped around his fist. They also maced me, blinding me. The pain in my eyes made me drop to the ground, and they cuffed me as I laid there.

Chaos reigned, and as more police arrived, they drew their guns and forced everyone back inside. Monica showed up and freaked out. The cop I'd punched actually acted pretty decently, at least at that point. I had about twenty grand on me and five phones. He never questioned why, and even passed everything off to Monica before they hauled me away.

Monica followed us to the hospital, where I got my eyes washed out. I had sheriff friends that tried to get the sheriff that I hit to drop the assault charges against me, but he still refused.

They arraigned me on second-degree assault on a police officer. I pled not guilty. I hired Tom Mooney to represent me and went to trial. The security footage from the restaurant captured the melee, but nothing distinctly showed me throwing a punch. Mooney also put about ten witnesses on the stand who testified I hadn't swung on the cop and that it was, in fact, the cops who beat me pretty good.

The jury found me not guilty.

A couple years later I found myself back in court on another assault charge, this time accused of beating up the coach of a rival AAU program.

It began when one of his players left his team for DCA. I knew the kid's father from my one season coaching at Dunbar, back in the '90s. The father decided to bring his son to Assault, and the other coach became the biggest asshole I'd ever encountered.

During a game at Oxon Hill High School, the other coach showed up. When his former player went to the free-throw line, the coach stood directly under the basket and heckled him. The kid was fourteen, and he had his ex-coach fifteen feet away giving him crazy looks.

After the free-throw attempts, the old coach left the gym. From the stands, I noticed the kid's father run out the gym after the ex-coach. I followed, and a few more people joined me. When we caught up to the coach in the hallway, we gave him a good old-fashioned ass whoopin'. We beat and stomped him down until he had nothing else in him. It reminded me of Stickman's work at the Landover Mall all those years before.

The coach told the police I had beat him and pressed charges. Suddenly, in the *Washington Post*, my critics questioned my fitness as a role model for the kids in DCA's program. The coach threatened to sue me for everything I had.

Once again, I turned to Tom Mooney to save my ass. We went to trial, where witnesses claimed I hadn't been involved in the beatdown in the hallway. The prosecutor could have nailed my ass if the security cameras caught me in the act. But the cameras hadn't been working on the day of the game, or the security footage couldn't be located. A happy coincidence for me. The prosecutor could not prove I'd left the gym or been in the hallway. Without any evidence, and with my witnesses defending me, I was again found not guilty. During the criminal trial, a witness I knew testified he overheard the coach saying he accused me in order to clean me out financially. That ended any hope of a possible civil suit.

I was now 2-0 at trial. I began to believe money and Tom Mooney could get me off any charge, especially in Prince George County, where I was practically a celebrity. In hindsight, I wish I'd apologized to the coach, maybe worked something out to help his program. It was wrong for his kids to see him hurt. It also damaged my own reputation among people who knew the truth. But the lesson I learned, at the time, was that Curtis Malone was fucking invincible.

How wrong I was.

Game Over

Psych and Cat Eyes explained their new transport method to me. Using an outfit in LA, they would fly the kilos on a private chartered plane to Baltimore. The cocaine would then be loaded into a car and driven to my door, or wherever I wanted it delivered.

"We're going to increase quantity big-time, which is why the boss wanted to know whether you can move more," Bald Head explained.

"I'm ready, but how much you thinking?"

"Three to four times as much."

That turned out to equal 120-140 kilos a month. I suddenly had more cocaine than I knew what to do with. I expanded my crew a little bit and told them all they needed to step it up because things were heading to another level.

The new method worked perfectly. Security for private aircraft did not compare to TSA's for a commercial flight. Bald Head's people practically walked the cocaine onto the plane and carried the money back onto the flight at the other end. They could make runs more frequently, and with more product and less risk than anything we'd done prior.

I didn't necessarily want to expand my operation—it created the risk of more people knowing my business—but in order to show my Mexican supplier I could handle the work, I didn't say no. For over a year, the money poured in.

My other life continued without pause. In 2010, DCA's sponsorship deal with Adidas came up for renewal. Jim Gatto, Sonny's successor, had treated us well and we had already renewed with him once prior. But I had heard from former DCA player Mark Karcher that a new athletic apparel company had emerged who wanted to make an entrance into the basketball shoe market: Under Armour.

They planned to follow the same model Sonny Vaccaro had created decades before by sponsoring top AAU programs. Under Armour planned to implement their strategy beginning regionally around the Baltimore/DC area.

I began having conversations with Under Armour reps during DCA's last year with Adidas. I first met founder and CEO Kevin Plank in the lobby of the Marina Del Rey Marriott while in LA for the Elite 24 tournament.

"I've heard really great stuff about DC Assault. We're very interested and prepared to take care of you guys," Plank told me.

The discussions progressed to the point that Damon Handon, our general manager who'd succeeded A. Brown, joined the talks. Joel Bell, who also knew and had connections to the company, agreed to serve as DCA's legal representative. Mark Karcher acted as a liaison, helping set up lunches between our two camps.

I still spoke to Sonny Vaccaro on occasion, so I filled him in on the discussions we had with Under Armour. He urged me to get Under Armour to give me stock options as part of the deal. Once again, Sonny showed his keen insight for identifying talent. Over the next five years, Plank led Under Armour to huge growth, becoming the second-largest athletic apparel brand behind Nike.

By the end of 2010, we had worked out a record-breaking sponsorship deal. Under Armour committed to $200,000 per year for travel costs, with a guaranteed $10,000 per year increase for five years. They also committed to $300,000 per year in gear and apparel, again for five years. The $2.5 million+, five-year deal was the largest sponsorship deal for an AAU basketball program at the time and solidified Under Armour's seriousness in becoming a basketball brand.

This meant DCA was no longer an Adidas program. I also no longer worked as an Adidas consultant or sat on their Super Six board. But the money promised by Under Armour was going to allow more DCA teams to travel for free, exposing them to better competition, while improving their skills as well as their lives and the lives of their families. I could now pay for more parents to travel, who couldn't afford it before.

My life had changed significantly since the 2008 draft. Over the previous two years, I'd expanded my drug empire, been on trial twice, failed in my dream of entering sports management, and ended my relationship with Adidas—the company which had given me so many opportunities.

I'd also watched Sydney develop into a strong, confident, and independent young woman; cheered on Nolan as he improved, year after year, to follow in his father's footsteps; and fell further and further into the dark hole of alcoholism.

In April of 2010, the Drug Enforcement Agency (DEA) began an investigation nicknamed Operation Snow Bird. The investigation centered on a small LA hip-hop record label, Behind da Scenes Entertainment, run by a guy named Ricky Brascom and his brother, Jerome.

The DEA had received information that the Brascom brothers received powder cocaine from the Sinaloa Cartel, then transported the kilos on privately chartered planes across the country, sending money back the same way.

On September 21, 2010, the DEA moved in on a private plane that had landed in Salinas, Kansas, to refuel. The agents searched the plane and found fifty kilos of cocaine. After no one claimed the kilos, they wrote everyone's names down and then let them go.

Shortly thereafter, the Brascom brothers came to pick up two suitcases of money from me equaling $1.7 million. Three hundred seventy-five thousand dollars of it was mine—payment towards my next shipment. I never heard from the brothers again. The DEA arrested them as soon as they landed in LA.

By November of 2010, the Brascom brothers were indicted, along with twelve others, including Charles Ransom, the pilot of the plane, on drug trafficking charges.

Then they moved in on my supplier.

Ultimately, the DEA seized 298 kilos of cocaine, which had a street value of about $6 million, along with $1.1 million in cash, two Aston Martins, a Mercedes, and a BMW, and shut down an operation that connected Sinaloa cocaine with dealers across the country. Snow Bird led to raids and arrests from LA to Baltimore to New York. Fallout from the investigation continues to this day.

Operation Snow Bird did not lead to my indictment. But I lost a lot of money, product, and connections. Almost overnight, my drug empire shrank.

On January 21, 2011, Joel Bell sued Mike Beasley for breach of contract. He claimed that Mike had wrongfully terminated him after Joel had negotiated the Adidas deal, so that Mike could avoid paying Joel's commission. Joel had worked tirelessly on the deal, securing Beasley a much more favorable contract than Nike had offered.

Then later that year, on September 27th, Beasley, acting vindictively, countersued Joel and named me as a third-party defendant. The lawsuit claimed Bell's firing came from his facilitating payments and gifts, both to me and to Mike and his family through me, in order to secure himself as Mike's agent. Of course, no proof nor paper trails existed tying anything from Joel to Mike or Fatima.

In Mike's countersuit, Fatima called me Bell's "runner"—an intermediary between players and potential agents. This I've never denied. I never hid my relationship with Joel Bell and believed he did good work for his players, no matter their professional potential. The suit also claimed Bell did not approach or deal with Nike in good faith. This was demonstrably wrong. Nike did in fact make an actual endorsement deal offer—an embarrassingly low one.

Fatima claimed that, while living in Kansas, her rent and car payments, as well as her move to Kansas, were made by an associate of mine—unnamed in the suit but clearly Greg Holloway—as gifts to further influence Mike's choice in agents. Again, a lie. Yes, Greg provided money to Fatima, and helped purchase Mike's used Tahoe as part of the $37,000 loan to be paid back once Mike went pro. Fatima and Mike knew all of this, and also that Joel was not involved in any rent or car payment facilitations, and definitely not involved with the move to Kansas.

The Sports Agent Responsibility and Trust Act, which went into effect in 2004, barred agents from giving players money or gifts in order to induce the player to sign with the agent. Beasley claimed Joel had violated the law by using me as the go-between.

The only truthful statement in the entire suit was Fatima's claim that I had told her Bell was not the best agent, but also not the worst. Completely true. Joel couldn't compare to Dan Fegan or Arn Tellem. He dressed sloppily, picked his teeth in the middle of dinner, and was a cheap prick. He basically ran a momand-pop agency, had no employees, worked out of his home, and never visited any of his clients in the cities where they played, only meeting them when they came to DC or close by for a game. He would meet them at the team hotel and treat them to a basic meal at the hotel's restaurant. But—and this is very true—Joel worked hard for his clients. What he lacked in polish he made up for in grit. I never would have worked with him, and risked my own reputation, had he done a poor job for his clients.

Joel and I had our own issues by this time. He'd stopped paying me my commissions on Dante Cunningham and Solomon Jones, among other players; money I deserved because I'd brought those clients to him. But Beasley's lawsuit made us allies again, if only temporarily.

Ultimately, Mike's countersuit was thrown out, and he settled Joel's claims out of court. Joel received about $500,000, which we split in half. After lawyers' fees and reimbursing Joel for money he had loaned me, I received about $130,000 from the settlement.

At the time the DEA executed Operation Snow Bird and my Cali connection dried up, I still had between $400,000-$500,000 saved up. I knew I could live off that money for a few years, but also knew we couldn't survive on it long-term.

Nolan had been drafted by Portland. He offered me a monthly allowance, but I declined. Instead, we agreed he could pay our mortgage—$2,200 per month—while looking out for his mother. We felt that she was the only one deserving of Nolan's hard-earned money.

After all the arrests and indictments, I had pretty much retired. But I still wondered if I was one of the unknowns on any of those indictments. In 2012, once I believed they wouldn't make a move to come get me, I turned to my old friend Mario to bring in cash. Pedro's brother still operated out of Miami. As we got back into business together, he drove about twenty kilos at a time up the coast in cars and trucks tricked out with special hidden compartments. He began bringing cocaine and then heroin, which had a much higher street value. I've never been a fan of heroin. It kills communities quicker than anything else out there. But it brought in better money and Mario wanted to move it.

His runs weren't that frequent, once or twice a month if that, but I made about $20K per run, marking up each kilo by a grand. The money allowed me to continue to help out DCA players and live a very comfortable lifestyle.

Part of that lifestyle included attending car shows. I went to Tysons Corner to test drive a new Jaguar that I had previously seen at one of them. I loved the Jag and told the salesman to clean it up. Then I called my financial guy and told him to meet me. I gave him $107K cash for the Jag, and he went to the dealership and purchased it for me.

Our crew at this time included my best friend Cat Eyes and my cousin Half. Cat Eyes came home from prison back in 2010 after serving thirteen years. His wife and I picked him up from Cumberland Federal Correctional Institution. Cat Eyes was my main man, and I had to make sure he was good, so I gave him the Tundra truck and took him on a $10K shopping spree to make sure he looked sharp, just like when he left. I asked Cat Eyes what he wanted to do. He told me he wanted to get some more money so he could eventually retire.

I called my connect and told him to send me 500 grams of China White (heroin) from his next shipment. Heroin was Cat Eyes's drug of choice. He felt that drug could make him rich the fastest. Once I received it, I gave it to him. He asked how much he owed me for it, but I told him because he's my main man and family, and that I love him, it was a gift. I also told Cat Eyes to get some money so that we could both retire. I knew we couldn't hustle drugs forever.

Cat Eyes worked out of the Clay Terrace projects in Northeast Washington. I just dropped off the dope to him and Half, then we'd split the profits. It became dead simple. All my life, I knew I was a damn good drug dealer. The drug game acted like a crutch. So long as I could lean on powder and pushing dope, I didn't need to figure out how to hold myself up legally.

But in truth, my failures weighed me down. My best chance to achieve my dream in the agent world had died with Mike Beasley and Joel Bell. Lamell and Earl's false offers had just served as salt in my wounds.

I was also failing in my marriage. For years, Monica and I had Sydney and Nolan to bind us together. I loved those kids, and they loved me. Whatever arguments erupted between Monica and me were forgotten, if not totally forgiven, in order to maintain our home. We were a wealthy, Black power couple with professional athletes, rich sports owners, and celebrities on speed dial. We wanted to keep that image. Part of this perfect picture included the kids: poised, articulate Sydney and polite, mature Nolan.

But by 2012, we had drifted apart. We no longer had trips to Durham to distract us. Petty arguments would blow up and resentment lingered for days. Monica probably felt neglected, disrespected by my lack of trust in her, so she nagged me over small things, instigating angry outbursts so she could feel some semblance of control. I avoided the conflict by staying away from home, further isolating her and pushing her away.

We discussed divorce, but it always came back to keeping the family together. We existed in some kind of frozen stasis, going through the motions of marriage without any real desire or effort. Every Wednesday, we kept up our date nights. Typically, we spoke less than twenty words to one another during our "dates."

Monica fell out of love with me, and it was my fault. My life, since 2008, seemed to be on a downward spiral I could not control. Like dominoes collapsing onto one another, bad shit just kept on coming. So, I turned to the two things that made me feel better: Bacardi and Diet Coke, and the streets. I felt neglected and unloved, which caused me to push even further away.

No matter what I went through in my marriage, I knew that the streets loved me. Life has ups and downs, but my family and friends got me through the bad times then and continue to stand by and love me to this day. These people were a part of my life before Monica and remained loyal after Monica. Most came from the streets.

My days took on a repetitive routine. I had breakfast at the Olde Towne Inn. After I ate, I'd take care of any pressing business, either drug or DCA-related, then go to Jerry's Seafood for lunch. I'd start drinking there and continued throughout the afternoon. I'd end my day at Jasper's, a bar where I'd often meet my entourage and begin to party, blowing up to a grand.

I'd always wanted to be more than a drug dealer. When that didn't happen, I fell back to the game I knew so well, the game I actually hated playing. My marriage gave me a boost; Monica really was a come-up. But as it disintegrated, little remained to make me happy.

A long-time friend of mine, Gail, counselled me to make my marriage work. Growing up as a kid, I never remembered seeing Gail in the neighborhood. I thought, "How could this pretty girl be from the neighborhood, and I don't know who she is?" Of course, she wasn't running around the streets like my fast, grown ass. Once I went to high school, I started to see her in the hallways at Parkdale and became close friends with, and a teammate of, her brother Eric. I thought her the sweetest and prettiest girl walking the hallways. I developed the biggest crush on her and didn't care who knew.

After Eric and I went off to Potomac State, we became the best of friends. Coming home on the weekends, we spent lots of time around one another's family. Gail and I developed a close friendship. We secretly had a crush on each other, but we also both had committed relationships, so nothing more ever developed between us. As we got older, we lost contact with each other, but every now and then would run into one another. It was as if we never missed a beat. Gail and I could always talk about anything. We also had the same sense of humor and seemed to be laughing and smiling whenever we caught back up. Once I got married, we still talked occasionally. Gail was also in a relationship at the time, but that never stopped us from being there for each other as friends.

Gail always told me the truth. She'd say what I needed to hear even if it wasn't what I wanted to hear. She knew Monica was good for me, that whatever problems existed in my marriage I probably created, and Gail advised me to do the hard work in order to stay together. Her friendship was invaluable to me, but her advice too little, too late. I believed Monica just waited for me to crash and burn one more time. I'd become self-destructive, and she'd decided I wouldn't bring her down with me.

In late 2012, Cat Eyes sold heroin to a confidential informant in the Clay Terrace projects. The rat gave Cat Eyes's name to the DEA, who placed wiretaps on his phone. In order to identify his supplier, the DEA had the informant call Cat Eyes to make another buy. He called me and then called the informant back to arrange the sale. The DEA had enough to get surveillance warrants on me. They tapped my phones and placed a video camera on a pole across from my house.

We didn't know this, of course, and continued with our business as usual. There were a few signs, had I not been blinded by alcohol and too arrogant to notice. On more than one occasion I thought I was being followed, and once I even observed a Ford Expedition parked down the street from my house.

My friend Rock and I got in my truck and acted like we were going somewhere, but then drove up right next to the Expedition. Rock quickly got out and knocked on the tinted window. The guy inside fumbled around with something and then took off. Rock jumped back in the truck, and we took off behind him. He hauled ass, speeding through traffic lights, ignoring road signs. We didn't want to risk injuring anyone, so we let him go. But I did get his license plate number.

I, of course, called my friend at the sheriff's department, and he explained to me that no name or address came up for the plate number, code for: It's the police or feds. I later found out the incident near my house with the Expedition caused the police to think my friend and I were headed to a drug deal, when in fact we had just tried to find out who was in a tinted car watching things on my street. I thought it could have been someone planning to rob or break in my house, or a neighbor's house. My actions that day triggered the police to obtain twenty-four-hour surveillance on me.

When the end comes, it comes quickly. On August 9, 2013, I was arrested.

With Monica in Atlanta visiting friends, I called Half and told him to come by and pick up two kilos that he had asked me to hold for him from the fifteen I had received earlier in the week. He didn't make it on the day I called him, August 8th.

The following day, the day of my arrest, I got in touch with him, and he came by and grabbed one kilo, intending to make a quick sale and bring the money back to get the other kilo. An hour later, I got a call from Half's mother. He'd been pulled over and arrested near her house, which wasn't far from mine. At the time, I thought the situation an unfortunate pain in the ass, but nothing I couldn't handle. I told her he was good, and I'd get him out as soon as we heard from him. Little did I know at the time, Half would eventually become my co-defendant.

I knew I'd have to help Half out, but I had other crap on my mind. Sydney and Alexus were staying at the house. We expected a plumber to show up to fix a leak, but I also needed to meet Cat Eyes over at Clay Terrace. I left the girls to deal with the plumber and headed over to meet Cat Eyes. I'd already been drinking for several hours.

I then went to my friend PB's company's warehouse. We counted out money for thirteen kilos, part of the fifteen I got earlier that week. Half had already taken one kilo, and he still had one waiting for him. Those two kilos were the only ones we hadn't received any money for yet.

We were now heading over to meet Cat Eyes at Clay Terrace. Or so I thought. I left my truck at the warehouse, so we took PB's convertible Mustang. I called Cat Eyes to make sure he was at Clay Terrace and to tell him we were on our way.

"I'm not there yet. Don't go down there. Wait until I call you back..." Cat Eyes explained.

Just as he said this, PB and I were pulled over on Eastern Avenue. A couple of plainclothes police officers approached the vehicle, ordered us out, and started speaking with us. They said PB could leave and that he could pick me up later from the station. I started to give him my phones, but the officers said there was no need for that, I'd be back out in an hour or two. I know that whenever cops say stuff like that, and tell you not to worry, it's usually a bunch of bullshit.

I wasn't worried, though; I thought this just a simple "All Hands On Deck." "All Hands On Deck" was a police program in DC where they rushed a neighborhood or projects and would pat-search everyone on the street trying to find drugs or guns. I thought being pulled over was related to this. Neither PB nor I had any drugs or guns on us, or in his vehicle for that matter, so I didn't worry too much.

The officers then put me in handcuffs and walked me over to a Dodge Durango with tinted windows and placed me in the back seat. The whole thing seemed strange to me. Still drunk, I kept pretty calm. That all changed when we drove off, and one of the officers turned around and showed me his DEA badge.

"This isn't about All Hands On Deck, Mr. Malone," he told me. "We've been following you all day. Nabbed Mr. Williams several hours ago. We know all about the cocaine you've been selling."

Half's arrest should have tipped me off. It would have, had I been a little less arrogant and more on point.

"So, let's drive around and talk, Curtis, alright?"

"There's nothing to talk about. Just do what you need to do," I told the officers.

"You sure, Curtis?"

"Yes, I'm sure."

"We're at your house right now, by the way."

I thought about the one kilo of cocaine I'd left in the basement, the one that Half didn't pick up because of his arrest, and I immediately wanted to kick myself in frustration and stupidity. How could I be so ignorant? Fuck. *Rule number five: Never keep drugs where you or your family lay their heads.*

Then I thought about what Sydney and Alexus must be going through. They were out running errands when the police arrived but showed up with the search underway in the house. Sydney and Alexus asked the officers what was going on, got some information, and then called Monica. The girls were a bit shaken up by these events.

A little later, at the police station, I saw a woman and her daughter. I knew both of them through Cat Eyes. Whenever I went over to see him, he was usually hanging out in their house, and we would chill there. They had been busted, so I knew something probably happened with Cat Eyes.

As he drove back to his house, Cat Eyes had spoken with his wife on the phone. Just as she began explaining what was going on, he'd realized the police had surrounded his house and were inside. They noticed him and immediately ordered that he pull over. Cat Eyes obeyed and pulled off the road. Then, right after the officer approached his window and asked for his license and registration, he just took off. He got into a high-speed chase with the cops and actually got away.

Cat Eyes ran for nine months. I got messages to him a few times over that period but didn't actually see him until he was arrested and brought into the DC jail where I was still in custody.

The next morning, a Saturday, at my initial appearance in court, the judge denied bail. He informed me my case would be transferred to federal court. After that took place, I was finally allowed my one phone call, which I, of course, used to call Monica.

I was arraigned the following Tuesday, August 13th, and charged with conspiracy to distribute at least a hundred grams of heroin and at least five kilograms of cocaine, and possession of a firearm during a drug-trafficking offense.

When I had called Monica on Saturday, August 10th, after my initial court appearance, I told her she didn't need to rush back from Atlanta, but hadn't really meant it. Had she been in any kind of trouble, I would have dropped everything to be with her.

At the arraignment in federal court on the thirteenth, Monica wasn't there. She'd taken my recommendation literally and didn't cut her trip short. This disturbed me quite a bit. I felt betrayed and let down. I'm sure she felt the same. All the problems in our marriage had eroded the relationship to the point that it could not withstand the challenge my arrest created. Once back in town, she finally came to see me.

"You're an embarrassment to me and my kids," Monica said later during one of our phone calls from the DC jail. Despite her disappointment, she did visit me a few times. About a month after my arrest, she came and told me she'd hired Billy Martin, a celebrity lawyer who had represented Michael Vick and Allen Iverson. Martin wasn't cheap; his retainer: $50,000.

"Nolan is paying for him?" I asked.

"No. I sold my wedding ring."

I sat silent for a moment. It was a nice ring, expensive, but not $50K expensive. The fact that she would tell me she sold the ring held more significance than I really wanted to face. I felt Monica had found her way out of our marriage.

My arrest sent shockwaves through the DC basketball community and the AAU world. Many ran from me as fast as they could, distancing themselves and downplaying our relationship. They spoke to the press and claimed they never liked or trusted me. They used my arrest as a way to forget what they owed me.

Joel Bell was one of those people. During our time working together, I'd brought him several pro players, including Dante Cunningham. Though Beasley's betrayal had caused Joel and me to sever our business relationship, he still owed me commissions on the players I'd brought to him. He took advantage of my arrest to screw me over and default on those payments.

To this day, Joel continues to ignore my letters and calls. He knows he owes me a few hundred grand and doesn't care about loyalty or how difficult life in prison can be.

I also ran into conflict with Damon Handon, DCA's general manager. My arrest had obviously led to a public relations nightmare for DCA. From ESPN.com, to the *Washington*

Post, to *Sports Illustrated*, my downfall, and my link to DCA, was publicized widely. To many, I *was* DCA. Damage control became Damon's top priority.

I wanted Monica to take my place as DCA's president. She had the business savvy to handle the relationships I had built and, as my wife, had met and rubbed elbows with all our sponsors.

Damon felt the program needed a clean break. He also probably saw an opportunity for himself. Having Monica step in was probably shortsighted on my part. Not only were we headed for divorce, but DCA was not my own fiefdom to act as dictator. For years, I'd been the face and driving force behind Assault. But a team, with many coaches, sponsors, and supporters, made the program successful. We'd grown from one team wearing a sneaker no one had ever heard of, to seventeen teams and one of the most prominent programs across the country. Damon had been there from the beginning. My own mistake forced me out of the program to which I'd dedicated so much time, energy, and money. DCA had been my baby, and I didn't want to lose it. Yet, my own poor choices cost me everything.

DC Assault complicated my relationship with Mike Sumner as well. Mike asked me to be his best man in his wedding, and I am the godfather to his son. Unfortunately, and sadly, we don't speak anymore. Mike sided with Damon and resented my reluctance to leave DCA in their hands.

Steve Reed also didn't do me any favors. In fact, the only thing I received from Steve was a bunch of lies. I never got the $100K for DCA. And he certainly has never answered any of my calls since I've been incarcerated.

Lastly, and perhaps the person's character who surprised me the most, is Frank Martin. He basically forgot how his life dramatically changed when I sent Beasley and so many other DC Assault players to Kansas State. Frank never even had to work for any of them. He used to give me birthday gifts every year while coaching Kansas State, one way to show how much he appreciated me.

Frank is now the head coach at South Carolina making millions of dollars a year. He won't answer any of my calls or return any messages. I would like to know how he's doing. After all, I did play a major role in changing his entire life. But I guess part of the reason Frank is not contacting me is because I'm of no more use to him now; I don't have any players to deliver to him from prison.

Other people in my life rallied to my defense. Sydney really stepped up, as if sensing the end of my relationship with her mother and wanting to save it, and became the link between Monica and me; Nolan, playing in the NBA, could have put distance between us in order to save face, but he never turned his back on me.

Greg Holloway remained a close friend. Troy Weaver still took my calls. DerMarr and Dalonte spoke highly of me in the press, as did other DCA alums.

My arrest shocked my parents and family. They thought I'd left the drug game back in 1992. They watched the rise of DCA, and my own success, with pride. They saw me as a well-known, well-connected, successful man who had everything—both materialistic and emotional—a man could want. Why couldn't I have been satisfied?

But my family didn't let their surprise and disappointment destroy the loving bond we enjoyed. My arrest may have been the exact thing my mother feared and predicted nearly twenty years before, but both my parents worried more about my mental and physical well-being.

And many times, as I laid in my bunk in my small jail cell, I struggled with accepting my new reality. Getting arrested triggers a grieving process much like a death does. An arrest is, in fact, like a death: the death of a lifestyle. But it can also be a transformation—from what a person has been to who he will be. I'd lay in the quasi-dark of my cell at night and let anger consume me, at the unfairness of it all. I denied my new reality (I'd beaten other charges in court before, after all); I wallowed in regret—if only I'd stuck with Fegan! If only I'd not trusted Fatima for so long.

But, ultimately, one must find acceptance and figure out how to live. That is not a quick process; I'm still going through it. But with the love and support of the people who see the good in me and refuse to deny it, I survive.

My initial charges carried a mandatory minimum sentence of five years. Had I gone to trial and lost, the government could have enhanced my charges and pushed for up to ten to twenty years, a staggering amount of time. It sucker punched me in my gut. It meant my parents could die while I sat in prison, that my children would be grandparents when I was released, that I'd be in my sixties. It felt like a nightmare.

Trial was never a real option, but I pled not guilty and tried to get the best plea bargain I could. Billy Martin negotiated a plea deal that carried a sentencing range of sixty to a hundred thirty-two months (five to eleven years). A hearing was scheduled where I'd change my plea and accept the agreement. I hesitated and told the judge I could not plead guilty.

My mentality was part denial, part hope, that the government would make a better deal. Nearly seventy-five people wrote to the judge in my support, and several prepared to testify if need be. I still thought I had a good chance of forcing the Feds to narrow my sentence range. I at least knew that if I avoided trial, I'd avoid twenty years.

But the offer from prosecutors never got any better. Finally, on March 12th, 2014, I pled guilty to one count of conspiracy to distribute or possess with intent to distribute 500 or more grams of cocaine and a hundred or more grams of heroin. I also agreed to pay $150,000 in restitution.

On May 28th, 2014, Federal Judge Ellen Huvelle sentenced me to a hundred months, or eight years and four months, right in the middle of the five- to eleven-year range stipulated in the plea bargain. My nightmare became reality.

Reflections on Loyalty and Greed

These are just some of the hundreds of young men who are now alumni of DCA: Dwayne Anderson (Villanova), Ron Anderson (South Florida), Eric Atkins (Notre Dame), Michael Beasley (Kansas State), Tony Bethel (NC State), Keith Bogans (Kentucky), Eric Branham (Virginia Tech), Nate Britt (UNC), Val Brown (George Washington), Brian Chase (Virginia Tech), Quinn Cook (Duke), Anthony Cowan (Maryland), Dante Cunningham (Villanova), Mamadi Diane (Virginia), Jason Flagler (SC State), Austin Freeman (Georgetown), Donte Grantham (Clemson), Jeff Green (Georgetown), Josh Hairston (Duke), Cliff Hawkins (Kentucky), David Hawkins (Temple), Dalonte Hill (UNC Charlotte), David Holmes (Manhattan), Omari Isreal (Notre Dame/Loyola), Kris Jenkins (Villanova), DerMarr Johnson (Cincinnati), Lafonte Johnson (UNLV/GWU), Kris Joseph (Syracuse), Wally Judge (Kansas State), Mark Karcher (Temple), Tre Kelley (South Carolina), Damion Lee (Louisville), Rob Little (Stanford), Kevin Lyde (Temple), Travis Lyons (Manhattan), Chris Matthews (St. Bonaventure), Anthony McClain (Cincinnati), Rodney McGruder (Kansas State), Frank McQueen (JUCO), Al Miller (Central Florida),

Terrance Nixon (George Mason), Arinze Onuaku (Syracuse), Chinanu Onuaku (Louisville), Mike Pegues (Delaware), Roddy Peters (Maryland/South Florida), Bernard Robinson (Michigan), Ed Sheffey (Georgetown), Nolan Smith (Duke), Isaiah Tate (George Mason), Marcus Thornton (William & Mary), Tyler Thornton (Duke), Romelo Trimble (Maryland), Julian Vaughn (Georgetown), Christian Webster (Harvard), James White (Cincinnati).

Two of the most important lessons I've learned in my life are about friendship and loyalty. At the end of the day, you can know a person your whole life and that person can still turn his back on you, while a practical stranger will step up and show you the most loyalty. I learned you can try to give someone the world, but that doesn't mean they will do the same for you. Twin once warned me, "Curtis, stop thinking everyone else thinks like you." I never took him seriously until I experienced how my life changed.

In some ways I was very naive. I'd grown up with Twin, Irvin, Byrd, Freeman, and my parents as examples of loyalty and trust and, as a result, was often too trusting. The media claimed I used my players for my own gain. I disagree. Instead, I feel I was used by a lot of people around me, and I trusted them too much to realize it.

I feel the most let down by Michael and Fatima. The split that occurred between us led to everything else going to shit. I don't blame them; I made bad choices and there were other factors, but I do feel betrayed and hurt. I loved Mike as a son. I spent more time with him and gave more of myself to him than I did my own daughters (for which I am sorry, Tanay and Alexus). When he emerged as a top prospect, it seemed to me as if Fatima realized he was her lottery ticket. Caught between his mother and his adopted parents, I understand how conflicted Mike must have felt. At that time, he wasn't old enough or mature enough to deal with the situation.

But years have passed. He is no longer an immature child. He could reach out and explain all the things I still don't know, like what he was being told and why he believed all of it.

I also wish I'd dealt with the situation with Fegan differently. He outgrew me, but I still could have helped him. I could have compromised. I could have restructured our deal to maintain the relationship. Fegan died in a car accident in 2018, so he'll never read these words, but I continue to look at him as the epitome of class and professionalism. He was everything I aspired to be.

With Joel Bell, I saw opportunity. He offered me the chance to grow and possibly become a legitimate partner. But, like Lamell McMorris with Nolan, Joel's friendship and offer rested on my ability to deliver Beasley. I thought we were stronger than that. Many people warned me about Joel's character. People called him a conman, a shyster. But I gave him the benefit of the doubt, in part because of greed, and in part because I, too, had been demonized and put down by others who never knew the real me. I wanted to believe in Joel. Ultimately, though I respect how he represented his clients, his personal character is exactly as I was warned it would be.

Rising to terrific heights, then falling down, beaten and bloodied, forces you to take a long look at your own failings. I do not believe myself a failure. In fact, most everything I've done succeeded. Had Mike not fired Joel, I may have, indeed, become his partner. Mike would have led to more lottery picks or first-round level clients, and I never would have fallen back into drugs the way I did.

But not being a failure is different than being perfect. I am not perfect. I have character flaws like everyone else. Growing up a popular kid should have led to self-confidence, but at some point, that confidence led to arrogance, though I'm trying to fix that. The more success I achieved—whether with DCA or in the drug game—the more arrogant I became. I believed myself untouchable, until I found myself in the back seat of a Durango with two DEA agents.

And I'm lazy, in a way. Oh, I hustle. I put effort in when I benefit from it. But ultimately, I look for easy solutions. As my marriage fell apart, I never tried analyzing what I was doing or responsible for. Instead, I figured it would fix itself. I write that I'm not a failure, but, in my marriage, I did fail.

Ultimately, greed became my biggest vice. I always want more. And when greed combined with laziness, I returned to the quick, easy money found in drugs. So many other options existed, but why put in the hard work when I knew how to make lots of money selling cocaine?

I learned from a young age that money equaled power, respect, stature. I watched Twin or Irvin dole out wads of cash and knew I wanted to be just like them when I grew up. And wasn't I? Instead of passing a hundred bucks to some neighborhood kid to use at the mall, I clothed and housed kids like Frank, DJ, Dalonte, and Mike…I not only emulated my childhood idols, I surpassed them. My whole self-image, my personal definition of who Curtis Malone was, depended on having money. Lots of money.

Yet, I hold few regrets. In life, we all have moments of choice we wish we'd done differently. But, despite what my critics say, I never used my players. I loved my players. And I loved providing them a path to success. Maybe my means did not justify the ends. Or maybe they did. My legacy is that long list of players at the beginning of this chapter. Each escaped their circumstance for something better, each got the chance at higher education.

I've seen friends reinvent themselves: DJ returned to Cincinnati to get his degree after his shortened career; Dalonte climbed back up after a few DUI arrests had knocked him down. I have always picked myself up in life. I will again.

I have a plan: a basketball academy that combines skill development with private tutoring. My focus has always been, and will continue to be, basketball in pursuit of education. And I have support. Gail, my longtime friend who always encouraged me to work things out with Monica, is now my girlfriend.

Once incarcerated, I reached out to Gail because I wanted my friend to come see me. At that time, I also felt as if my marriage was over. Once she came to visit me, I knew in the back of my mind that I wanted to make her my lady. But still being a married man, I wanted to be respectful of both Gail and Monica, so I decided to file for divorce.

When Gail and I became committed to one another, she became very close with my family as if she'd known them forever, and has built great relationships with them. She has also shown tremendous support and love to all of my loved ones. From day one, Gail demonstrated to me what it's like to have a strong woman in my corner at the lowest point of my life. For this, I am grateful. I thank her every day for loving me unconditionally and still having confidence in me when a lot of people don't. She is what any man dreams of having during times like these. She truly is a "ride-or-die" woman. I'm so lucky she's mine.

Through it all I am still Curtis. Older. Wiser. More aware of my faults, but also dedicated to increasing my strengths. For years, I led two lives, both nearly intersecting one another. A public life as a mentor and a powerbroker helping to land city kids in colleges, and a private life moving kilos. I was duplicitous.

Now, I've laid myself bare, to be judged by anyone. Now, I am just me, trying to love, continuing to be loyal, moving past my greed.

Acknowledgments

I'd first like to thank my Lord and Savior, Jesus Christ. Without you, none of this would be possible—the good or the bad.

To my parents, Herman and Rosa Malone; my grandparents, Ella C. Mitchell and Coles Terry; my sisters, Sharon, Brenda, and Beverly, thanks for all the tough love and ass whippings; my brother, Andre Malone; my other siblings, Lola Stevenson, Marie Forman, and Marilyn; and my grandkids.

To my daughters Alexus, Tanay, and Sydney, and my son Nolan, who have all given and shown me unconditional love; my godsons, Dalonte Hill and DerMarr Johnson; and my nieces and nephews: I love you guys.

To my immediate family, who has always shown me love and support: the Hills, the Tinsleys, the Lassiters, the Blockers, the Nicholsons, the Galimores, Evelyn and Mike Reese, cousin Dave, Johnny, Herb, Mike, my favorite cousin Devonne, and Kathy (I didn't forget you).

My friends who have supported me loyally: Steve Gant, Steve Williams, Danny Hatcher, Preston Bailey, Chico Brown, Troy Weaver, Curtis Richardson, Carlos Williams, T-Dub,

Curtis Scoon, Steve Smith, Rockefella, Greg Holloway, Dave Kontaxis, Darian King, Fat Cat and Kim, Quinton and Toni, Angel and Marisa, Ducky Vaughn, Chick Lyles, Stacey Robinson, Charles Ricks, Keith Stevens, Bruce Shingler, Mark Karcher, K-Dog, T-Harvey, Stubblefield, Mike Pegues, David Cox, Bob Huggins, DJ, Corey McCrae, Steve Marsh, Cliff Earl, Charles Smith, Mike Locksley, Lawrency, Moo Byrd, Tracy White, Johnette Tillman, Sheryl Anderson, Mariane Niles, and Gail Anderson.

To all of my DC Assault family, Adidas family, and Under Armour family, thanks for your love and support. Thanks, Sonny and Pam Vaccaro.

To my co-defendants, Cat Eyes, Half, Derico Williams, and Clarence Redd, for all being stand-up men.

To my extended family, who has loved and supported me unconditionally: 1320 Missouri Avenue, Palmer Park, Uptown, Landover, Clay Terrace, Loopy, Sean Harris, the Rustins, the Coffers, the Riverses, the Richardsons, the Whites, the Jacobses, Kenny Fairfax, Ms. Sherry, and Ms. Tillman.

A special shout-out to all the convicts and good, stand-up men who have helped me and taught me how to bid.

My list of the ones gone, but not forgotten: RIP Grandma Ella C., Andre Malone, Marilyn, Aunt Shirley, Harold Jones (Twin), Irvin Wallace, Ronald Byrd, Lee Mackins, Ms. Pearl, Ms. Gant, Mike Coffer, Ken Freeman, Uncle Munk, Jabouri McClamb, Randy Sutton, Ted Cook, George and Ruby Rustin, Maude Hamilton, Mr. Barksdale, Dave Jacobs, Uncle Tim Weaver, my Li'l man Carrington, Psych out of the Jungle, Lemeo and Lep, Beebo, Diamond Byrd, Butch Cherry, Dan Fegan, and Bret Bearup.

I want to thank Jake, JB, Dean, and the entire team at Cross MacBean for assisting me as I told my story.

I want to send a special thanks to my beautiful wife, Gail Malone. Thanks for all your love and support. You have shown over and over what a true friend is. Thank you for loving me unconditionally and riding out this storm with me. I couldn't ask for a better partner to have my back through thick and thin. My love and a big thank you to Momma Mary for allowing me to be your son-in-law.

About the Author

Photo credit: Shutter Up Warehouse

Curtis Malone is one of the most influential figures in grassroots basketball. In 1993, he co-founded DC Assault, a nonprofit organization dedicated to supporting young men ages seven through seventeen in their pursuit of basketball dreams and academic achievement.

Under Curtis's leadership, DC Assault helped over two hundred young men earn full college scholarships, with more than a dozen going on to careers in the NBA and NFL. Many others found success playing professionally or thriving in other professional fields.

In 2013, Curtis was convicted of drug conspiracy and served seven years of an eight-year sentence. Since his release, he has committed himself to mentoring youth by sharing his story and lessons learned. Curtis's ability to connect with and inspire young people has fueled his success as a speaker, engaging communities and academic institutions across the country.

Curtis is now a partner at CampusVR, a tech company and a partner and advisor at Good Favor Sports.